MW01014189

Immigration's Unarmed Invasion

Deadly Consequences

by

Frosty Wooldridge

authorHOUSE™

1663 LIBERTY DRIVE, SUITE 200
BLOOMINGTON, INDIANA 47403
(800) 839-8640
WWW.AUTHORHOUSE.COM

First published by AuthorHouse 07/16/04

ISBN: 1-4184-6387-6 (e)
ISBN: 1-4184-6386-8 (sc)

Printed in the United States of America
Bloomington, Indiana

This book is printed on acid-free paper.

IMMIGRATION'S UNARMED INVASION—DEADLY CONSEQUENCES
By Frosty Wooldridge

"Wooldridge opens the door for a debate of national importance, which few Americans realize at this time. His stark honesty, however grim in its reality, is the result of painstaking research. Every American needs to read this informative but shocking book." Joseph Kubiak, Manhattan Beach, California

"Every American must read this compelling book. Wooldridge makes a clear and readable approach to the severe problems facing this nation as a result of illegal immigration and its impact. Readers will be overwhelmed by Wooldridge's clear, intelligent and factual information on this critical issue. After reading it, follow his list on 'How To Save America.' You'll be doing it for your kids." Jan Herron, Evergreen, Colorado

"Among those struggling for a more moderate and democratic immigration policy, Wooldridge's no-holds-barred approach to this critical issue has quickly established him as one of the movement's most important observers of America's reckless immigration policies." Craig Nelsen, director, Project USA, Washington, DC

"Hispanic activists and politicians say Hispanics want high immigration and open borders. That is outrageous, just as it is outrageous for a handful of self-appointed Latino spokesmen and women to presume to speak for all Hispanics as if tens of millions of us hold the same views on this controversial topic. Most Hispanics want immigration sharply reduced. Wooldridge and others who speak through the pages of this book set the record straight on why immigration impoverishes America. We sell our nation's future down the river—socially, culturally, fiscally, environmentally—for no better reason than to provide business with a flood of cheap, taxpayer-subsidized immigrant labor. This nation's poor and minorities are hurt the most in the process. I urge all Americans to heed this book's warning." Corine Flores, Immigration-reform advocate, Santa Fe, New Mexico

"Wooldridge brings his vast experience gathered from first hand observations during his worldwide travel to the subject of immigration. Few authors have seen the links between immigration and so many of our pressing social ills. Wooldridge touches on all of them—-sprawl, disease, loss of environment, failing schools and hospitals. Through his clear prose and well-documented research, all Americans will learn the importance of getting involved in the immigration debate. Read his book. Urge your friends to do the same. Then get busy before it is too late." Joe Guzzardi, Author/ Former Candidate for Governor of California

"My son Mark used to talk about the 'invasion' in California. What had once been orderly was now a disaster area. Today, the invasion has arrived in Nevada, BIG Time! It's moving swiftly to all parts of our country. If anyone seeks answers to this immigration invasion nightmare, this book is THE best. If something is not done, our nation will become a Third World country. If you are a die-hard American like I am, and you want the facts, I strongly recommend this book. Wooldridge tells the story like it sadly is — the unimaginable invasion of our nation." Judy Singer, Las Vegas, Nevada

"When I was born 50 years ago, there were 140 million Americans. Today, we approach 300 million. In my daughter's lifetime, we could reach a "China-like" billion Americans! Most Americans concerned that ours not become a nation as polluted and overcrowded as many other nations, have shown their support for a bright, sustainable future through a near replacement-level birthrate. 'IMMIGRATION'S UNARMED INVASION—DEADLY CONSEQUENCES' gives voice to reasoned arguments and outrage against what is being done to our country. Read this book as if your children's futures depend on what you will learn. Their futures do depend on exactly that!" Kathleene Parker, Los Alamos, New Mexico, Writer, publisher and immigration-reformer

"This must-read new book about the immigration invasion of the United States rings ironically and powerfully as we citizens are told how our government is protecting our homeland against attack. Wooldridge brings to readers of all ages an urgent message demanding Americans of all ethnic and cultural backgrounds stand up and scream for prompt reform. Mr. Wooldridge, a world traveler and keen observer of the global dilemma which excess human numbers generate, has written a highly readable book explaining America's many faceted excess immigration problems with a clear and chilling certainty. His bottom line message: Greatly reduce immigration now or end the America we now enjoy within no more than one generation. His exhaustive listing of the ills brought, and the problems created by this invasion of our homeland make earlier efforts seem tepid." Donald A. Collins, Board Member, Federation for American Immigration Reform

"The shocking reality of the words in Wooldridge's book are intended to move the readers into action. As citizens of this great land, it is our duty and our obligation to "sound the alarm" about the unspeakable violations and crimes our own government leaders continue to ply upon us. If we know and still do nothing about this invasion and these obscenities, then we are also guilty of our own destruction. My son Kristopher William Eggle and patriots and heroes from all across our land deserve to be respected and honored for what they have sacrificed in the name of freedom. Thank Wooldridge for his work in the field of immigration reform and speaking out about our unsecured borders. May he be blessed for his teachings, his writings, his personal contacts, his spiritual guidance to others, and for wanting America to once again become that bright and shining city on the hill!" Bonnie Eggle, Cadillac, Michigan

"If you only do one thing this year, read this book! Wooldridge writes in concise, clear and all too real language about the sad tale of the decline of our great nation due to massive, uncontrolled illegal immigration. He lays out in graphic detail the results of the colonization of our country by illegal aliens. I worked as an Obstetrical Nurse in southern California, just after the 1986

Amnesty to End All Amnesties. The effect was a massive influx of illegal aliens into our country. I watched pregnant illegal aliens flood into the hospital Labor and Delivery units. These babies became eligible immediately for all the social services and safety nets our country had to offer. Women openly admitted to me their reason for crossing the border was to have an American citizen child. I was shown many fake social security cards; some women had two or three cards, each with a different name. While I nursed these women my own children went without health insurance because insurance rates had climbed too high for me to afford. Wooldridge explains this insanity in dialog you can't ignore. Listen well, for our future and the future of our children is at stake." Stephany Gabbard RN, CLNC, Hungry Horse, Montana

"This book presents Americans with critical information whereby U.S. corporations are the tail that wags the dog. It shows how Mexico's Fox parlays his millions of refugees sent to America to enrich his own coffers without changing his own corrupt government. As an Hispanic immigrant, I am watching the destruction of my own adopted country. The point where Wooldridge interviews a man from India is particularly disturbing. The man said, "You Americans have an artificially high standard of living and it's about time you drop to the level of the rest of the world's poverty." Wooldridge responded, "Would you consider the fact that you have an artificially low standard of living because, with 1.1 billion people, you have an artificially high overpopulation crisis?" To that I say, "Why should we become the next India, China or Bangladesh with horrible population problems?" Haydee Pavia, legal immigrant and proud American, Los Angeles, California

"It is obvious that illegal immigration negatively alters the direction of this country. This author provides essential background and statistics showing how we arrived at our irresponsible national policy. Every concerned citizen needs to read this. Both our borders need to be militarized. We don't have much time to lose on this national tragedy that will affect our children's lives in horrific and unimaginable ways." Helen T. Kempski, Cleveland, Ohio

"In times of terrorist threats worldwide and political apathy concerning illegal entries in the United States—violence and crime continue escalating on our Southern Borders. Border Enforcement Agencies, which include National Park Rangers, Border Patrol, Customs, Sheriff's Departments and local police, encounter a constant invasion in this nation. Human and narcotics traffickers to thousands of illegal, undocumented aliens from Mexico as well as other nations cross at will into United States territory. For anyone that is concerned with the future of this nation, Mr. Wooldridge presents the facts in a "politically correct" America." John W. Slagle (Ret) Special Agent, Anti-Smuggling Unit U.S.B.P. Senior Intelligence Analyst 9/11/2001. Author of "ILLEGAL ENTRIES."

IMMIGRATION'S UNARMED INVASION:

DEADLY CONSEQUENCES

BY

Frosty Wooldridge

DEDICATED TO:

Article IV, Section 4 of the U.S. Constitution

"The United States shall guarantee to every State in this Union a Republican Form of Government, and shall protect each of them against invasion; and on Application of the Legislature, or of the Executive (when the Legislature cannot be convened) against domestic violence."

AND

"Pressures resulting from unrestrained population growth put demands on the natural world that can overwhelm any efforts to achieve a sustainable future. If we are to halt the destruction of our environment, we must accept limits to that growth."

—World Scientists' Warning to Humanity, signed by 1600 senior scientists from 70 countries, including 102 Nobel Prize laureates, November 18, 1992

AND

"A person (including a group of persons, business, organization, or local government) commits a federal felony when she or he: assists an illegal alien she/he should reasonably know is illegally in the U.S. or who lacks employment authorization, by transporting, sheltering, or assisting him or her to obtain employment, or encourages that illegal alien to remain in the U.S. by referring him or her to an employer or by acting as employer or agent for an employer in any way, or knowingly assists illegal aliens due to personal convictions." Federal Law—Section 8 USC 1324(a)(1)(A)(iv)(b)(iii)

FORWARD

This book exposes Americans to the accelerating consequences of mass legal and unrestricted illegal immigration into the United States. It examines individual communities and lives across this nation that have been undermined by the 1965 Immigration Reform Act.

Before that time, an average of 178,000 people legally immigrated into the United States each year. They learned English, educated themselves in our school systems, became contributing members of society, swore loyalty to their new country and assimilated into the American way of life. Since 1965, however, more than 60 million people including their offspring immigrated into the United States. Since 1990, 1.1 to 1.3 million legal immigrants and 800,000 to one million illegal aliens have poured into America annually without pause. Our population rose from 200 million in 1965 to 292 million in 2004 and will exceed 300 million in this decade—on its way to a half billion past mid-century.

These immigrants arrive from countries that avoid family planning. Across the planet 10,000 babies are added hourly, 240,000 daily and over 80 million people, net gain, annually. (Population Reference Bureau) All the while, an endless human line waits its turn at America's portals.

Most come from Third World origins that lack basic education and skills for viability in the United States. Millions come from countries that clash with our culture while practicing rituals Americans consider barbaric. Female genital mutilation was unheard of in the United States ten years ago. Today, states struggle with this operation performed on baby girls with razor blades or broken glass. Cock fighting and dog fighting continues in old Mexico, but today, those 'sports' play in backyards across the Southwest or wherever Latin immigrants enclave. Worse, horse tripping by Mexican cowboys known as 'charros' grows inside the United States wherever immigrants from south of the border gather. Animal sacrifice rituals known as 'Santeria' find thousands of Third World immigrant devotees in the United States.

On the disease front, immigrants bring afflictions such as leprosy, Chagas Disease, tuberculosis, Exotic New Castle Disease and hepatitis. For example, 16,000 new cases of incurable multi-drug resistant tuberculosis migrated into the United States in the past five years in the bodies of illegal aliens. Over 7,000 new cases of leprosy in the past four years invaded this country via illegal aliens from India, Brazil and the Caribbean. We suffer tens of thousands of hepatitis cases.

On the felony scene, illegal aliens as well as legal immigrants represent a growing crime wave embedding itself in our cities and towns. Drug trafficking into the billions of dollars moves through the 20,000 member "18th Street Gang" in Los Angeles as well as the "MS-13 Gang" spreading to 28 cities in the United States. These gangs kill and extort business owners as well as addict our children with drugs.

This immigration invasion's consequences supersede any threats from Al-Qaeda, Iraq, North Korea or any other country. Why? You can define those enemies. Not today's immigration aggression! It resembles a multiplying parasite. It feeds on us as the host country as it consumes the foundation of our republic that makes our society viable.

This book addresses how this invasion destroys America day by day, week by week and year by year. Political elites, churches, cheap-labor-seeking companies and corporations drive this invasion. Their goals require maximum money, power and influence at the expense of American citizens. It's been a slow death over the past thirty years, but it's quickening. As a nation, we're losing our national unity that kept us vibrant, cohesive and viable for over 200 years. The fabric of our country frays and rips with mass immigration's serrated sword.

Legal and illegal immigrants displace American workers and depress wages. Their numbers grow so fast that many regions find 'city-states' growing isolated against the American Way of life. English is no longer adopted or accepted among these newcomers.

Illegal aliens remain in our country as criminals. Employers hiring them break federal statutes. The excuse is, "They do the jobs Americans won't do." Unfortunately, they take millions of jobs that Americans will do, but we can't raise a family on 'indentured slave wages' and won't live 15 to a trailer. Illegal aliens 'colonize' meat packing plants, paving, construction, dry wall, hotel, janitorial, home building, landscape, fast food, retail and many more labor arenas. They work under the table with one-third to one-half not paying taxes while using our infrastructure. A few Americans accumulate wealth at citizen expense. We stomach a $7 trillion national debt. Americans suffer $2 trillion consumer debt. Fifteen to eighteen million Americans can't find work.

When is enough immigration enough? We are being colonized by the Third World at the command of our national leadership. It makes no sense and foments a nation-destroying agenda. Since our elected leaders provoke it and won't stop it, American citizens must step up.

With 80 million people added to the planet annually, it is time delinquent countries become responsible for their populations.

On the environmental front, America via immigration evolves from a stable, sustainable society to one fast approaching unsustainable as its numbers reach a half billion past mid-century. Rampant immigration creates unsolvable problems, which move America toward a non-functioning society. Once the numbers of people multiply beyond carrying capacity, they manifest an irreversible crisis.

Many warnings abound from the brightest minds in the world:

"Pressures resulting from unrestrained population growth put demands on the natural world that can overwhelm any efforts to achieve a sustainable future. If we are to halt the destruction of our environment, we must accept limits to that growth."

—World Scientists' Warning to Humanity, signed by 1600 senior scientists from 70 countries, including 102 Nobel Prize laureates, November 18, 1992

This book is not about race, creed or color. Americans of all races suffer this onslaught. It will become worse for all of us. As one man from India wrote me, "You Americans live an artificially high standard of living...it's about time you come down to the rest of the world's poverty." He wasn't kidding. One look at California demonstrates his statement.

From extensive world travels, this author appreciates that every human being on this planet paddles his or her boat the best he or she can. Every religious faith is doing the best it can. However, overpopulation does not care about such things. It weds misery and suffering for every person within its clutches. Overpopulation is relentless once humans are caught in its grip. It stems from 'exponential growth.' It's the reason you see no one fleeing to Bangladesh, China or India. In these pages, the International Human Suffering Index will be discussed as well as its escalating numbers.

This book addresses carrying capacity and sustainability. It addresses a viable United States versus a country that is headed, like a steaming, brakeless locomotive, toward the edge of the Grand Canyon.

Although the focus of this book addresses the ramifications propagated by immigration, the salient factors boil down to social chaos and crisis brought about by incompatible cultures and languages as well as overpopulation. No one can escape that crisis once it manifests itself in a society. As Americans, we command the right and the obligation to future generations to arrest this crisis and place it under control, while we can—in our own country.

If we are perceived as a world power and leader in enlightened environmental consciousness, our responsibility on this issue also serves as a model to other countries.

Ironically, the greatest calamity of unrestricted immigration driving American population momentum is being ignored by the brightest minds in the White House and Congress. Fifty years ago, the leaders of China, India and Bangladesh ignored their exploding populations. Today, they suffer in every quarter of their societies with problems they cannot solve. Why? Because they chase population momentum that keeps gaining.

Immigration forces the United States into being the third fastest growing nation in the world. The dilemma of overpopulated countries will be our crisis within 50 years. Globally, people flee misery, poverty and suffering in their countries. However, as their numbers accelerate, they transform America into the nations they fled.

Even if we absorb two million immigrants annually, that means we relieve $2/80^{th}$ of the annual world population gain. If we absorb $4/160^{th}$ in two years and 6/240th in three years, you can see how hopeless the situation remains. We can't save the world, but we can destroy our country. Why? Because the line exceeds carrying capacity for water, arable land, animal habitat, landfills, clean air and non-renewable resources.

Do enormous complexities surround this issue? You betcha! The author understands the intricate complexities in every realm. He understands the duplicities of his own government. He appreciates the role of religious networks in the United States, Middle East and the Vatican that tenaciously cling to the past as they arrest family planning in developing countries. Thus, they ensure continuing poverty and unwarranted suffering for millions. He realizes the United States has supported puppet dictatorships, undermined other countries, plundered Third World resources and started wars without merit. He understands this 100-year 'Age of Oil Orgy' is moving toward a condition of scarcity. He is aware that alternative energy 'hydrogen power' resembles the Powerball lottery. He understands terrible climatic, species extinction, global warming, water shortages and many other aspects of this growing crisis.

He realizes that no matter how many immigrants we absorb, we cannot and will not solve this global crisis. He warns that the more extreme our numbers the more extreme our children's consequences. He further appreciates that thriving economies or communities are not sustained by growing numbers; rather, they ultimately suffer collapse. Balance and population stability are the only factors that will retract us from this crisis.

However, if the United States doesn't act, who will? When? How? This book examines major impacts and consequences to this growing American and world predicament. It offers alternatives for Americans who want their children to grow into the American Dream instead of the American Nightmare.

As you will see in the pages of this book, our country is in serious trouble.

At the end of this book is a section, 'HOW TO SAVE AMERICA.' It presents ideas from Americans on what we must do to maintain our country before it careens out of our ability to control our destiny.

It's time for the Thomas Jefferson's to start writing, Betsy Ross' to start stitching, Ben Franklin's to start creating, Eleanor Roosevelt's to vocalize, Susan B. Anthony's to march, Dr. Martin Luther King's to lead and Barbara Jordan's to speak up. Whatever your talent, this is your nation and your kids' future. The worst decision you can make is to feel that you can do so little that you do nothing at all. You can and will make a difference in the future of your country by taking action. The Internet may save this country because 75 percent of Americans are connected to it. For starters, join www.numbersusa.com and join tens of thousands of fellow Americans as a faxer. It's fast, easy and effective. Go to www.securedbordersusa.com and sign the petition. Also, check www.asapcoalition.org and www.balance.org. Additionally, go to www.frostywooldridge.com for action items listed for your state and nationally.
Frosty Wooldridge
July, 2004

TABLE OF CONTENTS

CHAPTER 1—

THIRD WORLD MOMENTUM
IN AMERICA

"The one absolutely certain way of bringing this nation to ruin, or preventing all possibility of its continuing as a nation at all, would be to permit it to become a tangle of squabbling nationalities."

President Theodore Roosevelt

The United States suffers an unarmed invasion at its borders 365 days a year. This incursion originates from 100 countries around the world. It is as constant and ceaseless as the tides. It is a gathering storm. You can 'see' it on the horizon of every state in our nation. It is an unending line of people crossing our borders around the clock. Its implications reach beyond America's borders and promise a dangerous future for this nation.

Each day, 4,100 immigrants land in America legally. Another 2,200 and more, cross illegally through Mexico, primarily, and to a lesser degree, Canada. Other visitors over-stay their visas. Chain migration, diversity visas, work visas and a host of other methods for entering the United States await millions of desperate people. An average of 300,000 women annually cross our borders and deliberately birth their children on United States soil—in order to gain citizenship. Those 'anchor babies' become wards of our welfare system. It costs American taxpayers billions of dollars that could be used for our own children.

Why do immigrants come to the United States? Desperation! For example, Mexico City like most overpopulated Third World cities is a living nightmare. It features appalling, unsustainable numbers of people estimated at over 22 million. It stands neck deep in a crisis verging on breakdown. Pollution of its air and water stand at lethal levels. Sanitation sinks to the depths of filth. Disease spreads like wildfire. Crime and corruption equal pandemic levels. Tourists are kidnapped. Gangs rob restaurant patrons. Bandits rob passengers on trains and busses. Even more distressing is the fact that police and security guards collude with criminals. Multiply that crisis to dozens of countries. That's why they come to America.

Unfortunately, legal and illegal immigrants arrive speaking in excess of 300 languages. Once immigrants gain a foothold in the United States, it's called 'chain migration' whereby they immigrate hundreds of relatives. Their growing numbers add 1.99 to 2.3 million persons to our country annually. At current growth rates created by immigrants and their offspring, our nation will add 200 million just past mid-century.

Incursion into America by massive immigration affects every state, city, town and family in an explosion of detrimental and accelerating consequences. Unless brought under control, it will overwhelm this nation's ability to remain a functioning society.

A recent report by FAIR stated that America is, "Being 'swamped' by immigration." The flood rose from 19.8 million in 1990 to 31.1 million a decade later. Six cities now encompass at least 51 percent more foreign-born inhabitants than American citizens. Among them are Hialeah and Miami, Florida along with Glendale, Santa Ana, Daly City and Elmonte, California. Not far behind with at least 40 to 50 percent foreign inhabitants are Los

Angeles and Garden Grove, California along with Elizabeth, New Jersey.

"America's immigration policies have launched us into a risky experiment never tried by a modern day country," said Dan Stein, director of the Federation for American Immigration Reform, based in Washington, DC. "What remains to be seen is if this country has the capacity to accommodate and assimilate an unending wave of mass immigration. Failure to do so will result in a balkanized, fragmented, strife-torn and dysfunctional America."

Their numbers negatively impact American lives by the millions. Wages are depressed, jobs lost, schools overwhelmed, hospitals suffer bankruptcy, tax bases vanish and billions of dollars are sent back to countries of origin—thus draining America of hard currency—to name a few consequences. Even worse, the most cohesive aspect of American society dwindles in the process—English as our national language.

More important, a First World republic and functioning society needs an educated population with a similar moral and ethical foundation pulling in the same direction with a single language. America is losing all four points for this nation's vitality. Furthermore, we add unsustainable numbers of people. The American writer Asimov said, "Democracy can not survive overpopulation."

Additionally, clashing cultural conflicts arise in states across our nation. Immigrants wave their own country's flags, promote polygamy as a cultural right, female genital mutilation, home school in their own rituals and create enclaves that are fast balkanizing. As more and more Americans see their jobs, schools and communities overwhelmed with immigrants that lack any investment in America as their 'home,' American citizens demand answers and action. What is that action? The only way to gain a handle on this crisis requires a 10-year moratorium on all immigration into the United States. It will allow this nation to regain its footing and put its own house in order. Without such action, we will forever be the dog chasing his tail until he and this country collapse from futility.

3

Financially, the United States suffers from a $7 trillion and growing national debt. That equals a $23,500.00 debt plus accelerating interest for every man, woman and child within the United States. This debt's severity could bankrupt the United States. Consumer debt totals $2 trillion. The average credit card balance averages $8,000.00.

To create even more jeopardy for American citizens, illegal foreign nationals and growing immigrant populations send $56 billion dollars annually back to countries of origin, thus draining money away from the American economic engine. Mexico received $15 billion, Latin America $25 billion and Asia receives $16 billion in 2003. This financial drain rides atop the average $110 billion dollars exiting the United States in the form of drug traffic annually. Coupled with an annual trade deficit over $400 billion, the citizens of the United States are being financially bled to death.

Drugs, gangs, diseases, corruption and a host of other problems continue spreading throughout America due to unrestricted immigration from around the world. Immigrants flee horrid conditions in the Third World. Unfortunately, these newcomers create Third World Momentum in America.

This causes a phenomenon of sheer numbers of people immigrating into our country at such high rates of speed—they cannot and do not absorb into the American Dream. They enclave into cities and sections of the country that support their exclusion within America. Along the way, entire cities suffer from established and violent gangs.

From an environmental standpoint, Third World Momentum gains speed with every passing day. In 1985, Border Patrol agents were hamstrung by Congress. Third World slums, called 'colonias,' sprouted up on the American side of the border from Brownsville, Texas to San Diego, California. The term 'colonias' is Spanish for 'new neighborhoods.' In reality, these shantytowns expand daily like a cancer inside their host. In this case, America is their host country.

They resemble a never ending line of broken-down trailers, cardboard shelters nailed together with wooden pallets, or metal buildings like ice fishing shanties. But there is a catch. They pass no housing codes, do not feature electricity nor do they enjoy toilets or running water. They stand in the desert without paved roads, sewer or power lines, water or garbage disposal. Trash piles grow putrid in the summer sun. Rats multiply in the refuse. Diseases proliferate.

Those diseases include dysentery, hepatitis, tuberculosis, Chagas Disease, leprosy, ringworm, skin rashes and cholera. Illegal aliens, who make up most of the residents, transport water in 55-gallon drums. El Paso Health Director Dr. Lawrence Nickery said, "Those industrial water drums are contaminated with fecal bacteria and every carcinogen on the list."

I have seen them on my bicycle travels through the Southwest. They look worse than the slums surrounding Mexico City and are as miserable as the millions living in shocking poverty in Bangladesh. But instead, they're here in America. To see them jolts one's senses. Upon riding through an encampment in the 1990's, I said while gasping for emotional breath, "My God, what are we doing to ourselves?"

In 1985, their numbers reached 170,000. By 1995, they exceeded 500,000. By 2000, they reached one million. At the current rate of growth, colonias will exceed 20 million people by 2021 according to a report in the New York Times. It's as if millions of people on the outskirts of Mexico City transplanted themselves onto American soil.

While they grow, they create another crisis for Americans. As conditions worsen, citizens flee out of border areas. Wages continue depressing while functioning towns and cities rock back into Third World slums. Unfortunately, as conditions degrade in the colonias, residents seek aid and shelter in outlying towns. Like a dandelion spreading its seeds, those refugees migrate into our cities.

Since they were unchecked at the border as they crossed in the dead of night or inhabited the colonias for weeks, months or years, they unknowingly carry within their bodies a mixed bag of diseases.

If current lack of border enforcement of our immigration laws continues, as well as continued massive legal immigration of people from Third World countries—American citizens in every state of our nation will eventually suffer in some way due to the onslaught of this invasion.

What is Third World Momentum? Examples abound in Bangladesh, India, South America, Mexico, Africa, the Middle East and China. Their people suffer unrelenting poverty, filth, degradation, relentless misery, starvation, lack of education and health care. Their educational systems falter because their sheer numbers overwhelm any possibility for governments to correct them. Inside that vacuum of ignorance rise dictators who grab power while wielding it for their own benefit.

In the case of oil rich Saddam Hussein of Iraq, the man could have used billions to enrich and educate his people. Instead, he built palaces, drove luxury cars, yachts and enriched his inner circle. He killed people, used torture chambers, gassed his countrymen and built an army to maintain his iron-fisted power. In short, he was a thug.

Nevertheless, he had plenty of goons for inspiration. Kim Jon II of North Korea represses his people using terror like an art form. Millions starve and suffer daily from his actions. Machiavelli would be a Mr. Rogers in comparison to Jon's cruelty. Than Shwe of Burma crushes human beings like stepping on bugs. Hu Jintao of China controls all media, uses spies and executes 4,000 people annually at his whim. Mugabe of Zimbabwe has killed, tortured or displaced 70,000 people since coming to power in 1980. Crown Prince Abullah of Saudi Arabia, at age 80 is number five on the list of the "World's 10 worst Dictators." He's a 'prince' of a man, but oppresses woman, arrests anyone at will and tortures them without hesitation. His people live in fear of him. He would make Hitler and Stalin proud.

Third World Momentum is the reason immigrants overrun Europe. Desperate people by the millions invade First World countries. Why? Those nations maintain functioning societies. But as Third World immigrant numbers grow beyond sustainable 'carrying capacities,' First World societies cannot and will not sustain themselves. Again, why? It's simple. The line grows by 80 million annually.

In the United States, we naively opened our borders with the 1965 Immigration Reform Act, which, by the way, was not debated or voted upon by the American public. It opened the floodgates to the Third World. They have poured in without pause by the millions for nearly four decades. The caveat of this action concerns the fact that none of the countries using the United States or Europe for an escape valve will take responsibility for family planning or their burgeoning numbers of human beings.

In 2004, however, their continued flooding into our country creates severe damage to our functioning society. Everything they fled, they manifest in our country. Without controlling immigration into our society, Third World Momentum will prove the undoing of America.

CHAPTER 2—

JUST HOW FAST ARE THEY INVADING OUR COUNTRY?

"You don't know my people—the squalor, superstitions, the fatalistic sloth that they've wallowed in for generations. You don't know what you're in for if that fleet of brutes ever lands in your lap! Everything will change in this country of yours. They will swallow you up."

Jean Raspail "The Camp Of The Saints"

Raspail's novel depicts a rusted, flea-bitten ship of ragged, illiterate, diseased and slothful refugees headed toward the 'Promised Land.' Their own country suffered war, disease and hopelessness. They escaped, much like Moses toward revelation and a new beginning. However, instead of moving toward their destiny, on their own and by their design, their destination was another country that enjoyed a working civilization. Like a lamprey leeching off a larger fish, the haggard mobs in Raspail's novel targeted another culture for their survival and revival.

Little known to most Americans, in 1987, Population Crisis Committee, headed by Kathleen Mazzocco produced a graph that depicted the 'INTERNATIONAL HUMAN SUFFERING INDEX.' It explained human suffering worldwide. This index (no longer in print) illustrated various states of 'suffering' by different people and countries around the globe.

The Index was presented as a color poster with countries ranked in order. It showed linkage between high suffering and rates of population increases.

Extreme Human Suffering—registers at 75-100. This includes 27 countries with eight percent of the world's population encompassing 430 million people. The list included Mozambique at 95, Angola, Afghanistan (average life span 41 years), Chad, Mali, Ghana, Somalia and Niger.

High Human Suffering—included 56 countries with 65 percent of the world's population encompassing 3.5 billion people. They registered between 50 and 74 on the Human Suffering Index.

The Index followed with 'moderate human suffering' and 'minimal human suffering.' Factors included 10 measures of human welfare encompassing economics, life expectancy, daily calorie supply, clean drinking water, infant immunization, schooling, GNP per capita, inflation, communications, political freedom and civil rights.

The least suffering country was Switzerland at 4, followed by West Germany, Luxembourg, Netherlands and the United States.

The index also took note of whether citizens were free from government terror, free to travel, own property, marry and able to vote for more than one political party.

Sharon Camp and Joseph Speidel, the authors of the Index concluded, "The Human Suffering Index vividly shows that the majority of the world's people must endure lives of poverty and human misery."

They added, "Development efforts such as family planning, health and education could ease the suffering of millions...the responsible planning of births is one of the most effective and least expensive ways of improving the quality of life on earth—both now and in the future—and one of the greatest mistakes of our times is the failure to realize that potential."

Wouldn't it be better for First World countries to give aid, assistance and family planning in countries of origin? Compassionate care would make financial resources work at optimum levels.

Unfortunately, that won't happen in countries where major religions inhibit family planning. The Vatican's Catholic Church hides behind centuries of dogma too thick to crack with a plow. The Pope won't budge on birth control. Being the mouthpiece of God, he condemns millions of the world's Catholic poor to unending overpopulation and suffering. Islam operates on similar dogma created centuries ago. Even many Protestant leaders cling to the past regarding birth control. Their actions create more suffering.

It's estimated that nearly three out of six people on the planet, at 6.2 billion human beings, live in some degree of misery. The World Health Organization estimates that 38,000 children under the age of 10 die daily of starvation or related diseases 365 days per year. It results in an excess of 12 million deaths annually. Additionally, diseases such as tuberculosis kill two million adults annually and millions more adults die of starvation. In Africa, three million died of AIDS in the last few years while another five million contracted the disease. Orphans out-number parents in many areas from the AIDS pandemic.

Third World countries suffer overpopulation, disease and famine at unrelenting levels. What is the cause? It boils down to illiterate populations, lack of education, lack of resources and no family planning. It's the chicken and egg syndrome. They suffer cyclical poverty so deep, their own hands cannot solve it. Thus, it cycles endlessly into 'misery' for all citizens. To make it worse, competing tribes or brutal leaders savagely grab top spots while fomenting violence at all levels. It is for millions—Darwin's hell of survival at the lowest common denominator.

Yes, you will hear from high level politicians that more aid is needed in the form of medical, educational and monetary investment. But, in reality, most financial aid from other countries ends up in the Third World rulers' Swiss bank accounts. "Foreign aid is the redistribution of wealth from the poor of a rich nation to the rich of a poor nation." Unknown

One need only look at Emelda Marcos' 3,000 pairs of shoes to find the answer to where foreign aid ends up. It's the same for any country in the world. The top dogs take it all, live in luxury and people starve in the streets. You may inspect such countries as Iraq, Saudi Arabia, Iran, Argentina, Ecuador, Egypt and Mexico for starters.

You may ask yourself: How fast is this immigration invasion overtaking America? How quickly will it devastate this country? Governor Lamm illustrates our dilemma in Chapter 3 where shows us, 'HOW TO DESTROY AMERICA.'

To bring it into perspective, the United States totaled 199 million people in 1964. In 40 years, due mostly to runaway immigration levels, we added 93 million people. If you look at the last page of this book, you will see a graph showing our severe population growth created by immigration. The American female stands at 2.03 fertility level, so it's not us doing to ourselves. It's our politicians doing it to us.

Realize this sobering demographic fact: From the current 6.2 billion, the predicted population of the earth by mid-century is estimated to be a low of 7.9 to as high as 9.8 billion people. Along the way, the 'human suffering index' explodes out of control.

As foreign countries can't handle their poor, uneducated citizens, desperate people hire international 'coyotes' to bring newcomers, in mass, across our borders. Presently, it's estimated that 2,200 illegals cross our Florida, Mexican and Canadian borders daily every day of the year. The majority crosses over the Rio Grande.

'SER,' which in Spanish means, 'To Be,' is a secret underground railroad with 80 safe house centers across America where they are given forged documents and jobs in all sectors of our country. Legal immigrants land on our shores at 4,200 per day. Along with our population momentum created in the past 39 years by massive immigration, we grow by a net gain daily of 8,200 people. That equals 3.0 to 3.3 million added each year. Past mid-century, we shall add a staggering 200 million totaling a half-billion people.

It begs the question. Fifty years ago, Bangladesh, China and India ignored their exploding populations. Today, China bursts out of its demographic britches with 1.3 billion people. India hit 1.1 billion. Bangladesh, a country no bigger than Ohio, houses a bone crushing 129 million people. Their hopelessness exceeds what most Americans can imagine. Those countries wallow in such quagmires of humanity, such piles of bodies—that their 'suffering index' sets new benchmarks on the scale.

What do they do? They flee to Europe and America. I talked to a citizen of Bangladesh who immigrated to the USA in 1990. He was my cab driver in Seattle, Washington in 2002. I asked him about his country's population. He said it sickened him so much that he would not go back. I asked him why? He said his Muslim religion encouraged every woman to have as many children as possible. I noted that his country exceeded its carrying capacity and that such massive population overload would destroy any hope of 'quality of life' and 'standard of living.'

"Why not practice family planning?" I asked.
"It would go against Allah's wishes," he said.
"But it creates such human misery," I said.
"One must not go against Allah's wishes," he replied.
"How many kids do you have?" I asked, in frustration.
"Seven with one on the way," he said, proudly.
"How many do you expect to have?" I asked, calmly.
"That is for Allah to decide," he said.

Having lived in America for 12 years, this man had not made the connection concerning quality of life and number of children. Having been influenced by America's educational system, he was as out of touch with reality as if he had remained in Bangladesh. His story stands as an example why Third World immigrants continue large families of five to eight children when they immigrate to First World countries.

This is a graphic example of Third World Momentum. The more we import the poor and hungry of the world, they maintain their rituals, traditions and mores.

How fast are illegal aliens invading America? A quick review shows between three and four million reside in California. An average of 1,500 people adds to California's population daily. They house nine million legal immigrants. More than 600 cars are added to their highways daily. It may be noted that the cost of educating illegal alien children exceeds $2.2 billion annually. California suffers a $38 billion debt. Additionally, two million of their students attend classes in trailers. Even more sobering, one new school must be built daily, seven days a week, 365 days a year to keep up with the influx of students. Added to that, they must hire teachers who can speak up to 100 languages. To make matters worse, at current growth rates, California will add 20 million people in the next 30 years. Like a horse being loaded with too much weight, its legs buckle and it fails under an impossible load. California children are failing from classrooms being overcrowded, violent, antagonistic and dangerous.

Their new movie star Governor Arnold Schwarzenneger may be likened to a man in a rowboat. He won the California governor's chair by his image as a man with an invincible body. Let's face it, 'The Terminator' was one bad dude! Arnold's task of 'rowing' that state out of its budget crisis resembles a man who has volunteered to row his boat up the entire length of the Colorado River. You can imagine him furiously rowing up river against Lava Falls Rapid (Class 5 and really ugly with nine foot rollers and I've rafted it screaming for dear life!) of the Grand Canyon and pushing against all odds to make the headwaters of the legendary river. With his amazing strength and rhetoric, yes, he's making progress, but, he's being swept downstream to ultimate exhaustion and failure. He will never reach his goal. Little wonder that California once held the top spot as the nation's best educational system but has plummeted to one of the worst. Who loses? American kids! Your kids!

Texas, with 1.5 million illegal aliens, suffered in 2001, $86.6 billion in total state debt. Source: Texas Bond Review Board. Like Arnold, they can't succeed no matter how hard they row because immigrants continue 'flooding' into their state without end. Last year, the Lone Star State suffered teacher shortages.

They hired non-professional baby-sitters for classrooms across the state. Consider what happened to education for Texans' kids.

Colorado, with 144,000 to 200,000 reported illegal aliens, suffered a loss of $140.6 million to educate illegal alien offspring. Source: Colorado Department of Education. That state is nearly $1 billion in debt. Colorado's problem stems from the lack of water. With the projected additions of five million people by mid-century, they won't have enough water for drinking let alone floating a rowboat.

Do you see a pattern? Similar figures mount for Georgia, Florida, North Carolina and many other states. Most states run a budget crisis. Look at the 'CHILLING COSTS OF IMMIGRATION' in Chapter 25 for a greater perspective of the costs to you. Illegal alien migrants make a lot of money for a few people in high places, but you pay escalating costs in the process.

How fast are illegal aliens advancing and what is the terrorist threat? In 2002, according to 27-year veteran Border Patrol Special Agent John W. Slagle (retired), the U.S. Border Patrol captured 37,000 non-Mexican border crashers. They average 1 in 4 captured. Of those 37,000, a staggering 7,500 arrived from terror-sponsoring countries like Iran, Saudi Arabia, Iraq, Afghanistan and other Middle Eastern countries.

I stood on the Mexican border in Arizona in April, 2004. When it comes to Homeland Security, it's a joke. Anyone can walk or drive across the border at will. What's more, they DO, by the thousands daily!

These questions astound my senses: Why would Democrats and Republicans support this invasion? Why would they break their sworn oath of office? Why don't individual senators and congressmen/women see what is happening? How can President Bush turn a blind eye to recent polls that register 85 percent of Americans want illegal immigration stopped and legal immigration sharply reduced to under 200,000 per year as it was before the IMMIGRATION REFORM ACT OF 1965? Why don't they comprehend the destruction to our school systems, language and medical care? What happens when diseases such as leprosy, TB, Chagas and hepatitis hit their children?

It's simple. Bush comes from the wealthy class. He's never struggled to meet a mortgage payment or grocery bill in his life. His kids never battled through multiple languages and incompetent or exasperated teachers in their schools. In a recent book, titled: "BOY GENIUS," page 73, published in 1999 by Dubose, Reid, Cannon, Texas Governor George Bush said, "If they can wade across the Rio Grande, they can stay." That alone gives you an idea of his stance on illegal immigration. More sobering, none of the democratic hopefuls addressed illegal immigration. John Kerry won the nomination, but he equals Bush in his disdain for addressing our immigration laws. Kerry's senate voting record illustrates his lack of representing American citizens. He supports legalizing illegal aliens and will not address stopping this invasion.

Most Senators and House members come from an elite class, although not all. Other than Tom Tancredo of Colorado and Senator Charles Norwood of Georgia, few in the Congress have lifted a finger to stop illegal immigration before or since 9/11. We can thank Teddy Kennedy for authoring the destruction of our country via his 1965 IMMIGRATION REFORM ACT. As can be imagined, Kennedy has never stepped foot into real life America in his 'forever' senate career. He remains insulated, isolated, aloof and privileged during his storied life. Chappaquiddick not withstanding! Such senators as John McCain, former Senator Spencer Abrahams of Michigan, Representatives Kolbe and Flake of Arizona—encourage illegal immigration by taking no action against it. Colorado representative Mark Udall as well as Diana Degette support massive immigration and do nothing to stop illegal immigration. Senator Orrin Hatch in Utah and Congressman Chris Cannon do their best to assist illegal aliens in any way they can. Nancy Pelosi of California works in favor of illegal alien immigration. The list is endless showing our elected officials not doing their jobs. They support of the Dream Act, which helps illegal aliens' offspring with millions of our taxpayer dollars—thus encouraging more illegal immigration. When they didn't enforce our immigration laws in the first place, they support giving our money to those who broke them. Additionally, they supported H-1B and L-1 visas which have displaced over one million American workers. They support endless 'chain migration,' 'diversity visas' and 'anchor babies' by their having done NOTHING to stop them. Who pays? You do!

Is there any wonder why illegal aliens cross our borders? Who is helping them? President Bush and Congress, that's who.

Are your senators and congressmen assisting this incursion? More than likely! How can you tell? It's easy because the majority of Congress isn't doing anything to stop this invasion.

CHAPTER 3—

HOW TO DESTROY AMERICA: IMMIGRATION DESTROYED THE ROMAN EMPIRE AND IT IS DOING THE SAME TO THE UNITED STATES

"If we don't persuade Congress to lower immigration to traditional levels of 175,000 per year, we'll condemn Americans to lives of increasing sprawl, congestion and economic failure."

Roy Beck, IMMIGRATION BY THE NUMBERS

History dictates that no great nation lasts forever. None have withstood the vagaries of time. Looking back through the hourglass of years—Rome, Persia, Egypt, Spain, France, Britain and Germany—all of them—rose to triumphal status only to plummet into defeat via war or they coasted into mediocrity. The historian

Arnold Toynbee observed that all great civilizations rise and fall. But it's their method of demise that creates an intriguing point. He said, "An autopsy of history would show that all great nations commit suicide."

Ironically, massive numbers of Vandals marched up Rome's superbly engineered roads and swept into the center of the empire—destroying everything in their path. While Nero fiddled, Rome burned. Roman armies, long since fat and lazy from being king of the hill for too long, suffered 'mongrel hordes' attacking from every direction.

In a recent movie, "TROY," starring Brad Pit as Achilles, the King of Troy (played by Peter O'Toole) asked for advice from his chief counsel on whether or not to bring the Trojan Horse into the city. The king's son said, "Burn it here on the beach." In the years before, the Greeks could not penetrate the walls of Troy. The head counsel, much like present day Karl Rove the chief counsel to President Bush, said, "Bring it into the city as a sign from the gods."

As you know, once inside the gates, Achilles and his men jumped out of the bowels of the horse and burned Troy. The same thing is happening to modern day America with immigration.

An historical connection and exact duplication of the overthrow of Rome can be equated with September 11, 2001 when Muslim terrorists flew our own airliners into the World Trade Centers in New York City. They used our own flight schools to learn how to fly our own aircraft. Our lack of enforcement of our immigration laws over the past 20 years assisted the deadly attack that killed 3,000 innocent people. Atrocity struck because our FBI, CIA, president(s) and Congress became complacent.

But another form of national suicide manifests itself in the destruction of America. In October of 2003, former Colorado Governor Richard D. Lamm stood in front of a group of civic leaders with a spell binding speech. He said, "I have a plan to destroy America. If you believe, as many do, that America is too smug, too white bread, too self-satisfied, too rich, let's destroy America. It is not that hard to do. History shows that nations are more fragile than their citizens think."

"Here is my plan on how to destroy America," he said.

"We must first make America a bilingual-bicultural country. History shows, in my opinion, that no nation can survive the tension, conflict, and antagonism of two competing languages and cultures. It is a blessing for an individual to be bilingual; it is a curse for a society to be bilingual. One scholar, Seymour Martin Lipset, put it this way: "The histories of bilingual and bicultural societies that do not assimilate are histories of turmoil, tension and tragedy. Canada, Belgium, Malaysia, Lebanon—all face crises of national existence in which minorities press for autonomy, if not independence. Pakistan and Cyprus have divided. Nigeria suppressed an ethnic rebellion. France faces difficulties with its Basques, Bretons and Corsicans."

"I would then invent "multiculturalism" and encourage immigrants to maintain their own culture. I would make it an article of belief that all cultures are equal: that there are no cultural differences that are important. I would declare it an article of faith that the Black and Hispanic dropout rate is only due to prejudice and discrimination by the majority. Every other explanation is out-of-bounds.

"We can make the United States an "Hispanic Quebec" without much effort. The key is to celebrate diversity rather than unity. As Benjamin Schwarz said in the <u>Atlantic Monthly</u> recently:

> "...the apparent success of our own multiethnic and multicultural experiment might have been achieved not by tolerance but by hegemony. Without the dominance that once dictated ethnocentrically, and what it meant to be an American, we are left with only tolerance and pluralism to hold us together."

"I would encourage all immigrants to keep their own language and culture. I would replace the melting pot metaphor with a salad bowl metaphor. It is important to insure that we have various cultural sub-groups living in America reinforcing their differences rather than Americans, emphasizing their similarities.

"Having done all this, I would make our fastest growing demographic group the least educated-I would add a second underclass, unassimilated, undereducated, and antagonistic to our population. I would have this second underclass have a 50 percent drop out rate from school.

"I would then get the big foundations and big business to give these efforts lots of money. I would invest in ethnic identity, and I would establish the cult of Victimology. I would get all minorities to think their lack of success was all the fault of the majority–I would start a grievance industry blaming all minority failure on the majority population.

"I would establish dual citizenship and promote divided loyalties. I would "celebrate diversity." Diversity is a wonderfully seductive word. It stresses differences rather than commonalties. Diverse people worldwide are mostly engaged in hating each other—that is, when they are not killing each other. A diverse, peaceful, or stable society is against most historical precedent. People undervalue the unity it takes to keep a nation together, and we can take advantage of this myopia. Look at the ancient Greeks. Dorf's <u>World History</u> tells us:

"The Greeks believed that they belonged to the same race; they possessed a common language and literature; and they worshipped the same gods. All Greece took part in the Olympic games in honor of Zeus and all Greeks venerated the shrine of Apollo at Delphi. A common enemy Persia threatened their liberty. Yet, all of these bonds together were not strong enough to overcome two factors . . . (local patriotism and geographical conditions that nurtured political divisions . . .)

"If we can put the emphasis on the "Pluribus," instead of the "Unum," we can balkanize America as surely as Kosovo.

"Then I would place all these subjects off limits–make it taboo to talk about. I would find a word similar to "Heretic" in the 16th century–that stopped discussion and paralyzed thinking. Words like "racist" and "xenophobe" halt argument and conversation.

"Having made America a bilingual-bicultural country, having established multiculturalism, having the large foundations fund the doctrine of "Victimology, I would next make it impossible to enforce our immigration laws. I would develop a mantra- "that because immigration <u>has been</u> good for America, it must <u>always</u> be good." I would make every individual immigrant sympatric and ignore the cumulative impact."

No applause followed. A chilling apprehension rose like an ominous cloud above each person at the conference. Every American in that room knew that everything Lamm enumerated was proceeding methodically, quietly, darkly and pervasively across the United States today. Every discussion is suppressed. Over 100 languages rip the foundation of our educational system and national cohesiveness. Barbaric cultures that practice 'female genital mutilation' and 'Santeria' are growing as we celebrate 'diversity' over unity and assimilation. American jobs vanish into the Third World as corporations import the Third World into America—take note of California and other states—to date, 10-13 million illegal aliens and growing.

It reminded me of George Orwell's book, '1984.' In that story, three slogans are Engraved in the Ministry of Truth building. "War is peace," "Freedom is slavery," and "Ignorance is strength." It dawned on everyone at the conference that this great republic is in profound trouble and worsening fast. If this immigration invasion is not stopped soon, like the Vandals that overran the Roman Empire or the Greeks who burned Troy, the United States will soon find itself in the dustbin of history.

Unless Bush stops fiddling and starts leading, and Congress does what it was elected to do, and that is to 'defend and protect' from enemies both 'foreign and domestic,' this nation will not survive. Finally, the most powerful leaders of America are its citizens. It's been said, "Democracy is not a spectator sport." Americans must take action with a collective voice and passion like their forefathers who charged up the gangplanks with intent to stop taxation without representation. They forced the issue with the now famous Boston Tea Party.

It is up to 21st century Americans to carry their great passion into action in order to preserve our nation, which is so woefully NOT being served by our president, state governors, mayors and Congress. Instead of serving illegal aliens rights groups, immigration lawyers who obstruct our laws, corporations hiring illegal aliens, allowing illegal alien crime syndicates to continue untouched, and allowing violent groups like LULAC, MALDEF and La RAZA to gain power—we must take action. In Chapter 9, you will see the drive and seriousness of these organizations.

It's time for another Boston Tea Party. This one needs to be called "A TEN YEAR MORATORIUM ON ALL IMMIGRATION PARTY."

CHAPTER 4—

OH WHAT CHAOS WITHOUT A COMMON LANGUAGE!

"The key to a cohesive community stems from the fact that neighbors can talk to one another. If they don't speak the same language, they become strangers. That leads to mistrust, animosity and alienation. California is a perfect example. Los Angeles is no longer an American city. Very few speak English. You can't understand people from your own country. That's because they aren't Americans and they aren't from America. They've invaded our country."

Sandi Lynn

In his speech in front of an audience of the Federation for American Immigration Reform in Washington, DC, October 19, 2003, former Colorado Governor Richard D. Lamm informed a stunned audience that one of the best ways to destroy America would be to make it a multi-lingual country. He presented examples from nations around the world that failed because of incompatible languages.

One look at France will show you a nation that has imported more Middle Eastern people, so much so, that given time, they will be speaking Arabic, not French. France will no longer be France. What is even more puzzling is that they did it to themselves. Not enough people spoke up before it was too late.

Norway embarks on the same path of self-destruction on a smaller scale. They've imported 400,000 Middle Eastern immigrants in an attempt to 'multiculturalize' their four million Scandinavian mono-ethnic society. Already, they suffer horrific consequences of increased crime, female genital mutilation, drugs, enclaving and language conflicts from immigrants who refuse Norway's culture and language.

But what the idealistic social planners who usurp power don't realize and do not consider is their own isolation from the harsh realities they force on their countrymen. The same thing is happening in the United States as men in power force this massive immigration crisis into this country. Men like Senator Ted Kennedy, Senator Orrin Hatch of Utah, Senator Wayne Allard and Representative Mark Udall of Colorado or Nancy Pelosi of California have never been down in the dregs of society or had their kids attend schools with extensive language conflicts, drugs, gangs and fellow students who could care less about school or anything else for that matter. It is nasty in inner city schools. I formerly taught there and couldn't wait to escape.

As Lamm said in his speech, "The histories of bilingual and bicultural societies that do not assimilate are histories of turmoil, tension and tragedy."

Already in California, millions of adults and kids from south of the border speak only Spanish, wave only Mexican flags and render their allegiance to other countries. Their enclaves welcome only those of their language. All others are excluded. Stick a feather in the cap of 'multiculturalism.' It's growing like a malignant cancer moving through California with increasing speed. It's infecting Miami, Houston, Chicago, Detroit, Atlanta and hundreds of other cities at breakneck speed. It pits itself against our nation while Americans lose their jobs, homes, communities and the rule-of-law. Little wonder 800,000 California residents fled the state in 2003. At some point, there will be no place to run.

In his book, "America Extinguished: Mass Immigration and the Disintegration of American Culture," Dr. Samuel T. Francis states, "Nothing is more basic to assimilation of immigrants in a foreign culture than learning its language. But many Hispanics and other immigrants are not learning English, a strong sign they haven't assimilated and don't intend to. Moreover, many Hispanics have a militant race consciousness and identify with Mexico, not America."

But as this loss of our single most important cohesive aspect of America falls prey to dozens and even hundreds of foreign languages, what does it mean to average American citizens?

What if your neighbor on the left spoke only German? And, the one on the right spoke only French? What if they had no intention of learning English? What if the one across the street spoke only Russian. What if the only theater in town offered movies in Spanish? What if you spoke only English?

Would you feel a part of a meaningful community?

Fans of Thornton Wilder's "OUR TOWN" will remember Mrs. Webb's daydream of taking a trip to far-off exotic climes, *"Where they don't speak English and don't even want to."*

"BIENVENIDOS" — The large sign over the entry to an elementary school in Escondido, California welcomes all that enter. Below that enthusiastic salutation, second billing is given in smaller letters in English—"GREETINGS." All who enter know which language is most valued.

"We are NOT a Minority" is emblazoned below the fierce-faced Indo-Hispanic on a billboard in Los Angeles. An American citizen visiting the City of Angels would be mortified to see dozens of foreign languages on billboards and storefronts everywhere in Southern California. Even more frightening are T-shirts that read, "Go back to where you came from Gringos." Among the logos scattered through the high school textbook, "THE MEXICAN-AMERICAN HERITGE," are clench-fisted, open-mouthed figures declaring "Viva La Raza" (long live our race) and

25

a picture of an artist atop a ladder leaning against the Statue of Liberty. He has already carved 'AZTLAN' across Lady Liberty's base and adds traditional Mexican symbols across Liberty's gown. He's reaching for her crown and flame. His actions represent a symbolic 'taking' of America from Americans—which is not lost to young Hispanics.

On the other side of our nation, a Mexican Indian girl, illegal alien immigrant—whose infant has been taken from her custody, is suing because the Alabama child welfare agency didn't give her custody advice in her native Mayan tongue of K'iche. She speaks neither Spanish nor English. Another Mexi-Indi woman is suing a hospital for not providing her with translations in her Indian language.

Jorge Ramos, Univision anchorman and author of "NO BORDERS: A JOURNALIST'S SEARCH FOR HOME" was asked why Latin American immigrants are retaining so much of their culture, while Irish or Italian immigrants, for example, in the past have tried so hard to assimilate?

"I think it's particular to Latino culture. The new wave of immigrants and the second generation Latinos are truly transforming this country, underlining that it is a multi-ethnic, multi-racial country. The country is going through an incredible demographic revolution. **By 2025, there will be more Latinos than (non-Hispanic) whites in this country. This will be a Hispanic nation,** *and we are in the middle of this process. In this process of Latinization, Latinos are affecting everything. Spanish is being spoken in every corner of the country."*

One of the most powerful methods for America's destruction is to allow immigrants to keep their own language without adhering to America's language and culture. The ensuing confusion, conflict and violence will dismantle our nation's ability to communicate with ourselves. Given enough time, it would be like the computer inside the Star Ship Enterprise not being able to communicate with itself and all systems becoming inoperable—thus a complete breakdown ensues.

That's enough of describing the growing situation in America today. What would English-speaking Americans, who created, fought and died for this country, have to say about the invasion of our nation by those who have no intention of becoming a part of the melting pot? Indeed, anti-American immigrants give ample indication on taking over America for their own purposes.

The California recall election was a last gasp effort to bring that state back from the abyss. Texas and Arizona are not far behind. Michigan, Georgia and North Carolina struggle with 100 different languages in their school systems. They are failing.At what point will too many finally be enough? When will all the meatpacking plants gain enough illegal labor? How long before all construction jobs speak nothing but Spanish and all American construction workers stand in unemployment lines? How will cities maintain a tax base for the estimated 1,500,000 illegal alien students who speak only foreign languages?

At what point will we begin to pull our country out of our $7 trillion bankruptcy debt? How will we survive environmentally and socially as we overwhelm our 'carrying capacity' if another 20, 50 or 100 million legal and illegal aliens cross our borders?

Alarming facts show our country in trouble. California and many other states suffer from the Tower of Babel. Those immigrants DON'T want to learn English. They're not concerned or eager to become Americans. Can we survive as a nation of 10, 20 or 100 languages? The evidence from thousands of years verifies that we cannot.

If every immigrant with a different language moved into America while demanding his language be placed on road signs, it would be impossible to fund or execute such a project. Commensurately, what if every immigrant demanded schools offering books and teachers in his language? How about demanding Americans start driving on the left side of the road because those immigrants came from a country that drove on the left side? Imagine the chaos! As it is, they demand driver's license tests in their languages. Worse, we comply. What if they wanted their country's money used so they feel more at home in our country? How about their weights and measurements? How can we incorporate their driving practices of running red lights, which is a norm in Third World countries I have visited?

In the latest ballot for governor of California, a multitude of languages was placed on the election ballot, thanks to a law President Clinton signed before leaving office. He opened a Pandora's Box of problems that we must suffer.

If we accept one, two or a dozen languages within our country, what are the prospects for our continuing self-governance if we lose the common currency of language? How will we debate in unison for our growth as a nation without the ability to talk among ourselves?

It begs the question? Whose country is this, anyway? English has been our official language for over 200 years and it's worked perfectly. It is the single most important adhesive aspect of American life and unity.

However, we hear about Mr. Bush and politicians pandering for the Hispanic vote. What about the American vote? American Hispanic voters fall prey to this immigration invasion as much as Black, White or Native Americans. Our jobs vanish as our wages depress to Third World levels. All of us suffer from the loss of our English language. Terry Anderson, an African-American radio host in Los Angeles is so angry at the loss of jobs, destruction of schools and English for fellow blacks in his area that he broadcasts once a week on his radio station that, "We need righteous indignation because this is our country, not theirs!"

Governor Lamm made a compelling point when he said, "America has been successful because we have become one people. There is a 'social glue' of a common language, a shared history and uniting symbols that tied us together. We live under a common flag, which we honor and salute. We can remember Cinco de Mayo, St. Patrick's day and Oktoberfest, and we can buy more salsa than ketchup without endangering our national soul. But we must avoid becoming a Hispanic Quebec; we must stay one people and one nation. A nation is much more than a place on a map. It is a single state of mind, a shared vision, and a recognition that we are all in this together. A nation needs a common language as it needs a common currency. You have to share something with your neighbor besides a zip code.

We need many things to tie us together, but one indispensable element must be that we all speak one common language."

If you look around this strife torn world, former Governor Lamm's words ring true. If you take a second look, we are quickly losing English as our national language. Our problems multiply with every single immigrant, legal or illegal, that comes into this country without speaking English or desiring to learn it. As more people cannot speak English, confusion reigns. That leads to conflict and finally, when people are unable to understand one another, they resort to separation and violence. It is further inflamed via disparities of multiculturalism.

We slide further into Third World Momentum.

CHAPTER 5—

ALL CULTURES ARE NOT EQUAL OR COMPATIBLE

"Why is it in Iraq that the Sunnis, Kurds and Shiites are all living in the same country, but try to kill or suppress each other in the name of their ethnocentric sense of self-righteousness?"

American citizen

In his speech on how to destroy America, Governor Lamm said, "Invent 'multiculturalism' and encourage immigrants to maintain their own culture. I would make it an article of belief that all cultures are equal.

"Pretend there are no cultural differences. I would make it an article of faith that the Black and Hispanic dropout rates are due to prejudice and discrimination by the majority. Every other explanation is out of bounds."

While sitting in that Washington, DC audience, I understood exactly where he was heading with his points for destroying America.

Multiculturalism is an ideal whose time will never come. It may seemingly work in the rarefied air of a college campus where intellectual order dominates; however, it breaks down quickly in the general population. It breaks down even faster in an uneducated population. Mixing cultures runs counter to humanity's nature. Races barely tolerate each other in the best of circumstances, but incompatible cultures, no matter how good the climate, do not mix.

"Diversity within a nation destroys unity and leads to civil wars. Immigration, a benefit during the youth of a nation, can act as a disease in its mature state. Too much internal diversity in large nations has led to violence and disintegration," said Garret Hardin. "We are now in the process of destabilizing our own country through the unlimited acceptance of massive immigration. The magic words of the destabilizers are "diversity" and "multiculturalism."

Beirut is a manifest example. At one time, the diversity of that city was beautiful. However, as the proportions of disparate ethnic groups changed, peace vanished.

It's been proven throughout history. It's been proven in America numerous times.

Yes, America celebrates different cultures. We honor all walks of life. The Germans celebrate Oktoberfest. The Italians champion opera, Columbus and pasta. The Irish celebrate leprechauns and green beer. Africans celebrate hip hop, jazz and blues. Hispanics enjoy Cinco de Mayo. The list is endless.

However, after every cultural celebration, Americans celebrate themselves as Americans first and ethnic origin second. Previous to 1960's, no hyphenated-Americans existed. Everyone spoke English.

Today, elites, churches and corporations force a culture crisis into the United States like never in the history of this country or any country. Before the 1965 Immigration Reform Act, only 178,000 immigrants moved into our country annually. They spread across the nation while quickly absorbing into the general population. They eagerly learned English because they wanted to become Americans. Even if they originated in poverty and illiteracy, they framed their goals by entering into the American Dream.

With over two million arriving yearly, that's all changed. Worse, they're arriving from countries with incompatible cultures and practices beyond the scope of a First World nation.

France, Germany, Norway, Holland and Italy today struggle with massive influxes of Muslims whose treatment of women and children run counter to anything known in their societies. The question asked is, "How far can Europeans bend to accommodate so many immigrants with such diverse and in many cases incompatible cultures?" Marzia Monciatti, a Florence city official said, "Certain cultural traditions are at such odds with Italian values that accepting them in any form is impossible." She said that having Romanian Gypsy immigrant girls forced into marriage at 13 was unacceptable. She could not and would not accept genital cutting of girls.

Norway grapples with its own burgeoning Muslim population that practices female genital mutilation in what most educated persons consider a barbaric act.

In her book, "THE TROUBLE WITH ISLAM," Canadian Muslim Irshad Manji wrote, "My cause is the democracy of thought and freedom of expression...I want to give my fellow Muslims permission to think...can you tell me why Islam is at the heart of terrorism and human-rights violations?"

At the center of Islam's message is that all other religions and their followers are 'infidels' and to be converted or killed. It is an antagonistic, imperialist religion rooted in the Dark Ages. It is said that 'Islam' means 'peace.' In fact, it means 'submission.' It means to gain the submission from all, if necessary, by force.

The Quran, Sura 5, verse 85, describes the inevitable enmity between Muslims and non-Muslims: "Strongest among men in enmity to the Believers wilt thou find the Jews and Pagans." Sura 9, verse 5, adds: "Then fight and slay the Pagans wherever you find them. And seize them, beleaguer them and lie in wait for them, in every stratagem of war." Al-Ma'idah 5:51.11 says: "O ye who believe! Take not the Jews and the Christians for friends."

Sura 2:193 states: "Fight them until Islam reigns supreme." Sura 8:12 demands: "Instill terror in the hearts of unbelievers...cut off their heads and cut off the tips of their fingers."

Recent videotaped beheadings of Nick Berg in Iraq and Paul Johnson in Saudi Arabia and barbaric violence to civilian Americans bear witness to the seriousness of followers of Islam.

The Quran insists that all nations must be fought "until they embrace Islam."

It is little wonder the WTC martyrs flew airplanes into the towers. They are promised 'Paradise' (Heaven) where "There will be gushing fountains...therein are bashful virgins whom neither man or jinnee will have touched before...virgins as fair as corals and rubies." (Sura 55) "The smallest reward for people of Paradise is an abode where there are 72 wives...."

Islam believes in a theocratic state ruled by religious law inflicting horribly cruel punishments such as the ones perpetrated under Prince Abudulla of Saudi Arabia.

Once gaining majorities in sheer numbers, Muslims don't fool around. They take over. Additionally, they play only by their rules. Their rules, as we have seen, decree brutality in most parts of the Islamic world.

In Belgium, Muslims have reached such numbers in their new adopted state that, instead of assimilating, they are calling for their language to be included as one of the official languages of Belgium. Their main goal is to stop government policy from integrating Muslims into Belgium society. Muslims have created their own 'citizen militia' that patrols Antwerp streets. The web site of the European Arab League explodes with anti-Semitic propaganda. In 2003, arsonists attempted to burn down an Antwerp synagogue. The Muslim immigrants openly ignore the mores and culture of their host country. As their numbers grow so does their boldness and disregard for their adopted country. They will force their religion on Belgium at some point because it is the nature of Islam. (Sura 2.193: "Fight them until Islam reigns supreme.")

What does that portend for the United States? It places American Christians, Jews and all other religions at risk. In most Middle Eastern countries where Islam dominates, no other religions are permitted. After having been enrolled in a 'madrassa' religious school, Manji wrote, "I imbibed two major messages—that women are second class, and that Jews are not to be trusted and are treacherous."

She demands that Islamic countries not blame the West and the CIA for their problems. Manji points out the brutal governments of Syria and Saudi Arabia, "Which sustain long histories of repressing, torturing and killing their citizens." It may be added those populations are kept in subservience by limiting their education.

If we inspect the top terrorist acts around the world in the past 15 years, they have come at the hands of Islam—Lockerbie Flight 103, Balli nightclub, WTC (twice), Pentagon, Pennsylvania corn field, Marines bombed in Lebanon, Berlin nightclub bombing, two U.S. embassies in Africa, bombing of USS Cole, sniper Lee Malvo, killing reporter Daniel Pearl, U.S. Army American Muslim soldier, Sergeant Hasan Akbar, who fragged senior officers—killing two in the first weeks of the Iraq War, train bombing in Madrid in March, burning, dragging behind cars and hanging of American corpses in Iraq, beheading of Nick Berg and Paul Johnson on television, Korean businessman Kim and, chillingly, many more to come.

In his chilling book, "Onward Muslim Soldier" by Robert Spencer, he unmasks basic aspects of Islam:

*Is jihad really a spiritual struggle? The traditional Muslim thinkers definitely refute this notion and argue that all Muslims must wage physical war against non-Muslims.

*Why the threat of violent jihad around the world is growing daily, despite claims that Islam is a "religion of peace."

*"We are not Americans. We are Muslims." The open hatred that many American Muslims display for the United States.

*"I want to see the black flag of Islam flying over Downing Street!" Why the influential British Muslim leader who said that may someday get his wish.

*"Bin Laden is a good guy. Everyone likes him in the Muslim world, there is nothing wrong with the man and his beliefs." Why these sentiments (spoken by a Western Muslim) are more

widespread among Muslims than American Muslim spokesmen would have you believe.

The big question here is, "Do we want to continue importing this kind of philosophy from the Dark Ages into our First World country? The emphatic answer is NO!

Additionally, America sets standards. Is it elitism or racism on America's part to subscribe to standards of sanitation, behavior and literacy for the majority? Is orderliness in neighborhoods condescending? Or, is this rational thinking and common sense prevention of social breakdown?

What will be the outcome of forcing incompatible cultures into an ever-closer salad bowl? What happens when multiple languages are added? What if illiteracy dominates the population?

Violence results! It's like throwing a cat and dog into the same cage. It's like adding gasoline to a fire. It's like pitting a scorpion against a moth. Scorpions seize and crush their victim with claws, immobilizing it by stinging if necessary. It's their nature.

Even with America's diverse population and known tolerance for diversity, can educated American citizens accept female genital cutting, Latin culture cock and dog fighting, Santeria animal sacrifice beheadings, horse tripping, bull fights or 13 year old girls being forced into marriage in certain cultures importing themselves into our Heartland? In Miami today, during holidays, Cubans fire guns off into the night for celebration. They possess no appreciation where the bullets fall or care who gets hurt. The police are powerless because so many people adhere to this cultural violence. It's another case of Third World Momentum engulfing America.

Lucky for the United States over the decades, if someone didn't like being around an incompatible group, the offended citizen moved to a new local. It's why African- Americans moved north after slavery to escape lynching. It's why white Americans fled to the suburbs as slums grew. It's why Californians flee their state today as three million illegal aliens invaded from south of the border.

35

But all that flight doesn't solve the problem of incompatible cultures. Additionally, it doesn't address enclaving.

Lamm might have noted in his speech that high schools and colleges in the most diverse states offer the most non-multicultural clubs in the nation. Instead of getting together to discover their similarities, high school kids form 'Philippine Pride Club,' 'Hispanics United,' 'Chinese Friendship Club,' 'Asian Student's Union,' 'Korean Unity Club,' 'Vietnamese Club' and a dozen others. One student tried to create a high school 'Caucasian Club' in order to explore her own roots. She was immediately vilified as a "racist."

Not mentioned by Lamm was the proliferation of criminal clubs such as the '18TH Street Gang' in California. This 20,000-member club ranks as one of the most violent, deadly and fearless organizations known since Chicago's Al Capone or any of New York's crime families. Worse, because illegal aliens and even legal immigrants, in many cases are uneducated with no hope for a job, they are welcomed into these 'crime enclaves' with open arms.

Also not mentioned are the Muslim enclaves forming in Detroit, Michigan, Freemont, California and hundreds of cities across America. Instead of becoming American citizens with Middle Eastern origins, they are remaining Middle Eastern entities while they create 'city-states' within America. They keep their own languages while eschewing English or American culture. In the process, they grow more fractious and disenchanted within our country. As the myth of 'multicultural pleasantries' wears off, we can expect dissension, separation and violence. What we've done is imported 'jihad' into our own country.

Another example even more pronounced is the fact that 9.2 million Mexicans have immigrated, both legally and illegally, into the United States. That figure represents nearly one-tenth of the population of Mexico, which has moved, wholesale, into America and has taken up residence. They have turned Southern California into a clone of Mexico. It's an example of immigration enclaves and balkanization.

Huntington Park, California, 15 years ago stood at 80 percent Caucasian citizens. Today, via illegal immigration, it is now 98 percent Latino. Rosairo Marin, the mayor, proudly calls

Huntington Park, "...the most Mexican city outside Mexico." It features an unbroken line of Spanish language stores and restaurants. More than eight of 10 residents are ethnic Mexicans and a large percentage are illegal aliens—numbering over 25,000 of the total of 65,000.

What happened as American citizens fled the invasion? The median income dropped by 40 percent. Unemployment rose to 8.6 percent. Schools burst at the seams and the dropout rates rocketed into the stratosphere. In 2002, less than 40 percent of Huntington Park High's original class graduated with a diploma.

Huntington Park's Latino street gangs monopolize the police department's time. As usual, thanks to Special Order 40, illegal aliens are not reported or deported.

Many of the few Americans left in Huntington Park resent what happened to their city. Louise Zeltner and her husband settled in the city 34 years ago. She reported that they are the only Americans left on their block. She fears going for a walk because of street gangs. "I have no one to talk to," she said. "Everybody's Spanish."

Another couple, immigrants from Mexico, Mr. Medina and his wife don't go out anymore for fear of being mugged. "It's too dangerous," he said. "We were mugged one night." This scenario plays out in every major city in America. Where immigrants move in with large numbers, Americans move out. When they can't move from old age or lack of income, they suffer as do the Zeltners.

At the current rate of immigration from over 100 countries with profoundly incompatible cultures, is it little wonder that this country is importing the seeds of its own destruction?

However, it begs the question. Who is behind this social experiment? What is their agenda and why are they forcing discordant cultures from Third World countries into First World America? Why would they force not only the immigrants into impossible odds, but their own American citizenry into untenable situations?

Finally why do illegal and legal immigrants come? The answer is to escape the miseries of their own countries, poverty, oppressive religions, to escape embedded corruption so deep that it is impossible to change, to avoid violence and war. They bring all they flee into the center of our own country. Unfortunately, this immigration line grows without end.

In time, it will displace and destroy the foundation of this republic by the very incompatible nature of the immigrants and their cultures.

CHAPTER 6—

WAR IS PEACE, FREEDOM IS SLAVERY, IGNORANCE IS STRENGTH

"We are facing more than a crisis. Our citizens need to become active and vigilant in the quest for our sovereignty. Our country is being destroyed before our very eyes and yet, we have a government that allows this destruction. People: It's time to take back our country and we must never forget that we are the government."

Jan Herron

Another method for destroying America occurs throughout the United States. Governor Lamm said, "I would encourage all immigrants to keep their own language and culture. I would replace the 'melting pot' metaphor with the 'salad bowl' metaphor. It is important to ensure that we have various cultural sub-groups living in America reinforcing their differences rather than as Americans, emphasizing their similarities."

A perfect example of the 'salad bowl' metaphor is Lewiston, Maine. It is a working-class community with high school sports, bake sales and car washes on hot summer Saturdays. It features the normal array of Christian churches.

Well meaning church groups, who ride high on idealism but under the wheel wells and mud flaps of reality, in the past several years sponsored thousands of Somalian Bantus from Africa bearing incompatible cultural traditions. They migrated in mass into the tiny berg of Lewiston. They brought language conflict, religious conflict, welfare needs, medical demands and food stamp requirements. They brought zero job skills. It must be noted that Somalian Bantus are one step out of their grass dwellings. They never used a toilet or washed their hands before being plunked down into America. They practiced no personal hygiene or sanitation.

Instead of being compatible immigrants, they brought tension, dissent and conflict to that once small town "Mayberry RFD." One of the customs they brought was their Muslim tradition of 'female genital mutilation.' Imagine the horror little girls suffered while being brought into Lewiston hospitals with genital infections from having their entire clitoris, labia major and minor, cut away with a razor blade or broken glass. Not only that, the ritual is not used in conjunction with any anesthetics. Conjecture the pain to a little girl under the age of five having her entire sexual being cut away at the hands of some clerical person. They use needle and thread to sew up the vagina. Later, American hospitals must treat the ensuing infections.

Why do they do it? Somalians and most Muslims amputate the prepubescent girl's clitoris as a means of keeping her faithful to her future husband. It makes her a non-being totally subjected to her husband's domination. Basic Muslim society forces its women to wear 'burkas' that totally hide their faces and bodies from view. In other words, women are so degraded by their men that they have little value in Middle Eastern society.

Later, as she grows into womanhood in America, we can't imagine what emotional, sexual and psychological crisis each female immigrant suffers from a 'clitorectomy' that completely 'desexualized' her. She will be living in an enlightened sexual society where she will not be able to respond to or be fulfilled by her natural sexual being.

What if your daughter married a man who insisted your granddaughter undergo this operation? The complications of this nightmare are endless.

Muslims are 'nice' while they are in a minority, but once their numbers grow, they enclave and tolerate no differences in their midst. Worse, their prime directive is to convert or kill non-believers. Their most ardent believers pick up this kind of directive. They act on it. It's happening in a suburb of Detroit, Michigan where latest reports show them demanding to broadcast via loudspeakers from Mosques across the city with the five daily calls to prayer toward Mecca. Freemont, California is now known as 'Little Kabul' and other cities around America are being overwhelmed.

We might look at what is happening in Holland where Muslims will not assimilate into Dutch culture. After years of pandering to the multicultural ethic, the Dutch are closing down their borders to immigrants. They enacted a four-year moratorium on immigration. A local official said, "These immigrants have the highest incidence of unemployment, domestic violence, disability payments, truancy and crime."

Worse, Norway began immigrating Middle-Easterners in the 1990's. Norwegians are dumbfounded at the 'female genital mutilation' and violence now running wild in their major cities. Their rapes, killings, drug gangs and welfare have risen to unheard of levels.

France, now filled with five million immigrants, recoils in a panic. They have discovered the growing zealotry, intolerance, colonizing and imperialistic streak demonstrated by Islam. Few immigrants intend on becoming 'French.' President Chirac ended the wearing of the female headdress, hijab, as, "An aggressive act against the host nation." Already, the French public is in for a rough ride as Muslim numbers grow in strength. Spencer, in his book, "Onward Muslim Soldier" shows, "How non-Muslims in Muslim societies still suffer today under a system of legalized oppression that flows from the theology of jihad." France is in trouble.

In a bold statement in Great Britain, a cleric said recently that followers would turn the United Kingdom into a Muslim State. Instead of enjoying their newfound lives in a free society, they demanded that municipal swimming pools have special times for women-only swimming and men-only. As their numbers grow in enclaves, they will force their traditions onto a once free society.

As Europe's immigration invasion advances, several countries have said "NO" to further immigration. The Dutch are shutting their doors. Denmark is shutting down its borders. Danish prime minister Andres Fogh Rasmussen said he would support legislation to stop the practice of Muslim parents sending their sons back to home countries for longer periods to become familiar with the traditions of their parents' homelands. He's trying to minimize the impact of immigrants attempting to usurp the customs and cultures of their new chosen country.

After three decades of multiculturalism slammed down their throats, many of Europe's First World societies and enlightened civilizations have had enough.

The real question for America is, do we want primitive, female abusive and violent religions developing in our First World country? As they grow into the millions, at what point will they demand we accept their traditions? Will we have to separate our swimming pool times for men and women? Doesn't that harken back to our own Dark Ages of separate schools, pools, restaurants, drinking fountains and bathrooms? Will we be compelled to allow them to force their women to wear burkas, which cover their women into 'non-beingness?'

Americans remain incredibly naïve to this growing crisis. It's not in their hearts, experiences or minds to even conceive of such traditions as 'clitorectomies,' forcing 13 year old girls into marriages with 40 year old men, burkas or hijabs that cover a woman into non-being, or the total domination of men against their women.

Another 'cultural' tradition practiced by these incoming immigrants, both legal and illegal, is an 'honor killing.' It is still practiced in countries from Gibraltar to the Indus and further. Relatives arrange for the assassination of women who have become pregnant out of wedlock or commit adultery—in order to satisfy the honor of the extended family. The killing is performed by a younger son. He may face a short jail sentence. When released, in-laws will give him cash, land, employment and an arranged marriage.

What happens when the first of these cultural practices hits American cities? What happens when so many hit cities and states they won't be able to contend with the volume? What happens when they demand their cultural rights to continue such practices? Guess what? It's already happening.

What about immigrants coming from Saudi Arabia where they hire 'morals police.' In one instance while seeing schoolgirls fleeing a burning dormitory, the morals police in Saudi Arabia used their canes to drive the girls back into the flames. Why? The girls were not properly clothed.

This kind of Third World behavior pathologically crosses over to the dark side. It could be seen as something beyond amoral and felonious in American society. One man remarked, "It's down right sickening!"

What happens to separation of church and state? What occurs when enough Muslims demand Islam become a part of the governing process? That's what they demand because their religion has dictated how they have been governed since the beginning of Islam. Where has it gotten them? If you look at the Middle East today, their way of life has given them dictators, violence and Third World misery! Do we want this kind of situation in America?

Another crisis of the 'salad bowl' metaphor raises its ugly face resulting from language differences in classrooms in Lewiston—leaving American students limited in their learning.

When the mayor of Lewiston pleaded with Bantu leaders to stop urging more Bantus to immigrate into his city because they were flat broke and didn't have further social services to serve the immigrants; he was immediately branded a 'racist.' This further illustrates how immigrants and their lobbyists use Americans against themselves. Immigrants and their lawyers learned how to use the system to their benefit while imploding health care for American citizens who sustain it.

For example, it's been shown in California where the hospitals are so backed up that Emergency Rooms feature a four to eight hour waiting period. Some victims on gurneys have died while awaiting attention. Worse, 77 hospitals on the Border States suffered bankruptcy from serving thousands of illegal aliens being dumped on their doorsteps. They were forced to serve them without being paid. Further compounding the crisis, Senator John McCain of Arizona and supported by Senator Kyle, added a $1.4 billion Medicare appropriation rider to bail out the hospitals via taxpayer dollars. Instead of solving the crisis by putting troops on the border or stopping benefits to illegals, they encouraged more of it at the expense of taxpayers.

When the other 12,000 Bantus imported into America by church groups were forced onto cities across the nation, one city in North Carolina said, "NO, we don't want them." They were immediately branded 'racists.'

Even more disconcerting is the sponsoring church groups that bring them. They are supposed to be responsible for supporting the immigrants. But in fact, quickly, such unskilled and uneducated immigrants become wards of the state where they touch down. Each new immigrant becomes another drip in the draining of the financial tank of the United States. In February, 2004, the national debt exceeded $7 trillion as it rockets out of control with the Iraq War. Even more sobering is the fact that Americans pay $240 billion annually on the interest to service the debt. It means you are paying part of your paycheck for the $600 million dollars a day in interest.

This situation imposed on Lewiston begs the question. You could also make the case for the disaster being visited upon Austin, Minnesota or Boone, Colorado. Macon, Georgia is being invaded by a jumble of languages. Manhattan Island, New York suffers an influx of Russians who keep riding welfare as if it's an art form. The Chinese in major cities are bringing in more of their countrymen than anyone in this country can imagine. This invasion's extreme fruition is 'Little Mexico' as Los Angeles has been turned into a 'colonias' (new colony) of Mexico. Los Angeles and Chicago's legal Hispanic immigrant population continues hiding their illegal population. The Third World Momentum network of cockfighting, dog fights, gangs, child prostitution and crime as a way of life manifest themselves in America with every added illegal alien. Even legal immigrants from incompatible cultures bring a deadly mix to the melting pot.

What happens as immigrants in greater numbers retain their languages? What happens when they retain their allegiance to their former countries? What happens when enough of them cannot or do not get along with Americans or other immigrants?

As can be seen in demographic responses, Americans become the first to flee. They must retreat from a deteriorating community situation in their own country. What's left is a degrading condition in that community that further spirals into Third World Momentum.

Who instigated this massive invasion of incompatible 'salad bowl' ingredients? What is their purpose? Is there a master plan for destroying America? What possible benefit will it be to the 'rich' who live in this country like the rest of us everyday folks? Do they want their own country and children in the middle of multiple languages, incompatible traditions and cultural antagonisms?

Finally, have these power elites looked around the world recently? Aren't there enough examples where mixed cultures and languages don't work? Is it not apparent that France is headed for a violent confrontation with its ethnic minorities especially with religion in their schools? Why has Holland voted to cut immigration decisively since their language and too many unassimilated immigrants usurp Dutch culture? What about the violent differences of Palestinians and Israelis? What happens when enough of that 'violent passion' imports itself into the United States? Can anyone think that the Kurds, Sunnis and Shiites of Iraq will ever live in peace and harmony?

Dozens of examples of incompatible cultures and languages abound throughout the world. So why are our leaders propelling Americans into this nation-destroying experiment?

What is in it for corporations other than money and power? What is in it for our president and Congress? Why are Representatives Norwood and Tancredo the few outspoken men

45

against this invasion? Why are so many Americans asleep at the wheel? When they wake up, will they be able to get America back on the road?

THE CRISIS OF BEING POLITICALLY CORRECT

The driving aspect of this crisis is the term, PC, or, "politically correct." It might, instead, be defined as 'personal catastrophe' for an individual or nation. Government agencies cover up escalating consequences, obfuscate horrible things happening to American lives and lie about what is happening in the cities, towns and states of America. Fear strangles open discussion.

Again, let's reach back in time to George Orwell's book, "1984." In that story, three slogans are engraved in the Ministry of Truth Building: "War is peace" which was used for validating an unprovoked war in Iraq. Even with no weapons of mass destruction found nor any sign of Al-Qaeda connections by Saddam Hussein, a sitting president of a free country recklessly forced war on a sovereign nation 10,000 miles away. Never mind that Saddam was not much more than a thug with no ability to harm America in any way, shape or manner. Never mind that if the USA is going to be a policeman for all the world's thugs, we would have to attack North Korea and a dozen other countries. Never mind that a sitting president would not let inspectors finish their jobs. Never mind that the top United Nations inspector Hans Blix said there were no weapons of mass destruction. Don't mention that a top man in the U.S. Government, David Kay, said there were no weapons of mass destruction and that, "We were all wrong." Never mind the 9/11 Commission in June of 2004 stated that Iraq and Saddam had no connection with Al-Qaeda. Secretary Colin Powell remarked that if he knew before the war what he knew 10 months later, he would not have supported the attack that has killed over 800, as of this writing, U.S. service personnel, with several thousand wounded and over 10,000 Iraqi civilian deaths. Don't mention that the cost of the war created a $544 billion deficit for the U.S. taxpayer in 2003 with more added by the day.

Democrats and Republicans bear full responsibility for this encore to Vietnam.

The second slogan on the Ministry of Truth Building: "Freedom is slavery," which means that our government, corporations and the power elite use it for various means to justify their actions. Our own senators and congressmen pander 'outsourcing,' 'insourcing' and 'offshoring' of millions of jobs to other Third World countries. They import the Third World population into the USA by courting illegal alien labor to the detriment of American citizens. They coerce millions of uneducated and unskilled Third World people upon us without our consent or vote. They force American citizens into depressed wages and few choices because millions of hands are ready to take that job at any wage.

The third slogan on the Ministry of Truth Building: "Ignorance is strength," which is another way for them justifying the destruction of our republic. Again, you may appreciate that a 'democratic form of government or a republic,' in order to exist, demands an educated population with a similar moral and ethical code while speaking the same language. America loses all those aspects in an accelerating immigrant population. What is left of our schools is a dumbing down, a loss of one language, growing linguistic conflict, enclaving and a loss of Americans pulling in the same direction. Graphic examples follow in later chapters.

Governor Lamm's wisdom rings to an American's heart, "A nation is much more than a place on a map. It is a state of mind, a shared vision, and a recognition that we are all in this together."

The fact is, with this immigration crisis, we lose a cohesive "state of mind," "shared vision" and "recognition that we're all in this together."

CHAPTER 7—

DEVELOPING A VIOLENT UNDERCLASS IN OUR COUNTRY

"In the beginning of a change, the patriot is a scarce and brave man, hated and scorned. When his cause succeeds however, the timid join him, for then it costs nothing to be a patriot."

Mark Twain

In his approach for destroying America, Lamm elaborated on the fourth method for ensuring a painful degradation of our country. "Having completed the first three points, I would introduce the fourth aspect to make our fastest growing demographic group the least educated. I would add a second underclass, unassimilated, undereducated, and antagonistic to our population. I would have this underclass suffer a 50 percent drop rate from school."

A quick look around our country shows exactly that crisis occurring around America, today.   In Denver, Colorado the failure and dropout rate of students in the Denver Public Schools system reached 51 percent in 2000. Headlines in the states' two major papers announced the calamity. Has it improved since then? Not much!

Likewise, the educational crisis in California, again, makes that state the bow of the Titanic. New York, Georgia, North Carolina and Florida may be considered the stern. Each state reels from the onslaught of illegal alien students.

California, harboring three million illegal aliens, suffers a $2.2 billion annual cost for teaching alien children. American taxpayers pay $7.4 billion for educating children of illegal aliens according to the U.S. Census Bureau, August 20, 2003.

Worse, teachers are not equipped to instruct children speaking in excess of 100 languages. There is no standard from which to teach. When a teacher is faced with such monumental challenges, it's no longer a challenge; it's impossible. When it faces schools in 50 states, it's a "fait accompli" for disaster.

For example, a teaching friend in California said, "We've got so many kids from so many backgrounds, we're warehousing them while teaching 'cultural appreciation.' In other words, we can't teach in their native languages. We don't have enough teachers who can relate with them in their own cultures. They mill around at school until they are discharged at a functionally illiterate level."

Millions of illiterate parents can not hope to assist their children in education. Those parents do not possess the educational background. Additionally, they arrive from other countries, whether legally or illegally, thus the children enclave in the schools, which isolates them further. They gravitate toward their comfort levels in a growing version of educational balkanization.

Further, immigrants and their children account for over 65 percent of communicable diseases. Tuberculosis, rubella, leprosy, chickenpox, malaria, dengue fever, West Nile virus, hepatitis, Chagas disease and head lice run rampant in legal and illegal immigration populations.

One of the most irritating problems stems from head lice, which are transmitted to American children. The immigrant kids are referred to medical care, but after being diagnosed and given medication, the parents don't possess education or understanding to fulfill the regimen. Thus the lice return as super-lice which then re-infect their classmates.

On the world stage, tuberculosis kills more than two million people annually. In the fall of 2003, according to a report in the Detroit Free Press, 30 children and 4 teachers tested positive for tuberculosis in a small town in the thumb of Michigan. Delray Beach, Florida suffered more tuberculosis cases in one year than the last 20. One illegal alien infected 56 other people in Santa Barbara, California, which was reported by the Santa Barbara Press News on April 24, 2004 titled: "Anatomy of an Epidemic." In schools around the USA, children tested positive for tuberculosis and many other diseases. One can only imagine how frightened American parents have become for their children. Why? Tuberculosis was virtually extinct in America by mid-1990.

What this disease crisis created was anger, frustration and finger-pointing toward immigrant children and their parents. Many American parents did whatever they could do to send their kids to private schools. The rest were/are left with growing consequences.

"How could any national community maintain a minimum wage, a welfare system, subsidized medical care, or a public school system in the face of unlimited immigration?" wrote Herman E. Daly in "Globalization and Its Inconsistencies."

The fact is, we can't. We're failing and sinking fast.

What becomes of such educational problems throughout America? What kinds of responses occur? Who is to blame? Who is blamed?

As our nation imports millions of people from incompatible cultures, languages and uneducated backgrounds, they separate into antagonistic camps. The ones who arrived legally suffer because they are lumped into the morass of all those who didn't. The ones who arrived illegally have no intention of becoming Americans. They're here for the economic benefits. Their antagonisms know no bounds.

But the single salient aspect of their growing numbers is their lack of education. It relegates them to the most menial jobs, the lowest standard of living and they are the most susceptible to crime, drugs or welfare. It's the reason you see 20 to a house and five cars parked in the front yard. It's why litter and trash overwhelm the neighborhood. It's why loud music and fist-fights erupt constantly.

The example of the '18th Street Gang' sporting 20,000 members in Los Angeles is enough to run a chill up any citizen's spine. The Honduran gangs in Washington, DC expand by the day. Florida's Cuban gangs place everyone at risk. Chicago can't keep up with its gangs.

What do those gangs do? They funnel drugs into our schools. They recruit more kids for crime. They run child prostitution rings. They commit honor killings. They organize cock fighting, dog fighting and worse.

Since they have no other educated skills, they turn to anything and anyone who will support them. A gang is family. Crime is easy. Purpose is turf. Protecting it is paramount. Belonging to it is like being on a little league team. Only, in this case, the coach sends you out to kill people. Or run drugs. Or recruit more members. Or, to kill a cop. Los Angeles is its worst manifestation in America, but many cities fall into line like steers in the chute at the slaughterhouse.

Unfortunately, several groups have formed to not only support disparate Mexican immigrants now numbering 9.2 million legal and illegal in the USA, they are openly encouraging insurrection.

The underlying gist is that illegal Mexicans are not inclined to form organizations outside the extended family. They have a low level of trust in their fellow men, thinking that everybody is out to exploit them, which is a reality in much of Mexican history. So, Mexican-American civil rights and ethnic pressure groups were created for them by rich liberals on the model of black organizations.

Groups like the Southern Poverty Law Center—$36.3 million annual budget, National Council of La Raza—$30.9 million annual budget and Mexican-American Legal Defense and Education Fund—$10.9 million annual budget, are funded by the $9.5 billion Ford Foundation (not the car company).

The Ford Foundation developed as an outgrowth of the black civil-rights movement in the 1960s. However, it is fundamentally different. African-Americans wanted social justice in America as Americans.

These Hispanic advocacy groups want more of their own group taking over. Dan Stein, executive director of Federation for Immigration Reform, said, "I don't think there's any question that the principles involved in the Ford Foundation now have an objective to destroy the immigration controls of this country, and they have funded organizations, litigation, ethnic lobbies, and others that have worked for 30 years to dismantle and destroy U.S. interior immigration law enforcement."

"The Ford Foundation is destroying the traditional canon of American history," Stein said. "It can't succeed unless it changes the ethnic base of the society. Ford's objective is to radically overhaul the ethnic basis of American society to bring about the change they desire."

What you see developing is an underclass funded by rich organizations that can manipulate it to their political designs. In "OUT OF THE BARRIO," Linda Chavez noted, "Until recently, there was no question that each group desired admittance to the mainstream. No more! Now ethnic leaders demand that their groups remain separate, that their native culture and language be preserved intact, and that whatever accommodations take place be on the part of the receiving society."

Which means, unfortunately that our First World educational systems, health care, infrastructure and culture are at risk of being destroyed by this invasion. If they get their cultural ways, i.e., horse tripping, dog fighting, cock fighting and other practices of the Third World—it means other cultures will gain rights for their cultural practices, i.e., female genital mutilation, forced marriages of 13 year olds to 40 year olds, polygamy, violence to women and worse.

What emerges is an America with a free-for-all loss of American standards of civility, law, humanity and education.

Third World Momentum advances across America gathering speed and destructive power with each added legal and illegal immigrant. It's been said that each perfect snowflake in an avalanche pleads innocence. Nonetheless, its collective rampage destroys everything its path.

CHAPTER 8—

INVESTING IN BECOMING ANYTHING BUT AN AMERICAN IN AMERICA

"Illegal is anything that is against the law including drug trafficking, smuggling, terrorism or crossing the border into our country. Undocumented is anything that can no longer be verified including unemployed American workers who no longer qualify for unemployment benefits and are no longer counted in statistics. What a sorry nation we have become when we allow corporate political correctness to pervade our daily speech. Illegal means illegal."

Peter Romanenko, Waco, Texas

The fifth point for destroying America empowers the first four. Lamm said, "I would get the big foundations and business to give these efforts lots of money. I would invest in ethnic identity and establish the cult of 'Victimology.' I would get all minorities to think their lack of success was the fault of the majority. I would start a grievance industry blaming all minority failure on the majority population."

A gander across our nation shows major corporations undermining America for their maximum profit for a few. Immigrants, at the invitation of the meat packing companies, have overrun the plants formerly worked by Americans. Construction contracting firms hire eager illegal aliens at slave wages. Contractors pay under the table to save on taxes and benefits. Paving crews, once fully American, hire cheap illegal immigrant labor. Fast food chains formerly hired high school and college students, but now hire illegal aliens. Illegal immigrants flood farming areas. Large chain stores hire illegals for janitorial jobs—and then say, they didn't know illegals were working for them. Federal officials, in 2003, caught Wal-Mart in the act of contracting firms who hired illegals. Wal-Mart officials pleaded ignorance. Landscape companies hire illegals before Americans. Car washes hire illegals first, Americans last. In Texas today, an American who can't speak Spanish can't get a job at most fast food eateries. Illegal aliens have colonized the jobs with foreign languages.

Why? It's simple; illegal aliens won't complain. They accept cash payment. They don't ask for benefits. They live a dozen to a trailer. They increase profits dramatically for the business that hires them.

Along with that skullduggery, Americans who raise questions or confront what is happening in the jobs arena, education or medical services—are shut down. Legal and illegal immigrants are being taught how to use, abuse and defraud our system. They are taught how to be effective victims.

The first thing you hear from news sources is the standard, "They come to America to work for a better life." Nothing is mentioned about how they make Americans' lives worse.

If you look at the major immigration groups—LULAC, LA RAZA, NALEO, MALDEF AND MECHA, they promote the concept of 'Victimology.' They also push their agenda of taking back the Southwest section of the United States into the enclave of Mexico.

'Victimology' transforms into 'Entitlement.' As we see in following chapters, immigrants discovered how easy they could use our food stamps, assisted housing allowances, medical services, school, police and fire protection. Those immigrants from communistic or socialist countries find our benefits easy pickings. All the while, they push their own agenda.

Several books promote the Aztlan and Reconquista movement. They are "PUSHING OUT WHITEY," "WE HAVE BEEN WARNED," and "RECONQUISTA UPDATE."

To illustrate the speed of this incursion, it's being instigated in our public schools to the children of immigrants being educated with our tax dollars. Instead of being assimilated in American life, those children are being taught an adherence to Mexican life. Instead of being an 'Hispanic-American' they are being taught to be a 'Mexican-American' which leads to being a 'Mexican-Mexican' while living, working and having citizenship in America. That entitlement provokes more allegiance to another country than loyalty to America. It's the perfect recipe for national suicide.

What's more mind numbing comes from Mexico's President Fox sending Spanish books up to our schools to teach their kids at our expense in their language and historical perspective. It's breathtaking in pure arrogance!

Therefore, any contention or war with America with any other country, disloyal citizens in our country will not defend and may subvert our country.

Recently, Juan Oliverez published a book, "ABC's OF CHICANO STYLE." Instead of promoting assimilation into America, it promotes separation. For instance:

'A' is for Aztlan, which is a mythical land in the American Southwest stolen by Americans from Mexico. 'B' stands for Barrio for Mexican neighborhood and 'C' is for La Causa or their 'cause' which has nothing to do with America's cause, but instead promotes Chicano as being, "A political state of mind that includes all Spanish speaking people who are conscious of their history."

The conspicuous aspect of these major separatist groups is their long-term goals, which are being implemented day by day, week by week, month by month and year by year. It brings to mind the old wives tale concerning how to cook a frog. First, you throw the frog into the pot of water and turn up the heat. The frog will keep adapting to the rising temperature until it boils to death. If you throw a frog into boiling water, it will jump out immediately.

Likewise, the American people watch this incursion into their country and many even welcome it as a sign of good will. Many Mexican reconquista leaders have noted "How gullible and stupid" Americans are!

Our four Border States are the states most profoundly manifesting the breakup of America as a single nation. Schools promoting clubs that give more credence to other countries than being a part of America evidence this crisis.

But let's not forget the rest of the country. Let's talk about Miami, Florida. Instead of a melting pot, it's a seething caldron of discontent. You as an American citizen are not welcome or safe in Miami. As a woman, you are in greater danger. If you own a car, expect to have it stolen. If you speak English, expect to be insulted. If you're proud of being an American in Miami, you can expect to be insulted in your own country. Is it Miami, USA or Miámi, Third World?

Miami stands as one of its victims. It's the corruption of the Third World digging a stronghold into our country much like a prairie dog colony. As more and more prairie dogs 'grow' their system, all members benefit because all members work for themselves and one another. Escape routes are known by all. They scan the skies for hawks and watch for approaches of coyotes. The more their numbers the bigger their colony and the more power they accrue to protect themselves as they grow even bigger. The more they grow the more they take over their turf until other creatures can not survive.

Again, the reason Third World corruption grips so many nations of the world stems from entrenched systems. Police live in the back pockets of politicians. Dictators maintain armies at their beck and call. A free press doesn't stand a chance in those countries. Therefore, corruption gains an ever broadening power base. Soon, it engulfs the entire country.

Education is plundered which creates an uneducated underclass. They are controlled easily by force and fear. Without a free press, no crimes can be exposed.

What is happening in Miami, Florida stands as an example of what is coming toward all of us around this country as we are undermined by this Third World Momentum. Over the past year, I have asked people to tell their story so I could gain a better perspective on this crisis and how it affects individuals.

Let me introduce, B.E. Brockett, who moved into Miami for a point blank salvo into his mind and mid-section as to the aspects of 'multiculturalism' and 'Victimology.' His story plays out across America and grows by the day in all our major cities.

Miami, USA or Miámi, Third-world Folly? – By B.E. Brockett

"Before we got here, Miami was nothing!" – An exclamation shouted by a Cuban-American at a local Miami TV news reporter's camera covering the Calle Ocho Festival, Miami-Dade County's biggest annual civic event in March 1990.

This was not the first time I had heard some variant of the quote above, but it is seared in my memory the clearest. That moment steeled my resolve that the immigration problem America had allowed to fester in South Florida for years had devolved to the point of intractability. After living almost my entire life within 50 miles of Miami and commuting there off and on for five years, my employer required me to live in the city.

That instant – seeing that man, his resolve and the matter-of-fact manner in which it was reported – was the instant I decided I could not and would not stay. It took a call from a lawyer to my company's top executive, who had issued the edict that I move there, but I was living "back in America" before my one-year lease expired.

An "Anglo" moves to Miami

In January 1990, I moved to Miami with a mix of trepidation and hope. To get over the fear I had of not fitting in and of the high crime rate, I selected a nice high-rise, high-rent apartment building with a great view near downtown Miami. It was situated in close proximity to a Cuban neighborhood, a Puerto Rican neighborhood, a Nicaraguan neighborhood and a black neighborhood. This mix made up the majority of its tenants. Since most of the people in the building were under-40-professionals with significant incomes, I expected that living in there would be enjoyable even though I was one of the few white, native born Americans there. Nearly all of the other "Anglos" were medical residents who chose the location for its proximity to their teaching hospital. I hoped that living with socioeconomic peers would be helpful to my fitting in; I tried to look forward to the whole experience as an adventure.

Unfortunately, that hopefulness was snuffed out soon after I moved in. I learned that each ethnic group in the building held disdain if not outright hatred for all the others. Conversations between neighbors of other cultures were non-existent, even though very few in the building lacked English proficiency. My "hellos" were met with stone cold silence. Almost every time I stepped on an occupied elevator, neighborly conversations between those of similar heritage quickly switched to other languages.

The white female medical-residents were constantly harassed, and often groped, by male Hispanics. Within the first 60 days of my moving in, we had several car-jackings in the parking lot, all carried out by Hispanic gang members from the surrounding neighborhoods. In a few instances, usually when the beer was flowing freely, I was physically confronted by Hispanic males in the building. For what? Who knows? Even though I heard these "professionals" speaking flawless English to each other every day, they only addressed me in Spanish. I only knew enough of the words that spewed from their mouths to understand that they were not inviting me to read the Watchtower.

On weekends the building became a living-hell of loud foreign music, drunken fights and domestic disputes. In speaking with black and white native-born Americans in the building, I learned that our shared experiences were comparable. We pretty much had to band together for safety. I served as an escort from the parking garage to the front door for some of the female medical students who often worked late at the hospital; problems and confrontation almost never happened when more than one American was present. As much as possible, I avoided walking the halls alone and began spending weekends with friends to the north of Miami-Dade County.

I found day-to-day life outside my building to be equally disturbing. The second day after I moved to Miami, I was cursed at in Spanish by a clerk behind the deli counter at the local Publix Supermarket for not being able to order my cold cuts "en Espanol." The newspapers reported daily on the various scandals, corruption, election fraud and other disturbing community traits. I would routinely read my morning paper on the balcony as headless chickens and goats floated by in the river. This was a product, I learned, of ritualistic slaughters practiced by priests of the Santeria religion. They were a regular occurrence at a nearby public park.

I spent most of my free time in Miami just being appalled and trying to remain inconspicuous.

While I kept my job and commuted for two more years after moving from Miami, I have been an active immigration reformer ever since. Living in Miami made me wake up, read about, research, and learn everything I could about this government-sanctioned crisis. There is no assimilation in Miami. The southernmost part of Florida now consists almost completely of various Balkanized un-American ethnic communities filled with hate and fear. In 40 years, the pandemonium has driven nearly every real American family from their homes and up the coast of Florida. As I'm sure you have learned in reading this book by now, our current immigration policy and lack of enforcement encourages similar sequestered and balkanized enclaves to spring up in new little pockets all over this land each day.

My views about Miami are not narrowly based upon the goings-on in a single dysfunctional building or brief exposure to a few American citizens of foreign birth who have no clue about what it means to be American. Prior to living there, I had worked in Miami and had gotten to know its leaders for the better part of five years. Living outside the area, I had successfully compartmentalized, tuned out and turned off the things that concerned me.

Until I lived within it, I viewed the predominantly Cuban culture, mores, ethics and politics as transitory; these people would become Americanized eventually. Now because of my experience and research, I doubt assimilation is likely to ever occur regardless of how many generations we are removed from Castro's revolution, the Cuban Adjustment Act and the rise to disproportionate influence of the Cuban-American National Foundation (CANF).

After looking at this situation from all angles, it is impossible for me to conclude anything other than that Miami's entire power structure and its American sovereignty has been usurped. It is unlikely that American values will ever matter there again.

Bring me your wealthy, corrupt and arrogant masses

To understand what laid the groundwork for the "Cubanification" of Miami, one has to trace the history of this "exile" group's rise to dominance. When Castro's revolution drove Batista from power in 1959, many of his closest associates were able to escape in advance with most of their assets, leaving only their homes behind. Some came directly to Miami, others headed for other countries, but most that did not come to America directly were drawn to Miami within a few years. The majority of the first Cuban refugees to land in Miami were members of or had tight connections to Batista's moneyed elite. To draw a parallel, if our government allowed Vicente Fox to pick up his entire financial base and its people, then relocate it to Illinois, within 20 years a large part of Illinois would be an adjunct of Mexico and there would be few native-born Peorian's left in Peoria.

As the exiles were arriving, the CIA immediately began creating a covert force to overthrow Castro by signing them up as agents, sending many of them to U.S. espionage schools, handing out oodles of cash and creating a separate economy for former Batista henchmen to operate within safely. To maintain secrecy, our government encouraged them to only do business amongst themselves; thus, our tax money did little for the greater Miami economy. Over time this practice helped crush thousands of long-standing American small businesses and force Americans to leave the area. Miami's Cuban, cloistered, U.S. Government-guaranteed business success gave rise to a distinctly arrogant attitude and superiority complex; it also created vast amounts of wealth in their little enclave that would come in handy later.

In her 1987 book Miami, Pulitzer Prize winning author Joan Didion explained how the Port of Miami was, during the early to mid 1960's, the largest covert American naval base in history. But the citizens of Miami were intentionally excluded from any profit from the operation. Of the early Cuban arrivals, many of those who were not already fully in tune with the corrupt ways of the government they had lost were quick to pick up the game; this group and their descendants still form the core clique that makes and breaks people in Miami. President Kennedy's abandoning Cubans in the CIA-run Bay of Pigs operation turned most of them into Republicans once they became citizens, but Republicans in name only. Party is virtually irrelevant in Miami; you have to kowtow to or be of the Cuban-American world-view to get ahead.

Today, after nearly 20 years of business and political dealings in Miami's Cuban community, it is clear to me that their collective ethos will never really fit in with America's. I'm a firm believer in the importance of Americanization for every immigrant before they are given the privilege of citizenship. The window of opportunity for America to assimilate most Cuban-American families, to make them truly American, has passed. What began with our government's encouragement for them to remain separate, today's sheer numbers and determination maintain. While I have had many friendships with Miami's Cuban-Americans over the years, the hyphen always gets in the way. Forty-five years after losing their nation because of corruption and ineptitude at governing, Cuban-Americans are still attempting to build in Miami an idealized version of a Cuba that never existed. They have little use, and often a lot of disdain, for things that are American. This is the seed that gives rise to arrogant proclamations like "before we got here, Miami was nothing." In a weird, distorted sense, Cuban-American leaders have created the equivalent of a cultural Disney World where instead of hugging Mickey and Goofy in the streets, the people clamor to embrace the puffed-up, suited pretenders they have elected to office or have gotten appointed other positions of power in Florida and in Washington.

Once I followed the money, understood the arrogant machismo, and recognized the fantasy world that permeates the collective Cuban-Miamian mind, it became obvious that Miami truly deserves its reputation of being a "banana republic." The plantains haven't fallen far from the Batista tree at all. While Cuban-Miamians may technically be American citizens, with relatively few exceptions they will never embrace Americanism.

Who "really" runs Miami?

Considering that people residing in Miami have voted for 20 years in numbers that would make them blush in Boss Daley's Chicago, it shouldn't come as a surprise that the two key men who really run today's Miami had both assumed room temperature by 1997.

The primary decomposing composer of today's Cuban-American power base, Jorge Mas Canosa, still wields tremendous influence in Miami through his legacies. The most visible of these are the "humanitarian" Cuban-American National Foundation; its lobbying arm, the Cuban-American Foundation; and its political action committee, the Free Cuba PAC. Even though Mas was the son of one of Batista's army majors, he was on the outs with Batista at the end of that regime. The common belief in Miami is that his hatred for Castro was what drove his actions. Actually, it was his thirst for power and money.

Recruited early by the CIA in its "get-Castro" operations, probably because he had attended an American college, Mas was most certainly a beneficiary of the CIA's largesse. But that isn't the "official" story. His claim to have started out dirt poor was a figment of his carefully crafted image. It is probably true that Mas started a wildly successful business career after purchasing a small company. But his claim that he that he got started with "borrowed" money is highly suspect at best. It doesn't take a rocket surgeon to figure out that the CIA continued to grease the skids for everything that happened for Cubans in Miami for several years after the Bay of Pigs. Jorge Mas Canosa was no exception.

For more than 15 years, Mas was invisible while he built his business, He emerged from his cocoon soon after Castro unleashed the Mariel boatlift upon our shores in 1980. The influx of 125,000 more Cubans, one in five of them criminals, put American - Cuban policy issues on the Congressional and Executive front burner for the first time since the Kennedy administration. Sensing opportunity, Mas founded the CANF in 1981. His meteoric political rise gave him disproportionate influence in just about everything he did. He cajoled, charmed, threatened, and intimidated Congressmen, Senators, Governors, newspaper publishers and the last three American presidents. Along the way, while having his way with our leaders, he secured Congressional funding for two big sucking money pits: Radio Marti and TV Marti, which are intended to be similar to the Voice of America projects. Regardless of what their propaganda programming may be doing to influence activity in Cuba, their key "success" is that they provide cushy jobs for friends of CANF.

Mas also successfully steered other costly, American taxpayer-funded projects in a manner in which they would financially benefit Miami's Cuban community. The most notable of these is the National Endowment for Democracy, which has grown into a $48 million annual boondoggle. The CANF leadership consistently responds to various forms of government generosity from which they benefit by re-circulating portions of funds they receive back to Congress as political campaign contributions.

I met Mas several times and had a few business and political dealings with him. Our meetings always involved my bringing others (employers, clients, etc.) to "kiss the ring" and gain some political or business favor from the Cuban community through him. I never walked out of the room without feeling as if I'd been taken for a ride; the cost of gaining the Cuban-American community support never equaled the benefit. He definitely had a powerful aura about him, but it became obvious to me that his main interest wasn't in Castro's demise. He had built up an unprecedented base of power and influence. He was the de-facto ruler of a community with a stronger economic base than Cuba's. Virtually no candidate in Miami Dade ever got elected without his endorsement. He held disproportionate influence for his station in life throughout Florida and in Washington. And he had it all simply because he learned to beat the drum of anti-Castroism better than anyone else.

If Castro had fallen or died during his lifetime, he would actually have had to do some hard work to rebuild Cuba, put his reputation on the line and risk tarnishing the humongous pedestal he had placed himself upon. Jorge Mas Canosa's main goal was obtaining power and money, not Castro's downfall.

He went out a winner only because he died with Castro still in power.

Today, two sons of one of Batista's closest supporters (and nephews of Castro by marriage) serve in the United States Congress. Representatives Lincoln and Mario Diaz-Balart have more than made up for any Cuban-American power that might have diminished after Mas died. Along with another Cuban-born colleague, Rep. Ileana Ros-Lehtinen, they are tireless, unabashed advocates for Cuba in Congress. Everything they do is filtered through an "is it right for Cuba" filter before what is "right for America" is considered. A similar situation exists with the Cuban-American caucus in the Florida legislature.

Throughout Miami-Dade County, people who run for office have a significant advantage and usually win if they can lay claim to being the grandson, nephew, cousin or other relative of someone who was associated with the Batista regime. While being able to draw such connections may become less essential for candidates in the future, it already has gone on long enough for Batista's mark on Miami to be as permanent as Jorge Mas Canosa's. The county now has a vast third-world Hispanic majority with a decidedly errant understanding of the America it continually encroaches upon as it expands northward.

CONCLUSION: MIAMI IS AND WILL REMAIN ANYTHING BUT AMERICAN

Language

Most Floridians know that the citizens of the state enacted a constitutional amendment that makes English the official language of the state by ballot initiative in 1988. Very few are aware that the amendment directed the Legislature to enact enabling laws. Even fewer know that, because of the growing influence of the Cuban-American caucus of the Florida Legislature, no such legislation has ever been enacted. Miami's Cuban-Americans will go to unbelievable lengths to keep the Spanish language alive as the primary language, even subverting the state's constitution.

Media

In the media, Mas took on the Miami Herald in the late 1980's and won by charging that its publisher David Lawrence wasn't anti-Castro enough. Today the paper tows the line, supports open borders and is accommodating to every stripe of illegal alien imaginable. The top TV and radio stations are Spanish language network affiliates. The incredibly popular Hispanic talk radio stations are soapboxes for indoctrination and assimilation resistance that make Rush Limbaugh's biting commentary seem like the yammering of Elmer Fudd in comparison. Broadcast outlets for "Anglo" audiences openly participate in encouraging the region's further devolution into a balkanized, multicultural mosh pit.

Public Institutions

Miami's schools, more often than not, teach kids about Cuban martyr-poet Jose Marti before they teach them about America's founding fathers. Women who arrive at Miami's public Jackson Memorial Hospital from other lands in airport taxies to give birth to American citizen anchor babies are heralded as heroes in spite of the fact that the cost shifting they exacerbate has helped Miami-Dade County become the home of a full percent of all the uninsured residents of America. That's right. One percent of America's uninsured population lives in one county: Miami-Dade.

The Dominance of Third-World Values

There are disturbing common values at work in the various contentious cultures that make up today's Miami. Miamians exhibit a tolerance for corruption typical in most Caribbean, Central American and South American countries. They doggedly cling to failed formulas for dealing with each other, and with outsiders. Historically this is precisely what has kept their homelands from maintaining stable governments and planted them firmly in Third World squalor. The differences between American and Miamian values descend from the worldviews of American colonists versus the Conquistadors.

I now consider the floating, decapitated goats and chickens I saw from my balcony to be graphic symbols of what has gone horribly wrong with Miami. The lunacy I experienced while living there is considered routine. The practice of Santeria and its cousin Vodun (or Voodoo) are widely accepted as "normal" by most residents. These two sects and other similar hybrids of Catholicism and African Animism draw no notice in Miami because deep superstition permeates every balkanized enclave we've allowed to take root there. In most middle and lower class Miami-Dade County neighborhoods, at least a few families keep sacrificial livestock in their back yards despite prohibitive ordinances, the odor and the serious health hazards they present.

Hundreds of South Florida supply stores called "Botanicas" specialize in the sale of both white and black magic supplies, religious icons, magical herbs, candles, incense, instructional books and potions of all sorts. There have already been court cases that have given Santeria priests the "religious freedom" to practice their barbaric rituals; I can only imagine what seeing farm animals have their throats slit at the climax of some bizarre ceremony would imprint upon any child's mind. And our government tells us these people are, or will eventually become assimilated and Americanized?

The Encroachment of "E Pluribus Pluribus"

I have barely scratched the surface of how dangerous to America's future and its sovereignty that the example of Miami has become. The proof that Miami's future is not an American one is overwhelming. The dogged separatism of Cuban-Miami has served as the template for how other groups of refugees and other aliens behave after they arrive. The Cuban power base is loathe to let anyone of non-Cuban origin in, so each new opportunistic ethnic group that moves to the area follows the Cuban example and develops its own aspirations to build an idealized version of the failed Third World dictatorship it fled—right here in America. Thus, the concept of Americanization has been turned on its head in at the southern tip of Florida. Every day it is further morphed into a fractious, un-American, Third World region where "E Pluribus Pluribus" is encouraged and enforced while "E Pluribus Unum" is ridiculed and discarded.

CHAPTER 9—

THE TROJAN HORSE AND THE TERRORISTS AMONG US

"A house divided against itself can not stand."

President Lincoln

The sixth point in the plan for destruction of America includes creating dual citizenship and divided loyalties. "I would celebrate 'diversity,'" Lamm said. "It is a wonderfully seductive word. It stresses differences rather commonalities. Diverse people worldwide mostly engage in hating each other—that is, when they are not killing each other. A diverse, peaceful or stable society is against most historical precedent. People undervalue the unity it takes to keep a nation together, and we can take advantage of this myopia.

"If we can put the emphasis on "Pluribus," instead of "Unum," we can balkanize America as surely as Kosovo," Lamm said.

Most Americans look at Israel and Palestine as an example of insane horror. How would you like to go to work every day on a bus, train or taxi and not know if you would come home alive? That's the condition of daily life in that area. In places like Saudi Arabia or North Korea, fear keeps people in line.

You may travel to many places in the world and find ethnic conflict. In Africa, the Hutsi's and Tutsi's slaughter one another with abandon.

The slave trade continues on the Barbery Coast of the Black Continent.

Sixty years ago, in America, another kind of seething hate transpired in much of the South. The Ku Klux Klan lynched African-Americans at the drop of a hat. The fear instilled in blacks caused thousands to escape to the north. Eleanor Roosevelt did her best to stop lynchings, and was hated for her work. The crisis came to a boil when Rosa Parks of Birmingham, Alabama, a frail black woman, refused to give up her seat and go to the back of the bus. This was a time when the South offered separate but equal drinking fountains and rest rooms. Black Americans could not eat in white restaurants. They couldn't sleep in white hotels or motels.

It took Dr. Martin Luther King marching and speaking until the federal government passed laws for equality. King was killed along with many other protesters.

Even today, a restless tolerance prevails across America in black/white relations. However, because of the rule-of-law that is enforced as well as a functioning society where most people are fed, housed and clothed, this country succeeds along with its racial challenges.

Nonetheless, many examples abound around the world where diversity fails and fails violently.

America imports incompatible cultures and religions into its belly as if it won't suffer a bleeding ulcer. It already suffers deadly violence in cities across the nation.

The entire stance and philosophy of Middle Eastern Islam screams like fingernails raking a chalkboard: against Christianity, women's rights and American culture. They are in direct conflict. As Muslim numbers grow and enclaving intensifies, we can expect consequences. Although Mexican and South American immigrants retain a Catholic Christian compatibility, they have no basic congeniality with being an American—as illustrated in Chapter 12. One look at Mexican dominated Los Angeles will give you living proof.

The most graphic self-destruction also occurred in the land of Socrates and Aristotle.

This invasion mirrors the Trojan Horse of Greek mythology. The Archaeans besieged Troy for ten years—failing. In the last year, Achilles killed Hector. But

Troy's walls could not be breached. A magnificent hollow horse was built with many Archaeans hidden inside and left at the gates of the fortress. The army and fleet withdrew to Tenedos, feigning to have given up the siege. Unwittingly, the Trojans pulled the horse inside the once impenetrable gates of Troy. That night, the Archaeans climbed out of the horse and opened the gates. Their fellow soldiers slipped into the city and killed the rulers. What do you know—Troy fell! Ironically, they did it to themselves.

Today, California leads our Union with its own Trojan Horse exceeding three million illegal aliens. What's even more disturbing, those illegals are supported by millions more who share the same ethnic background. It's called an 'ethnic sympathy.' Ethnic leaders who champion the Southwest United States' being returned to Mexico feed it. They are organized, funded, vocal and led by fiercely ethnic Mexican-American citizens who have no allegiance to the United States.

Even more sobering is the fact that if these people spoke like this during wartime, they would be arrested for treason. Yet, because of 'political correctness,' they are free to move forward on their agenda to take what they consider theirs and move it under the Mexican flag. Sheer numbers give them more power, and given enough time, they will plunder California, Arizona, New Mexico and Texas out of our Union.

If you don't think they are resolute, there is little doubt from the speeches provided below.

The California Coalition for Immigration Reform produced a CD with excerpts of radical, racist speeches by fifteen American citizens Latino elected officials, professors, students and community activists.

California Coalition for Immigration Reform was co-author and sponsor of California's Proposition 187 in 1994, and spearheaded its successful passage. For a history of what happened to Proposition 187, go to www.ccir.net. CCIR is a grassroots organization dedicated to educating the public and our elected officials on the devastation caused by unbridled illegal immigration.

The term 'racist' was used to describe these comments by Mexican-American officials. However, in several cases, the word 'treason' comes to mind. Make no mistake whatsoever about their intentions. These people aim to take Border States back into the umbrella of Mexico. They succeed daily by chasing Americans away as living conditions degrade to Third World levels. Additionally, they succeed by sheer numbers of legal and illegal Mexicans 'colonizing' neighborhoods and cities with no affiliation with what it is to be an American. Los Angeles (Little Mexico) and Freemont (Little Kabul), California as well as Miami, Florida top the list of cities no longer American.

These are the verbatim transcripts:

1)Armando Navarro, Professor of Ethnic Studies, University of California Riverside at Latino Summit Response to Prop 187, UC Riverside, 1/1995: "These are the critical years for us as a Latino community. We're in a state of transition. And that transformation is called 'the browning of America.' Latinos are now becoming the majority. Because I know that time and history is on the side of the Chicano/Latino community. It is changing in the future and in the present the balance of power of this nation. It's a game—it's a game of power—who controls it. You (to MECHA students) are like the generals that command armies. We're in a state of war. This Proposition 187 is a declaration of war against the Latino/Chicano community of this country. They know the demographics. They know that history and time is on our side. As one community, as one people, as one nation within a nation as the community that we are, the Chicano/Latino community of this nation. What this means is a transfer of power. It means control."

In the above speech, Navarro railed against Proposition 187 which California voters passed overwhelmingly to stop funding for illegal aliens. The state was/is going broke over funding for three million illegals. Instead of standing up for American and Californian legal voting rights, Navarro declared a 'war' on legal residents. In our own country, such leaders use our laws against us. Everything Americans created as to law and order, voting and citizenship does not compute for those who support illegal aliens who live illegally in our country.

2) Art Torres, former CA state senator, currently Chair of California Democrat Party at   UC Riverside 1/1995: "Que viva la causa! It is an honor to be with the new leadership of the Americas, here meeting at UC Riverside. So with 187 on the ballot, what is it going to take for our people to vote - to see us walking into the gas ovens? It is electoral power that is going to make the determination of where we go as a community. Power is not given to you. You have to take it. Remember: 187 is the last gasp of white America in California. Understand that. And people say to me on the Senate floor when I was in the Senate, "Why do you fight so hard for affirmative action programs?" And I tell my white colleagues, "Because you're going to need them."

Once a man like Torres assumes power, you have no doubt how he will treat your American citizenship rights. Worse, as you can see, he harbors no loyalty to the United States of America.

3) Jose Angel Gutierrez, Prof. Univ. Texas at Arlington, founder La Raza Unida Party at UC Riverside 1/1995: "The border remains a military zone. We remain a hunted people. Now you think you have a destiny to fulfill in the land that historically has been ours for forty thousand years. And we're a new Mestizo nation. And they want us to discuss civil rights. Civil rights. What law made by white men to oppress all of us of color, female and male. This is our homeland. We cannot, we will not and we must not be made

illegal in our own homeland. We are not immigrants that came from another country to another country. We are migrants, free to travel the length and breadth of the Americas because we belong here. We are millions. We just have to survive. We have an aging white America. They are not making babies. They are dying. It's a matter of time. The explosion is in our population."

Gutierrez is a man who created one of the most racist organizations in the USA. His organization is as vitriolic and dangerous as the Ku Klux Klan was back in the 50's. Much like the Taliban or Muslim extremists that are beheading Americans in Iraq and Saudi Arabia, this man offers no compromises. As it says in his organization, "Everything for anyone who is Mexican, but for anyone outside the 'race', nothing!" That means Americans. Feel a little chill running up your spine at the thought of Gutierrez ever gaining power?

4) Mario Obledo, founding member/former national director of Mexican-American Legal Defense and Educational Fund (MALDEF), former CA Secretary Health/Welfare on Tom Leikus radio talk show: "We're going to take over all the political institutions in California. In five years the Hispanics are going to be the majority population of this state." Caller: "You also made the statement that California is going to become a Hispanic state and if anyone doesn't like it they should leave. Did you say that?" Obledo: "I did. They ought to go back to Europe."

This man would spit on the American flag and burn it if given the chance.

5) CCIR commentary on Mario Obledo: When CCIR, the California Coalition for Immigration Reform, erected a billboard on the California/Arizona border reading, "WELCOME TO CALIFORNIA, THE ILLEGAL IMMIGRATION STATE," Mario Obledo, infuriated, went to the billboard location and threatened to blow it up or burn it down. Even after this threat to deny American citizens their freedom of speech, President Clinton awarded Obledo the Presidential Medal of Freedom, America's highest civilian honor.

<u>CCIR question to Obledo</u>: "Jose Angel Gutierrez said, 'We have an aging white America, they are dying, I love it." How would you translate that statement? <u>Obledo</u>:
"He's a good friend of mine. A very smart person."

<u>6) Joe Baca, former CA Assembly Member, currently member of Congress at Latino Summit Response to Prop 187 UC Riverside 1/1995 and Southwest Voter Registration Project annual conference in Los Angeles, 6/1996:</u> "We need more Latinos out there. We must stand up and be counted. We must be together. We must be united. Because if we're not united you know what's going to happen? We're like sticks - we're broken to pieces. Divided we're not together. But as a unit they can't break us. So we've got to come together, and if we're united, si se puede (it can be done) and we will make the changes that are necessary. But we've got to do it. We've got to stand together, and dammit, don't let them divide us because that's what they want to do, is to divide us. And once we're divided, we're conquered. But when we look out at the audience and we see, you know, la familia, La Raza (the family, our race), you know, it's a great feeling, isn't it a good feeling? And you know, I started to think about that and it reminded me of a book that we all read and we all heard about, you know, Paul Revere, and when he was saying, 'The British are coming, the British are coming!' Well, the Latinos are coming, the Latinos are coming! And the Latinos are going to vote. So our voices will be heard. So that's what this agenda is about. It's about insuring that we increase our numbers. We have got to increase our numbers because the Latinos are coming. We can't go back, you know, we're in a civil war."

<u>7) Antonio Villaraigosa, Chair of MEChA (student wing of Aztlan movement) at UCLA, former CA assembly member, former CA Assembly speaker, currently Los Angeles City Councilman at Southwest Voter Registration Project Conference in Los Angeles, 6/1997</u> "Part of today's reality has been propositions like 187 (to deny public benefits to illegal aliens, 1994), propositions like 209 (to abolish affirmative action, 1996), the welfare reform bill, which targeted legal immigrants and targeted us as a community. That's

been the midnight. We know that the sunny side of midnight has been the election of a Latino speaker - was the election of Loretta Sanchez, against an arch conservative, reactionary hate-mongering politician like Congressman Dornan! Today in California in the legislature, we're engaged in a great debate, where not only were we talking about denying education to the children of undocumented workers, but now we're talking about whether or not we should provide prenatal care to undocumented mothers. It's not enough to elect Latino leadership. If they're supporting legislation that denies the undocumented driver's licenses, they don't belong in office, friends. They don't belong here. If they can't stand up and say, 'You know what? I'm not ever going to support a policy that denies prenatal care to the children of undocumented mothers', they don't belong here."

8) Ruben Zacarias, former superintendent of Los Angeles Unified School District at Southwest Voter Registration Project Conference, 6/1997: "We have 27 centers now throughout LAUSD. Every one of them has trained people, clerks to take the fingerprints. Each one has the camera, that special camera. We have the application forms. And I'll tell you what we've done with I.N.S. Now we're even doing the testing that usually people had to go to INS to take, and pretty soon, hopefully, we'll do the final interviews in our schools. Incidentally, I started this very quietly because there are those that if they knew that we were creating a whole new cadre of brand new citizens it would have tremendous political impact. We will change the political panorama not only of LA, but LA County and the State. And we do that we've changed the panorama of the nation. I'm proud to stand here and tell you that in those close to three years we have processed a little over 78,000 brand new citizens. That is the largest citizenship program in the entire nation."

9) Augustin Cebada, Information Minister of Brown Berets, militant para-military soldiers of Aztlan shouting at U.S. citizens at an Independence Day rally in Los Angeles, 7/4/96: "Augustin Cebada, Brown Berets, we're here today to show LA, show the minority people here, the Anglo-Saxons, that we are here, the

majority. We're here to stay. We do the work in this city, we take care of the spoiled brat children, we clean their offices, we pick the food, we do the manufacturing in the factories of LA, we are the majority here and we are not going to be pushed around. We're here in Westwood, this is the fourth time we've been here in the last two months, to show white Anglo-Saxon Protestant LA, the few of you who remain, that we are the majority, and we claim this land as ours, it's always been ours, and we're still here, and none of the talk about deporting. If anyone's going to be deported it's going to be you! Go back to Simi Valley, you skunks! Go back to Woodland Hills! Go back to Boston! To back to the Plymouth Rock, Pilgrims! Get out! We are the future. You're old and tired. Go on. We have beaten you, leave like beaten rats. You old white people, it is your duty to die.   Right now we're already controlling those elections, whether it's by violence or nonviolence. Through love of having children we're going to take over." Other demonstrators: "Raza fuerza (brown race power), this is Aztlan, this is Mexico. They're the pilgrims on our land. Go back to the Nina, the Pinta, the Santa Maria."

10) MEChA (student wing of the Aztlan movement - motto: "For the race, everything, for those outside the race, nothing.") chants at national conference, Cal State Univ., Northridge, 6/1996 "Viva la raza (long live our race)," "Chicano power," "We didn't cross the border, the border crossed us," "Long live the revolution," "Esta es mi tierra, esta es mi lucha (This is my land, this is my fight)."

"Immigrant advocacy groups no longer promote legal immigration, citizenship, learning English or any other assimilation into this country. Hispanic-rights groups talk of reoccupation and repatriation of the southwestern United States," wrote Linda Bentley in "Paving the Way to Aztlan: With Propaganda, Politics, Racism."

She further states, "The League of United Latin American Citizens now supports the theory that Hispanics have been victimized by white people and are staunch proponents of illegal immigration."

California today manifests this crisis as it is well on its way to becoming America's first Third World State. It's overrun with lawlessness. It harbors over three million illegal aliens. In 2003, over 800,000 Americans fled the state. It's $38 billion in debt. Chaos reigns in its schools. Education is numbingly incapacitated. Fewer people speak English and fewer still are native-born Americans. It's chasing one crisis after another. California, for all intents and purposes, is no longer an American state in this Union.

One can only imagine what speeches radical leaders of Islam will be making in the near future as they see their numbers grow into voting powerhouses. One of the biggest enclaves in Detroit in time will wall itself off from Michiganders. 'Little Kabul' in Freemont, California will be a gateway for more Middle Easterners to set up their country within our country. Suicide bombers in the Middle East regularly prove the extent of Third World Momentum and more sophisticated bombers with more stealth proved it in the Madrid train bombing.

Only, 'they' are now here in America. Tom Ridge assures us that Homeland Security works as 10,000 airport screeners pat down little old ladies and make them take their shoes off to check for C-4 plastic explosives. In the meantime, members of terror cells cross our southern borders at will. How do I know? In April of 2004, I spent two weeks walking on the border from Texas to Arizona. Anyone can walk or drive across our southern border any day of the week. It's as open as the front doors of any mall in America, but in this case, it's open to terrorists 24 hours a day. At this moment, they are planning their next 'Madrid train bombing', but it's here in America.

It's only a matter of time before irate ethnic bombers leave their packs in malls and movie theaters throughout the United States.

"History is a vast early warning system," said Norman Cousins.

Our leaders ignore history at our peril.

CHAPTER 10—

WHEN HERETICS ARE RACISTS

"Whenever legislators endeavor to take away and destroy the property of the people, or to reduce them to slavery under arbitrary power, they put themselves into a state of war with the people, who are thereupon absolved from any further obedience."

John Locke, 1690

One of the great inventions created for the destruction of the United States is the term 'politically correct.' It instills fear into people in responsible positions—to not speak up, to not mention the obvious and to ignore the 10,000-pound gorilla in our kitchen as it destroys everything we've cared about or loved in our lives. As a collective network applied to the United States, the term PC might be changed to a national 'personal catastrophe.' PC inhibits enlightened discussion.

For Lamm's seventh point, he spoke about another method for destroying America, "I would place all these subjects off limits—

make it taboo to talk about any of them. I would find a word similar to 'heretic' used in the 16th century that stopped discussion and paralyzed thinking. Words like 'racist' and 'xenophobe' halt argument and conversation."

Today, illegal aliens procure forged documents at the drop of a hat by a well-oiled, efficient criminal network within our country. It's an underground counter culture of crime—and, it's growing. Social Security cards, birth certificates, driver's licenses, Mexican ID cards and other forms of documentation allow illegal aliens a 'valid' cover for remaining in our country. Even Mexican consulates numbering over 45 in our major cities across America operate for and by Mexico. They augment illegal actions of their citizens in our country. Why wouldn't they? Immigrants send $15 billion back to Mexico annually. Talk about a cash flow! What a deal even Bob Barker or Regis Philbin couldn't beat!

Fox starves, then drive his poorest citizens to our country. We're forced to educate their children, give them free medical services, lunch programs, assisted housing funds and much more. They, in turn, send our money back to his country where he taxes his citizens a paltry 14 percent. Mexico features 22 billionaires. As shown in the following chapters, you will see how we are being used against ourselves.

All the while, our citizens stand in unemployment lines as our nation spirals into horrendous debt.

Increasingly, a phenomenon operates across America today by illegal immigration advocates. It stems from employers who benefit from cheap labor. They pay in cash and off the books while escaping taxes. They pay below minimum wage, which increases their personal profit at the expense of our society.

"Because they are employed by the consulting firm that recruited them, many of these foreign workers are paid either in cash or by check. No money is withheld for U.S. income tax, Social Security, Medicare, state or local taxes," said Edwin S. Rubenstein, president of ESR Research.

Who profits? Companies hiring illegal aliens. Who pays? You do!

Additionally, in excess of 7,000 immigration lawyers (American Immigration Lawyers' Association) prey on aliens by using every contrived angle for keeping illegal aliens from being deported. Illegal alien advocate organizations use their growing numbers to swell their rolls for political power. They use this term for muzzling any discussion. They scream, "You are a racist!"

Generated in the 60's when Dr. Martin Luther King marched against social injustice, Americans recoil at being called racists. Ironically, they're comparing apples to bulldozers.

Much like the clergy of the 16th century, illegal alien advocates fear anyone discovering their secrets. Clergy didn't want Martin Luther questioning their 'truth' or 'perfection.' They didn't welcome a free discussion of philosophical thought. It's much like backward societies down through time. Those in power wanted to stay in power and their trump card was keeping the population illiterate. The less they knew, the easier they were deceived. The more they were deceived, the more easily they could be ruled. Not much has changed today. Most Americans sit back, watch, wait, listen and don't do anything until personally affected. As it is, immigration affects us all over the country at a growing rate of speed. However, the press camouflages this invasion by making illegal aliens, 'undocumented workers.' It runs fluff stories on their hardships. Politicians avoid this issue with the deftness of the 'Ali Shuffle.' They dance around it better than Fred Astaire. They escape it better than Houdini.

Politicians skulk like shadows around the halls of Congress. No one has taken responsibility for 9/11 and no one has been reprimanded, but the fact is, Congress and the president are responsible, because they didn't and won't enforce immigration laws.

Who are the victims of this charade? American citizens and their families!

What the immigration lawyers don't want you to know is that they represent foreign nationals who have broken our laws by coming into our country illegally. Illegal aliens are criminals. They are subject to deportation. Lawyers also know that it is against federal law to "aid, assist, induce, encourage or abet an illegal alien to remain in the United States no matter what your personal convictions." Yet, money is the personal motivating force of these lawyers to do everything in their power to obstruct our federal laws. It's little wonder their numbers grew from less than 100 in 1970 to well over 7,000 in 2004.

Employers also know it is criminal to hire illegal aliens. It's a federal felony. Nonetheless, they hire them to maximize their own profits. They usurp the rule-of-law that allows them operations in a functional and law-abiding country. They calculate they won't be caught because of such practices as 'Special Order 40' or the fact that our Congress won't appropriate funds to hire enough agents to arrest illegals once their inside our country.

In contrast, they know that illegal aliens cause a crisis in crowded classrooms, incompatible languages, under-financed schools, medical facility failures and non-funded infrastructure. Additionally, they know illegal aliens are not checked at the borders for diseases that affect American citizens, but hire them anyway.

Organizations like MECHA, LULAC, MALDEF, LA RAZA and others advocate illegal immigration for their purposes of 'RECONQUISTA OF AZTLAN' or retaking California, Arizona, New Mexico and Texas back into the auspices of Mexico.

If anyone tries to speak up, the first words out of their mouths, are, "Immigrants come here to work for a better life."

Not surprisingly, their name-calling works. Americans recoil. The rule-of-law is thwarted. Police are hamstrung. The '18th Street Gang of Los Angeles,' with 20,000 members, operates with impunity. MS-13 Salvadoran and Russian Mafia grow daily in power on the East Coast. Schools suffer overwhelming chaos. Illegals swamp and bankrupt hospitals around our country. Congress willingly stuffs itself into the back pocket of big business. President Bush, instead of upholding his sworn duty to protect us from enemies 'both foreign and domestic,' acquiesces. In fact, he favors it for his corporate cronies. Clinton and democrats supported this invasion with equal flippancy. Both parties, by their actions, stand in favor of destroying America's middle class.

The reality before and since 9/11 shows Congress and the President of the United States have done nothing whatsoever to stop illegal immigration on our southern border with Mexico. Despite 3,000 American citizens killed in the World Trade Towers, our leaders exhibit impotence on the border. Illegal alien Malvo was caught and released by the INS. Later, he used Americans as target practice out of the back trunk of his car. But our Congress STILL will not stop illegal immigration. After David Marsh, a police officer killed by illegals in Los Angeles, our Congress won't stop this invasion. After the horrific death of young National Park Ranger Kris Eggle, our Congress does nothing. They won't station troops on the border, EVEN with 75 percent of all illegal drugs smuggled across that border annually! They won't lift a finger to stop the 2,200 plus illegals marching across our borders every 24 hours, seven days a week and 365 days a year. They won't stop the denigration of our national English language. They won't stop the 'colonias' from growing into massive, disease-riddled shantytowns from Brownsville, Texas all the way to San Diego, California.

But they will kowtow, shrivel, shrink and crawl away from being called, "racists." When in fact, the ones calling them racists are the ones advocating illegality as a standard of behavior. Curiously, the same folks hiring illegal aliens to do the "Jobs Americans won't do" were the same ones engaged in the slave trade before the civil war. Their intellectual heirs still use the same slogan, but call everyone else racists. Who is a racist when our open borders relegate our poorest Americans to the back of the job lines? You be the judge.

"Finally, having made America a bilingual-bicultural country, having established multiculturalism, having the large foundations fund the doctrine of 'Victimology,' I would make it impossible to enforce our immigration laws," Lamm said. "I would develop a mantra that, because immigration has been good for America, it must always be good. I would make every individual immigrant sympatric and ignore their cumulative impact."

For his last point for destroying America, Lamm said he would censor Victor David Hanson's book, "MEXIFORNIA." That book is dangerous because it exposes the plan on how to destroy America.

CHAPTER 11—

IMMIGRATION'S DISEASE INVASION, DEADLY CONSEQUENCES

"Immigrants bring diseases into the United States that were unheard of a few years and the problem is—they are spreading to US citizens across the country. We are importing a multiple disease epidemic into this nation."

Stephany Gabbard, RN

Now that you know the eight methods for destroying America, this chapter deals with the first of four mechanisms even more devastating to U.S. citizens. These topics include 'DISEASES BROUGHT INTO AMERICA BY IMMIGRANTS;' 'THIRD WORLD CRIME WAVE BEING IMPORTED INTO THE UNITED STATES;' 'IMPENDING WATER SHORTAGES IN AMERICA' and the worst will be discussed at the end of the book, 'THE PLAGUE OF THE 21ˢᵀ CENTURY: OVERPOPULATION IN AMERICA.'

This chapter deals with diseases being brought into this country that may be considered as bio-terrorist attacks because illegal aliens crossing our borders avoid health screenings for diseases. Many legal immigrants slip through carrying undetected diseases in their bodies. For instance, tuberculosis won't show up on a chest x-ray for a child under 15. The full manifestation of this crisis is like a 'Time Bomb,' especially with the advent of mutated strains of tuberculosis. Once in this country, carriers spread their diseases like a silent, ticking 'Time Bomb.' Stephany Gabbard, a Registered Nurse, researched all aspects of this chapter.

America is a First World country. We earned it by creating a powerful educational system, sanitation standards, water quality integrity, air pollution management, health care systems and a population that adheres to the highest standards for health care in the world. Many Americans eat too much and are grossly overweight, but that's another book!

By 1990, tuberculosis was virtually extinct in this country. No one had ever heard of leprosy in the United States. Malaria did not exist here. Chagas Disease, what is that? If you asked someone about Exotic New Castle, they would have replied they saw it in a Disney movie.

The invasion of illegal aliens pouring over the borders of the United States takes a foreboding turn. They are not alone! Their bodies may carry Hepatitis A, B & C, tuberculosis, leprosy and Chagas Disease. Chagas, which is a nasty parasitic bug (T. Cruzi) common in Mexico and South America, infects 16 million people and kills 50,000 annually. More sobering is the fact that an average of 2,200 unscreened illegal aliens cross the Mexican border every day. It's nothing short of a health care crisis form of bio-terrorism. The date 9/11 won't hold a candlestick to the numbers of deaths suffered from diseases being imported into this country.

Illegal aliens, by avoiding health screenings at the U.S. borders, carry Dengue fever and the most serious MDR-TB, a multi-drug resistant tuberculosis. World wide, TB kills two million people annually. It creates a higher death rate then cancer. MDR-

TB occurs when Mycobacterium TB becomes resistant to the most powerful TB drugs, Isoniazid and Rifampin. According to the New York Academy of Sciences, 2002 update, "Ordinary TB requires a six-month regimen of four drugs for cure. MDR-TB requires up to two years of treatment with a complex regimen of much more expensive drugs to which the patient's TB bacteria are susceptible." Even with intensive therapy, a diagnosis of MDR-TB is usually a death sentence.

Many of these drugs have toxic side effects. A patient with MDR-TB will infect others with MDR-TB, not ordinary TB. "It has been called "Ebola with Wings," by Lee B. Reichman M.D., M.P.H., in his chilling book "TIME BOMB: THE GLOBAL EPIDEMIC OF MULTI DRUG RESISTANT TUBERCULOSIS."

"TB bacteria readily fly through the air, as when an afflicted person coughs. It's estimated that each victim will infect 10 or 20 or more people—in whom the disease will likely remain latent, creating the potential 'time bomb' effect," according to the New York Academy of Sciences, Update, January, 2002.

Legal immigration also poses a threat. The screening procedures in legal immigrants' home countries are not foolproof. They can be admitted to the US if they carry latent tuberculosis, which may be carried in their bodies for years before becoming active. According to the Center for Disease Control, five percent of all latent tuberculosis carriers will develop active TB. It can go as high as 10 percent. Even getting a chest x-ray may be rigged. There is a black market for clear chest x-rays that people can purchase. Illegal aliens are not screened at all.

If those in gated communities or exclusive neighborhoods think they can avoid this disease, think again. According to James R. Edwards in a National Review commentary, "An immigrant TB patient secretly being treated by Maryland public-health officers worked as a wealthy family's chauffeur. Another contagious immigrant was a resident nanny. As the New York Times put it, "TB can circle the world at the speed of a passenger jet and be transmitted by a single cough."

Political correctness distorts the picture and puts Americans at greater risk. Some health officials loath exposing the immigrant-disease connection. James R. Edwards states, "A Maryland public health officer told the Washington Post, "My greatest fear is that there will be this terrible xenophobic response to anyone who is quote-unquote a refugee or immigrant." What an outrage from a public official charged with our welfare! Instead of putting the health and safety of Americans first and foremost, officials worry about public image! Who are they working for? Whose lives are they guarding? Will our loved ones be forced into a deadly epidemic because that health officer worries about disease carrying immigrants?

"Unless Americans are willing to adopt draconian immigration policies, the likelihood is that with globalization, tuberculosis will again become epidemic here, in the same way that HIV moved from Africa to take root throughout the world," said Kevin Patterson, M.D., in "The Patient Predator."

To make matters worse, in excess of 7,000 new cases of leprosy (Hansen's Disease) have been diagnosed in the USA in the past three years. It is now endemic to the Northeastern United States for the first time, ever. Ironically, only 900 cases of leprosy were reported in the last 40 years in the United States. Immigrants coming from India, the Caribbean and Brazil are most likely to carry leprosy. When you visit the doctor only to find out you have TB or leprosy, who ya' gonna' thank? Ghost Busters?!

Chagas, sometimes called the kissing bug disease because the parasite favors the face as a route of infection comes in acute and chronic forms. The chronic kind can damage the heart, causing enlargement with subsequent heart failure and death. Chagus also damages the intestines. Sixteen million people in Central and South America suffer from Chagas. It kills 50,000 annually south of the Mexican border. Nine confirmed deaths have been reported in the USA. Its worst manifestation is when illegal immigrants carrying the parasite give blood in U.S. donor facilities.

This parasite now threatens our blood supply, yet no means to test the blood is currently available. Ironically the public health community has been aware of this danger for years. "Hundreds of blood recipients may be silently infected, experts say, and there is no effective treatment for them. After a decade, 10 to 30 percent of them will die when their hearts or intestines, weakened by the disease, explode," according to the New York Times, November

18, 2003 by Donald G. McNeil Jr. Three people received Chagas infected organs in 2001, the first such cases reported in the United States, ever! Two 30-year-old women recipients died. It is moving quietly through Los Angeles, California and Miami, Florida.

Dengue Fever, with reports of polio, and now, the first case of malaria in Texas trickle into the United States as the invasion of illegal aliens increases in numbers. This health care crisis threatens America's population including school children.

Undiagnosed disease due to uncontrolled illegal immigration is not confined to California and the Border States any longer. This health care crisis spreads daily across the entire nation. In 2002, Northern Virginia reported a 17 percent increase in tuberculosis cases. Prince William County alone reported a staggering 188 percent jump over the previous year. Health officials have attributed this out break to immigrants. They also give "new immigrants" credit for introducing MDR-TB (the drug resistant strain). In 2001 Marion County experienced an outbreak of Multi-Drug Resistant TB, which was investigated by the Indiana University School of Medicine. Their findings? Mexican Nationals, i.e., illegal aliens, flooding into the area caused the problem.

In Queens, New York the health department found that 81 percent of new TB cases in 2001 were those of "immigrants." The CDC reports that last year one-half of all new TB cases were attributed to foreign born people, who have an eight times higher incidence of TB. Recent outbreaks include Portland, Maine, Del Ray Beach, Florida and Michigan. The top five TB importing countries are Mexico, the Philippines, Vietnam, India and China.

In 1999 a health advisory was issued due to a Dengue Fever outbreak along the Mexico (Nuevo)/Texas (Webb County) border. Dengue fever is a virus spread by mosquitoes, causing high fever, muscle aches, nausea and vomiting. It is not usually fatal but there is a more serious strain called dengue hemorrhagic fever, which CAN kill you.

It gets worse. The U.S. government, which is sworn to protect American citizens, is in reality, aiding and abetting this health care crisis. Quoting a Fox News Report from April 4, 2003, Miguel, an illegal alien who worked construction on a subway renovation project for months, was able to change his status to legal permanent alien. There was only one problem, Miguel was infected with tuberculosis. This did not stop the federal government from issuing Miguel a health waiver under the Immigration and Nationality Act, a waiver that permits him a green card, even though his disease made him inadmissible for the waiver. Miguel, with a TB infected body, is now legally free to move about the country. Like the hepatitis infected onions allowed across our borders by lack inspection, the personnel U.S. government forces TB infected immigrants into our population. What would have been a better course of action for our officials? How about 'immediate deportation' for TB-carrying Miguel for starters! Something like this makes you wring your hands in disgust while wondering what bunch of nincompoops are in charge? How did they reach such levels of incompetence? Did they graduate from high school? Is theirs a practical joke on the American public? Would they like their friends working around Miguel so they could catch tuberculosis? Or, is it just you and your friends?

Americans are unaware of the Third World disease threat that insidiously invades our country because the main stream press ignores it. The subject is too explosive. Politicians won't discuss it because it means offending constituents and losing votes. Chinese officials did the same thing with the SARS epidemic in 2003. They suppressed it for as long as they could until it exploded out of control. The same thing is happening in the U.S. right now as these diseases pour across our borders and enter our classrooms, pools, supermarkets, churches, day care centers, playgrounds, hospitals and movie theaters.

The outbreak last fall of hepatitis 'A' in Monaco, Pennsylvania's Chi Chi restaurants stemmed from 14 'unscreened' employees testing positive for hepatitis. Thus far, three customers died and thousands of Americans were exposed. While green onions were pronounced the guilty culprits coming from farms in Mexico, the evidence points to a lack of federal inspections at the Mexican border. Little known to most Americans, millions of illegal aliens work in food service. They carry a salad bowl full of diseases. Their personal hygiene and sanitation practices would sicken you.

In Third World countries like Mexico where I have traveled extensively, septic systems will not tolerate toilet paper. Therefore, people throw their used toilet paper into a box in the corner. If there is no box, they throw it into the corner anyway. Additionally, they do not wash their hands after using bathroom facilities. It's a matter of cultural habit. Once they arrive in America, they do not magically change their habits. One restaurant worker from New York wrote me of an instance where the manager ran screaming obscenities out the back door with a box of clean hand-towels that was filled with used toilet paper. Immigrants working in the restaurant had thrown their used toilet paper into the hand-towel box. This kind of behavior occurs all over our country. Then, realize these immigrants, both legal and illegals, are the ones chopping your tomatoes and onions for consumption as they prepare your meals at fast food and other restaurants across America.

What does this mean to American citizens? It means your children suffer risk when attending school. It means that when a classmate from a foreign country sneezes or coughs, your child may be at risk for any number of diseases. It means the high health cost dollar responding to tuberculosis in the U.S. will not be available to root out the source of diseases in foreign lands. If you go to the movies, you're breathing air that may be carrying tuberculosis. If you eat at a fast food restaurant, a person infected with hepatitis could prepare your food. It means if you need a blood transfusion, the blood could be infected with Chagas Disease, a parasite that will destroy your heart and other organs.

What can you do? You may visit the principal of your school and insist that every child pass a complete health screening for tuberculosis, head lice and hepatitis. You may ask local health inspectors to check restaurants in your community to see that all employees are legal American citizens and have been health screened. The obvious course would be to secure our borders against illegal alien migration.

CHAPTER 12—

A MEXICAN-AMERICAN REGISTERED NURSE SPEAKS OUT

"Of liberty I would say that, in the whole plenitude of its extent, it is unobstructed action according to our will. But rightful liberty is unobstructed action according to our will within limits drawn around us by the equal rights of others. I do not add 'within the limits of the law', because law is often but the tyrant's will, and always so when it violates the right of an individual."

Thomas Jefferson

Ask yourself how fast this Third World incursion proceeds while Americans continue sitting in front of their television watching our troops killed in Iraq? Ironically, Americans protect dozens of other countries with bases around the world, but, thanks to a capricious Congress, our own boundaries go undefended. Now that you have a greater understanding of the diseases crossing over our borders, you might appreciate why.

Again, it's Third World Momentum moving into our country like a combine in a Kansas wheat field. Much like wheat being mowed down, sucked through the machinery and spit out the pipe at the back—Americans suffer their financial legs, health and school losses in the same way. We're cut down and spit out by corporations and our own leaders. But we're the ones that created the combine, planted the wheat and purchased the tractor. We built the barns, railroads and locomotives!

As stated earlier, all cultures are not compatible. Some don't like other cultures from a basic tribal or ethnic standpoint. The reason many cultures suffer diseases stems from their unsanitary cultural practices. When diseases strike, individuals in some cultures don't have a clue as to the origins.

This is the story of a registered nurse, Lillian Gonzalez, who is the daughter of Mexican parents who migrated to Indiana where Gonzalez was born and raised. She also moved back to Mexico for two years to experience first hand what it was like living in that country.

She served with honor as a United States Marine. Lillian Gonzalez, a Registered Nurse, gives Americans a bird's eye view into the Mexican culture and what it thinks about Americans. She also relates the shocking reasons for animal cruelty and diseases engulfing the Third World from a nurse's perspective. Everything she writes about supports everything written in the preceding chapter on diseases and why they spread. We may extrapolate the practices of Mexico are even worse in other Third World countries.

Lillian Gonzalez writes:

"I have insight into two different worlds-the world of Mexicans and the world of Americans. As an American-born woman of Mexican ancestry, I have been exposed to the true feelings of Mexicans about Americans and of Americans about Mexicans. I am proud to be an American and my first loyalty is to my country. And out of this loyalty, I feel a need to expose to other Americans the realities that are little known about the Mexican culture as the two cultures struggle to find a means by which to co-exist.

"My father, Mario, was the oldest of six children in a poor Catholic family in Northern Mexico, near Monterey. As a teenager in the '50's he and his uncle illegally crossed the border into the United States in search of work to send money back to Mexico. I remember he'd talk about his days of being a "mojado" meaning "wet." Wet is the colloquial term used by illegals from Mexico who swam across the Rio Grande River to get into the United States. My father told of a story where be bit into a concrete fixture to help him keep from drowning in a raging river. It made his front tooth crooked and I remember him whistling Mexican ballad tunes through that crooked tooth. He hated carrots and one day he explained, that for weeks, all he ate were carrots from a field while hiding from border patrol agents.

"My mother was born in Rosebud, Texas, the 10th child of 13. Her father was a Baptist missionary who spread the gospel in northern Mexico in the '30's. Though born in Texas, my mother was raised in Mexico and never learned to speak English. She was a devout Southern Baptist farm girl. At age 26 she was considered an old maid. The assumption for old maids in her culture was to care for the parents. But she broke away from that tradition and married my father in Veracruz, Mexico in 1960. They immigrated to Indiana where my father worked legally in an Indiana steel mill. I was born to them in 1961. Soon afterwards, my brothers Ramon and Javier were born.

"As I grew up, I realized vast differences between my parents. My mother had impeccable hygiene because growing up she had running water on her farm. She'd educate me about the importance of hand washing. She'd smell my brothers' hands to make sure they were clean. My father's family thought my mother was a sort of religious fanatic and ridiculed her "obsession" with hygiene.

"My father's family was poor. The men were afflicted with a universal problem – alcoholism. My grandmother, Dora, hid from my mother her addiction to gambling; perhaps feeling my mother might judge her.

"As a little girl, I dreaded visiting my father's parents in Mexico. They had an outhouse that smelled horrible. My mom would take me to the woods to do my business far from anyone–and far from that smelly outhouse. She always had a roll of toilet paper just for me. The rest of the family wiped with newspapers.

"I recall at about age five when grandmother Dora made delicious Mexican soup. I inspected it carefully and found a dead fly in it. She told me to just throw it out and finish my soup. My refusal was deemed as defiance of an elder's orders and as strange behavior. It was common in my father's family to overlook the infestation of flies and roaches.

"Growing up in Indiana, I remember my mother cried a lot. She was terrified of my father coming home drunk and demanding food to be perfectly hot and quickly served. He was impatient and said words in Spanish that neither my brothers nor I were allowed to say in my mother's Christian home. My brothers and I learned to cry silently because to cry out loud would annoy my father – and he was feared. When I was old enough to know what divorce was, I begged my mother to divorce my father. But that was out of the question. Not only was it considered a sin to divorce, but she believed no respectable man would marry me if I were the product of a divorced marriage.

"I was exposed to Anglo families in the Midwest and yearned for a life like theirs. But I knew that as long as I stayed home, I'd be destined to a life like my mother's. My Anglo friends and their moms seemed to have so much more freedom. They were allowed to come and go as they pleased. This was odd to me because unlike my brothers, neither my mother nor I were allowed to go anywhere without my father's permission.

"I knew I wanted out of that life. At age 18 I joined the Marine Corps. I had visions of being slapped around by drill instructors-like in the movies. I was scared. But I saw it as my ticket to freedom. I couldn't wait to leave so I wouldn't have to watch my mother subjected to my father's alcoholism and my brothers getting into trouble with the law. In spite of strong objections from my father-who believed women in the military were whores, lesbians, or masculine—I left.

"Two and a half years later, I married an Anglo Marine officer. Secretly, I never believed I would stay married. I knew the divorce rate was high and I almost intended to join that statistic. I couldn't see myself being trapped by a man, the way my mother was. So I never even bothered to change my last name. What was interesting was that my husband didn't care. I remember asking my tall, Gringo, husband for permission to call my mother long distance. He thought the request was odd and in his Marine Corps way he chuckled, "You're free, almost White, and 21. This is America. You can do whatever the hell you want!" We've been married 22 years.

"Although my mother was quiet and subservient to my father, I'm thankful to her for telling me to get out and see the world. And I'm thankful to my father that I never went without food, shelter or clothing. He provided well for his family. And I love his memory because he was my father and did the best with the knowledge he had. I got a glimpse of his kinder side, just before he died of cancer of the pancreas caused by his chain-smoking or by the years of exposure to toxins as he diligently worked in the steel mill to provide for us.

"That said, I feel a need to shed light on the psychology of the Mexican culture from the perspective of a daughter of parents from American culture, and as a person who lived for 18 months as an adult in Mexico.

"It's no secret that the vast majority of people who force themselves into this country illegally do so because they are desperately poor. But the masses bring with them belief systems that are rigid, archaic, and harmful to American citizens and legal residents who strive to better themselves and want to participate in the further evolution of a nation.

"One belief strongly held by Mexicans is their view that women are inferior to men. A Mexican relative of mine hides from Mexicans her divorce status. In Mexico, divorced women are chastised. In fact, this Mexican relative told me about her inability to get the Catholic Church in Mexico to acknowledge her divorce even though her husband had abandoned her for another woman.

"I lived as an adult in Mexico briefly in 1988 with my husband and two children. When interviewing for a position as a bilingual secretary in Monterrey, Mexico, I was subjected to demeaning interrogation tactics by male managers. With feet propped up on his desk, one manager asked me: Are you married? Do you have children? How many? Doesn't your husband object to you working? Are you pregnant? Do you intend to get pregnant? I kept waiting for the questions about my typing skills, software knowledge, and English abilities. Instead, he asked, "Are you happy in your marriage?" As an Americanized woman, I took offense at the line of questioning and responded, "Are you looking for a secretary? Or a mistress?" He put his feet on the floor as I stood up. And before he could tell me to get lost, I said, "I'm sorry I wasted your time." His perception of my Americanized attitude was probably as appalling as my perception of his sexism. This sexism is normal in Mexico. There, women who are outspoken and dare to have an opinion are castigated.

"At age 9, I recall my own father turning red in the face, angered that I had voiced an opinion. In front of visitors he humiliated me by shouting, "And who are you to have an opinion?" My father verbalized opinions about politics, religion, and society. But if my mother disagreed, she would discuss them with me in secret.

"American women are stereotyped by Mexicans as being sexually promiscuous. After realizing that I could never work in Mexico as a secretary, I became an English teacher for Mexican white-collar professionals who understood the value of learning English. These executives knew that in order to maximize their earnings potential, they would have to learn to speak English as they embarked on taking advantage of NAFTA. I heard some of these executives comment that they would "play" with American women, but would never marry one. Their reasoning is that American women are sexually liberal and thus not marriage material for any Mexican man serious about starting a family.

"Among many Mexicans, hygiene is not valued. One Mexican acquaintance of my family proudly showed his new home to friends – the fancy architecture, imported tiles, and detailed woodwork. When asked where the bathroom was, "Oh that?" he said. "That comes later."

"I went into a fancy funeral home with a well-educated, Mexican female professional. In the restroom, after we had both exited the stalls, she followed me to the sink where I scrubbed my hands. She kept chatting with me as I washed–and she didn't. Her toddler had recently sustained an infection.

"My father objected when I decided to go to nursing school. He took every opportunity to ridicule my education. He said as I studied for hours, "All that studying, just to learn how to wipe an ass." To my father, nursing was in a category with prostitution. I believe it was difficult for him to imagine his daughter catheterizing a grown man.

"Perhaps this mentality is why only two percent of all registered nurses in the U.S. are Hispanic, in spite of a national Hispanic population of 13 percent. Many of my Anglo nurse colleagues label Hispanic patients as "noncompliant." Often the issue is not compliance, but rather communication. Diabetes is an example of a disease that is prevalent among minorities. According to the American Diabetes Association, in 2002, the U.S. spent $132 billion on diabetes. There are many ways to prevent costs associated with this chronic, debilitating, and deadly disease. But until culturally competent nurses teach patients about prevention in terms they can understand, this disease and others will continue draining our country in both human and healthcare resources.

"As a postpartum nurse in California and Texas, I have provided care for Mexicans and other Third World patients. Often I was the only staff person who knew Spanish on these hospital floors. I did my best to educate about the importance of hygiene as I discovered piles of bloody and soiled toilet tissue in the garbage. Knowing that in their homes in Third Worlds they do not flush toilet tissue, I often found it a challenge to contain contamination.

"In a California county hospital, I felt like a foreigner. Seventy percent of all patients did not speak English. And groups of foreign educated nurses huddled to speak in their native languages of the Philippines, Asia, Africa and Europe. I spent much of my time educating patients in Spanish while these nurses bonded with each other. One English-only Anglo nurse commented to me with great surprise that on one of her shifts all three of her postpartum patients spoke English. I commented it was wonderful she had gotten so lucky. I was very surprised when she complained that, "They ask questions." I questioned myself: how can nurses educate patients when they cannot communicate with them? What will be the health and financial ramifications to this country when more and more patients leave hospitals as clueless about their condition as when they came in?

"My grandmother disowned me two days before my father died. It was his wish to die with dignity utilizing hospice-a first world philosophy that was incomprehensible to my Mexican relatives. Even though he verbalized his wishes to all, including my grandmother, I caught my grandmother and aunt force-feeding my father. He was in the last stages of cancer when he suffered a stroke that rendered him speechless. I saw my father arch backwards as the milk being forced into his mouth by these women went down his windpipe and he turned blue. He was fiercely shaking his head no and he looked relieved when he saw me enter the room. It was at that precise moment that I realized that the hours and days and weeks of my educating my grandmother about dying with dignity were futile. I had even gotten a Spanish-speaking doctor to speak with her and her daughter about hospice. To his face, they deceitfully agreed to comply because to disagree with a man, let alone a doctor, is culturally unacceptable. I forced her to leave Texas and return home to Mexico. She cursed me and wished death on my children so that I could feel the pain of losing a child. To this day, none of my father's family will have anything to do with me. And perhaps they never will.

"Make no mistake about it. Few Mexicans come to this country in hopes of adopting a new and better culture. Most are convinced that Americans are selfish, self-serving, elitists who exploit poor people and lack moral conviction. Perhaps this mentality comes from their own experiences with rich Mexicans. Middle class Mexicans are rare. Most are very poor and a few are obscenely rich.

"Two years after my mother passed away, my father remarried a woman who had been a lady in waiting for a former first lady of a Mexican state. I had the opportunity to stay in this home and got a first-hand view of the lifestyle of rich political Mexicans. It was luxurious and fully staffed with maids, cooks, chauffeurs and others. I noticed that these rich people were light skinned and had colored eyes. With the exception of my stepmother, the staff consisted of poor Mexican Indians - the types of persons that are more likely to illegally cross the border as they attempt to escape reprehensible poverty.

"Our founding fathers came to this country in search of freedom of religion. They sought to make this new land their home. By contrast, Spanish conquistadors came to the New World in search of gold. Their intention was not to make this New World a home, but rather to steal its gold and return it to their homelands. Those who enter our borders without regard for our laws come here to do the same: to exploit us. They bring with them customs and values that are difficult for U.S. citizens to understand.

"Mexicans feel that their beliefs are superior to American beliefs. They point to their country's lower divorce rate as symbolic of better social order and higher morals. Mexicans value freedom and rights differently. For example, I recall in grade school in my back yard in Indiana, my father objected to me learning how to cheerlead as I jumped and bounced. In Spanish he scolded me for "moving like that." He said he expected more from me than the "Gueras" (Whites). He criticized my Anglo friends as being "libertinas," (libertines). The word "libertine" as my father used it and as other Mexicans use it is derived from the root "liberty" but it is intended to be a derogatory reference to American culture.

"Human rights are infringed upon every day in Mexico. My grandmother was appalled that my father could not be forced to go to a hospital against his wishes. Neither she nor my other Mexican relatives could grasp the concept of patient rights.

"Mexicans make fun of Americans' love for pets and view it as a flawed value system. I've often heard the phrase, "I bet they treat their dog better than their parents." What Americans view as freedom to live ones own life, is criticized by Mexicans as a lack of loyalty to family.

"When will our political leaders stand up to leaders such as Vicente Fox who continues to put his hand out demanding American charity rather than attempting to clean up his own mess? When will Americans be outraged at the mentality of the Mexican leadership that Americans owe Mexicans anything? They make these demands even when they turned their backs on us as we declared war on terrorism. When will Americans stop trying to fix the problems of other nations instead of protecting its citizens?

"Toward the end of my father's life, I witnessed his Americanization. He gleefully recalled attaining citizenship under the Ford Administration. He was careful not to brag to other Mexicans what I believe he felt in his heart – proud to be an American. My father lived his dream to make a better life for his children. Then he lived another dream when he retired in Mexico. But it wasn't long before he yearned for the comforts of the USA. He criticized the Mexican public bathrooms and called his people "barbaric." He denounced the Mexican street police who stopped him while he drove only because he had American license plates. They'd shamelessly demand money from him to let him go. While retired in Mexico, my father bought a dog that had puppies. When one of the puppies got sick and died, my mother shed true tears of grief. My father coped with several bottles of Tecate.

"I am grateful to my parents that I was born an American. And I will do my part in defending it from foreign invasion, the way Mexican Texans protected the Alamo. I will expose the true nature of those who exploit my country at every opportunity. And as a registered nurse, I will do my part to educate about healthcare-in English, or Spanish, or sign language.

"I believe that by allowing the mass entry of illegals from developing countries– including Mexico—we are setting our country up for a setback. Instead of evolving further as a First World country, we risk stagnation-or worse, demoting our country to Third World status."

CHAPTER 13–

ILLEGAL IMMIGRATION'S THIRD WORLD MOMENTUM CRIME WAVE

"Let every American, every lover of liberty, every well wisher to his posterity, swear by the blood of the Revolution, never to violate in the least particular, the laws of the country; and never to tolerate their violation by others...let every man remember that to violate the law, is to trample on the blood of his father, and to tear the character of his own, and his children's liberty."

Abraham Lincoln

In the summer of 2003 in Boulder, Colorado, eight illegal aliens raped eight American woman. The aliens fled back to Mexico. One was caught. In a nearby city of Longmont, a used car dealer was driven out of business because he suffered unending theft from his lot that he bankrupted. An illegal alien killed a California Los Angeles cop, David Marsh, in 2003. Robberies and break-ins have become the norm in California. John Hessler, a former CU college quarterback, was hit head-on in Colorado in 2003 by two Mexican nationals who ran from the scene. They fled back to Mexico never to be caught. Hessler suffers from traumatic brain injury and sits in a wheelchair trying to regain his life. The personal tragedies go on and on and on. They've become the pattern in Florida, Georgia, North Carolina and dozens of other states. But the sobering realities concerning these crimes point to major culprits: illegal aliens. They import themselves into this country with a vengeance. They are deadly, pernicious and organized. They represent the worst of what is common in the Third World.

According to Heather MacDonald in her recent "THE ILLEGAL ALIEN CRIME WAVE," our country is being assaulted by a crime wave that grows steadily and viciously.

A full 95 percent of all outstanding warrants for homicide in 2003, which totaled 1,500 in Los Angeles, were issued for illegal aliens. Soberingly, two-thirds of all fugitive felony warrants, totaling 17,000 were for illegal aliens. To make matters worse, in 1995 a report showed that 60 percent of the 20,000-strong 18th Street gang in southern California was composed of illegal aliens. That gang collaborates with the Mexican Mafia on drug distribution schemes, extortion and drive-by assassinations. They commit assault and robberies every day of the week. A night of crime to them is like a day of work for American citizens.

How did this crime wave come about and why is it spreading? In 1979, Los Angeles Police Department Chief Daryl Gates enacted Special Order 40. As if insanity took the front row seat in their minds, leaders of dozens of cities from San Francisco to Miami and New York City—adopted this special order. This law prohibits police officers from arresting illegal aliens. In reality, it's a carte blanche invitation for crime to grow in our country—putting citizens at risk for their lives.

"If I see a deportee from the Mara Salvatrucha prison in El Salvador crossing the street in LA, I can't touch him," said a

Los Angeles police officer. "I can't arrest him for an immigration felony."

Boulder, Colorado practices the same 'sanctuary' policy for illegal aliens. The mayor of the city encourages illegal aliens by making sure the police chief cannot arrest illegals. Some of Boulder's immigration lawyers boldly offered publicly announced classes for illegal aliens on how to avoid arrest, detention and deportation by immigration agents. The result in that town shows a tripling of the illegal alien population as well as jobs taken away from citizens and the eight violent rapes in the summer of 2003.

Not far away in Denver in the autumn of 2003, an illegal alien, Javier Cruz-Caballero, purposely ran down police officer, Robert Bryant, while the officer operated a radar gun in a school walk zone. Witnesses saw the Mexican national rev his engine while taking dead-aim at the officer. Officer Bryant flew 30 feet through the air while suffering a broken leg and head lacerations. He could have easily been killed. Again, Special Order 40 adopted by the Denver leaders protected Cruz-Caballero from previous arrest and deportation.

At a greater level, New York's Mayor Bloomberg supports illegal alien crime by maintaining a 'sanctuary policy' in that city. Last year, four illegals raped and killed a New York jogger. That crime was one of thousands of crimes committed by illegal aliens who are protected from the law. More horrific from impact of this loss of the rule-of-law, former Mayor Guiliana practiced Special Order 40. He tenaciously defended illegal aliens in his city. Several of them protected by the 'Order' participated in 9/11. The death toll reached 3,000 while the impact on our nation reverberates today. Yet, Special Order 40 continues full force in protecting the estimated 9 to 13 million illegal aliens in our country.

Thousands of them kill, rape, rob and drive illegally in our country. They carry no insurance for their vehicles, which means they 'hit and run' or flee from accident scenes. You and I see our loved ones killed and we pay the damages. Over 400,000 deportees continue walking around free in our country. The ones that commit crimes and are caught comprise 29 percent of our prison populations. They cost American taxpayers nearly $1 billion annually to feed, house and care for them in our prisons.

And, yet, Special Order 40, continues as if it was a fig leaf for welcoming hardened alien criminals.

Most Americans have heard about the Bloods and Crips, which are Hispanic American turf gangs. Those guys play with teddy bears compared to the MS-13 Salvadoran gangs formed in the 1980s . They encompass 28 states as of this writing.

"MS-13 may, hands down, be the most dangerous out there," said Wes McBride, president of California Gang Investigators Association and veteran of the LA County Sheriff's Department. "They have no compunction about killing. MS-13 will kill a cop at the drop of a hat. They don't mess around. They've taken over the East Coast as the worst gangs. They swagger with more than 8,000 members."

Robert Ward, intelligence analyst at the Organized Crime and Violence Unit of the National Drug Intelligence Center, said, "They've spread to Seattle, Nashville, Houston, Dodge City and Shreveport, Louisiana."

They have become one of the most notorious gangs in the world. Members murder, rape, beat people up, carry out drive-by shootings, deal drugs, smuggle illegal aliens, traffic in weapons, prostitution, extortion and kidnapping.

"Gangs are like cancer," McBride said. "It's controllable if you get it early and stay on it."

The problem he voices has to do with importing more people enslaved in poverty. The gangs help them find an identity and respect. While our Congress is insulated from this crime wave, it's slithered into Washington, DC in the past few years. It's killing American citizens. In July of 2003, four persons were killed and five others wounded in the District in a series of shootings where gangs fought for turf. They feature names such as Street Thug Criminals and Vatos Locos, which means "crazy men."

Not far away in Fairfax, Virginia, police Lt. Culin said, "There are an estimated 3,000 members of the Salvadoran gang MS-13 in Northern Virginia. There are 82 gangs in Fairfax County. Two police supervisors and seven detectives work gang crimes full time in the country."

These examples of illegal immigrant crime depict a growing menace to our functioning society. While the American public

103

slumbers and our Congress refuses enforcement of our borders along with mayors adopting the 'sanctuary policy,' we citizens receive an average of 2,200 illegals every day, 365 days per year. Since the Amnesty policy was announced, the invasion intensifies with greater numbers. Some Border Patrol officers report a 15 percent rise in crossings.

The situation escalates, so much so, FORBES, June 7, 2004, reported an ever-growing crime network in a piece titled, "PREYING ON HUMAN CARGO," by Michael Maiello and Susan Kitchens. They researched how American companies subvert American law. Human smugglers make $7 billion annually. The network imports 10,000 Chinese illegally from Fujian Province into New York City each year. A coyote makes $9,000.00 in two days leading 15 people across the border, but that is a fraction of the $500,000.00 annual take. Illegal aliens arrive from every country imaginable. Only 4 percent of illegal aliens are apprehended crossing the Texas border. Target, Wal-Mart, Shop Rite, Clarion Hotels, Best Western and Dunkin' Donuts were implicated in the article. All firms pleaded that individual franchises made contracting decisions.

American citizens pay enormous costs while supporting this crime wave in ways they don't realize. Millions of these people do not participate or pay for operating this country. Illegal aliens send as much as 70 percent of their income to their home countries. They end up using our welfare, food stamps, medical facilities and infrastructure at horrific costs to us. Who benefits? A few people at the top! The rest of us pay and pay.

Where does that leave you? If you're in California, you're planning on moving to Idaho or Montana because it's already too late. The gangs are burrowed and connected into Los Angeles as deeply as the sewer systems. With over three million illegals, California's crime wave is beyond stopping. If you're in Georgia, you're probably stewing under your breath, but you don't have a clue that it will worsen. In Chicago, they take jobs, rob banks or organize drug, prostitution and theft rings. If you're in Miami, it is no longer an American city. Houston is just as bad. It grows worse in every city in America.

It's called "Third World Momentum." The key is to understand that in the Third World—corruption, crime, child prostitution, bashing in peoples' heads, torture and worse are the norm. Why? The rule-of-law no longer applies. Today, in America, concerning illegal immigration, our public officials who swore to uphold the Constitution, neglect their oaths of office. We're forced NOT to discuss it via political correctness, yet we are the victims of our own silence.

Because the American public still hasn't figured this crisis out or keeps thinking it will vanish on its own—IT IS GOING TO GET WORSE—and you or your loved ones will become victims given enough time.

To give you an idea of the extent of this crime wave, the following chapter will bring it to you from a police officer's squad car.

CHAPTER 14—

ILLEGAL IMMIGRATION FROM A POLICE OFFICER'S SQUAD CAR

"We have Nicaragua, soon we will have El Salvador, Guatemala, Honduras, Costa Rica and Mexico. One day, tomorrow or five years or fifteen years from now, we're going to take five to ten million Mexicans and they are going into Dallas, into El Paso, into Houston, into New Mexico, into San Diego, and each one will have embedded in his mind the idea of killing ten Americans."

Thomas Borge, Nicaragua Interior Minister
Quoted in Washington Times, March 27, 1985

Tens of thousands of illegal aliens drive without driver's licenses or insurance. Coyote smugglers drive without lights the wrong way on California freeways in the dead of night—only to crash into innocent American drivers who didn't have a chance as the human torpedoes hit them head-on in the darkness.

In Sequoia National Park last summer, $150 million drug plantations, run by Mexican drug cartels, and guarded by armed aliens that threatened backpackers, were discovered by federal law enforcement officials. Their brazen disregard for our laws exposed another problem: Our president and Congress refuse to enforce our immigration laws, thus encouraging more criminals toward bolder lawless behavior in every sector of our nation.

Many cities and states harbor illegal aliens and give them aid. Some states allow illegal aliens a legal driver's license with no background check. They could be the next terrorist flying a C-4 plastic explosives loaded single engine airplane into Hoover Dam, a college playoff bowl or an NFL football game.

In Miami last year, an illegal Honduran was arrested for lewd and lascivious molestation. He overstayed his visa. But, because he was not checked for immigration violations, he was set free. Later, he viciously and violently raped seven Miami women. He wasn't arrested in the first place because of the large Honduran immigrant population in Miami. This example graphically shows that immigration is no longer a policy driven by us, but our policy, driven by fear of what 'they' might do, is driving us by sheer numbers of illegal aliens. In other words, our laws no longer apply to anyone who is an immigrant, legal or otherwise. The 'tail' is 'wagging' the dog.

How bad is it? Below is the tip of a growing iceberg slamming into American cities. It's not getting better, but it is getting worse.

In the last chapter, we examined what is becoming an illegal alien crime wave across our country. But like everything we read in the papers or see on TV, it's not personal, that is, until it happens to us. That's why a police officer is the best source of what is REALLY going on with immigration chaos in America. This is a view that is up close and ugly. Meet Doug Hamilton, not his real name, police officer on the graveyard shift in a city much like your own. Dozens of other police officers offered to tell their stories from California, Houston, Dallas, Miami, Atlanta, Seattle, Cleveland, New York City, Chicago and Detroit.

Officer Hamilton filed the following reports from his squad car:

"At 05:30 today, I sat in my patrol car underneath the overhang of an office building. This was in a business area and I watched a car make its way down the road. Moving quickly from one side of the road to the other, the operator was delivering newspapers. He pulled into the parking area and delivered some papers. He was the same man I had written a ticket to twice before and had towed his car for driving without a license or insurance. I walked over to him saying, "I assume you must have gotten your license. May I see it?

"He gave me a blank look and stated he did not speak English. I asked if he remembered me and what I had told him several weeks earlier in this exact spot. "Delivering papers," was the response. He then gave me a Peruvian license, without an accompanying International License. Not that it would have mattered—he has been living in the US for over three years illegally. I had warned this illegal about driving without a license. It must have made quite an impression, because in addition to delivering newspapers he also got a job delivering pizzas. The empty Domino's pizza delivery bag on the back seat told the story. I could have let him go on his way. After all, he was just doing the jobs Americans won't do.

"The odd thing is that I know an American citizen who attempted to get one of these delivery routes, but he was not needed. I wonder why? The illegal immigrant's newspaper boss showed up and I told him that it probably wasn't a wise decision, from a liability standpoint, to hire an unlicensed driver to deliver his papers. He told me they weren't liable because drivers are considered sub-contractors. He was correct. I towed the car and wrote another ticket, wondering for the hundredth time why I bother?

"I drove home slowly after my shift because of the treacherous road conditions. It was still snowing and there were patches of ice all over the highway. I waited patiently as the road narrowed to one lane because of an accident up ahead. As I approached, I saw a green cleaning van heavily damaged and resting against the jersey barrier. Standing around it were three Hispanics. The van had passed me on the left earlier, traveling at a high rate of speed. Maybe they were here legally, but I doubt it. It just amazes me that we have so many illegal drivers, breaking traffic laws, causing crashes, and laughing at the dumb Americans that register their cars, pay for licenses, and carry car insurance."

This police officer, Doug Hamilton, is an ex-Marine. He served his country with honor. Now in his early 30s, he serves as an officer of what is known as the 'Thin Blue Line.' He's the difference between you being safe at night in your bed or being mugged on a city street or killed by a speeding drug dealer. He patrols a major city on the East Coast on the graveyard shift. He's like any American citizens—a husband, father, citizen and involved in his community.

"Nobody in the media will expose what is happening in every city in America," he said. "I couldn't possibly make any of this up. Of dozens of calls that were dispatched last night, two crashes involved Hispanics that fled the scene. One illegal was arrested. Later, a female from Peru, who did not speak English, was arrested for domestic assault with a weapon. I ticketed yet another unlicensed illegal for motor vehicle violations. As a police officer, I come into contact daily with people who are in this country illegally and who have no respect for the law or American citizens. Even when treated with respect and courtesy and being warned instead of being arrested, they again flaunt the law. The reason for this is that they know there are no federal repercussions after they are arrested even though it is discovered they are here illegally. They don't respect our laws because we don't enforce them. Period!"

Illegal aliens that suffer from tuberculosis, leprosy, Chagas Disease or hepatitis spread those diseases to other inmates. This causes further medical costs into the millions. Officer Hamilton spoke of a few examples:

"I stopped a car for a violation and discovered the operator was an unlicensed illegal immigrant who worked as a busboy in a Spanish bar," he said. "I allowed a licensed friend of his to drive him home and warned him he could not drive. Several days later while I was walking a foot post, I observed him about to enter a car. He looked at me, got in, and started to drive away. This time I towed his car and gave him a ticket. The very next week I again observed him driving and this time placed him under arrest. He posted bail. He was arrested again by another officer for operating without a license. He did not respond to court or pay any of his fines. He was arrested on a warrant, but did not serve any jail time. Every officer I know can relate similar stories. These are just the ones we catch."

"What would you say is one of your greatest frustrations as a police officer?" I asked.

He said, "This summer I observed a group of illegal male Hispanics drinking from beer bottles in one of our parks. I did not take action, but told them to the empty the bottles and then join their friends in the picnic area. Beer is allowed; glass is not. I parked a short distance away, but right in front of me, they returned to the vehicle and removed several beer bottles, drinking them a short distance away. I ended their party and wrote tickets. Why did they do this despite my presence? No respect for our laws."

"What are the dangerous aspects you encounter regarding identification?" I asked.

"This one drives me nuts," Hamilton said. "Illegals learn many ways to confuse the police and hinder them in their investigations. The most common way is to pretend that they don't speak English. Another common method is using several different names. If a man's name is Juan Sebastien Lopez-Garcia, he will use several variations of that name and often change his date of birth. He may use Juan Lopez the first time he is arrested. The next time he may use Sebastien Garcia. The intent is to prevent an officer from discovering a past arrest or warrant—and it does work. The reason is that rarely does an illegal immigrant have any true documentation of which they are, so it is much tougher to verify a person's identity. A better way is to make a custodial arrest and require photo ID before allowing release. Unfortunately these offenders are often released after showing dubious photo ID's that are easily obtained for a fee."

I asked, "What you're reporting is a complete lack of law and order or respect for the law. With millions more poised to be added with the Bush amnesty, what do police officers think about illegal immigration?"

"I gotta tell you," he said. "Many Americans are fed up with the current trend of our government turning a blind-eye to the massive problem of illegal immigration. We create immigration laws that are ignored and then, when enough people sneak into this country, we pardon them by granting amnesty. This encourages further violations. It makes you sick. It is also unfair to the thousands of people who have followed the proper immigration procedures to obtain citizenship. It also encourages these people to continue breaking laws while they are in the country, especially motor vehicle laws. Municipal and state law enforcement officials, like myself, are fed up with arresting illegal immigrants, only to have them released. We must re-arrest these individuals when they again commit a crime, as they invariably do."

"Are you saying that national security is ineffectual?" I asked. "Is Tom Ridge fooling himself and us? How great is our risk each day?"

"I can tell you," he said. "If an illegal wants to legally circumvent our driving laws, he can obtain a license from a state with minimal identification requirements. In Virginia, for example, if a person has a Virginia address and a photo ID, like a passport, he can obtain a license. Once an illegal has this document, he can now legally drive in this country and has legitimate identification. I discovered this after I compared notes with several other officers and learned that illegal immigrants would go to Virginia, get a license, and then use it to drive in other states that had stricter laws for obtaining licenses. This way when they were stopped, the only action an officer could take would be to write a ticket for failure to change address. This is what I do. I spoke with a cooperative illegal immigrant who told me that many of his friends would go to Virginia and that they all used the same address of someone they knew in Virginia, on the application. This was very common and most illegal immigrants knew how to do it. This is a tremendous hole in our national security system that needs to be closed—NOT opened by allowing illegal immigrants to obtain licenses as was recently proposed. Since 9/11, I believe that states have tightened up on this aspect, but I still receive Virginia licenses with regularity."

After writing a ticket to an illegal alien from Guatemala whom had no license, this officer said, "Guess what he is doing? Delivering papers. His job requires him to drive a car, yet he has no license. Unbelievable! But it gets better. I warned this same guy several weeks ago not to drive. I had been heading to a call and told him it was his lucky day because I did not have time to write him a ticket. I told him that if I saw him driving again, the next time I would tow his car. So after writing him over $400.00 worth of tickets, that is what I did."

Hamilton's shift ended at sunrise. What would go through one's mind if they were serving their state and country with their lives on the line daily while their own leaders would not uphold our nation's laws? It begs the question across America concerning the rule-of-law. If our laws are routinely disobeyed by illegal aliens at the federal level and then, at the state level—and finally, at the local level with impunity—at what point does a nation move toward lawlessness as the norm? What is the definition of law? How long before it breaks down to the point whereby so many disregard it that a community can't function or functions in fear. With 10 to 13 million illegal aliens operating in the United States, an amnesty will draw millions more just as a green light means 'GO' in traffic.

PART II—THE LOSS OF LAW AND ORDER

"Here is a question I have found myself asking numerous times," Hamilton said. "What exactly does the INS, now the Bureau of Immigration and Customs Enforcement do?"

"I know what they are supposed to do and it has something to do with protecting our borders and enforcing immigration law, but they don't do it," he said. "I know they now have a new name, and a wonderful new leader, but I still don't see any action."

Mr. Ridge are you listening? The only color code we need is green. You either have a green card or you don't. If you don't, then you need to leave, not register to work as our president has proposed. I learned early on in my career that an INS agent, or whatever they are calling themselves now, virtually never shows up when called about an illegal alien. I assumed that they only responded to very serious felonies, but this doesn't seem to be the case either.

"I learned about an example of this from a fellow officer last night during my shift," Hamilton said. "We were talking about the massive problem of illegal immigration and the ineffectiveness of the BICE when he told me about a call he had several years ago. He had stopped a truck for a motor vehicle violation and discovered the truck was uninsured and unregistered. The operator was a previously deported felon and was placed into custody for the motor vehicle violations. While the car was being searched, a loaded handgun was found under the passenger seat. INS was notified and said they weren't interested, but to call back if he was convicted. Interesting! A deported felon with a weapon is in police custody, but they are not interested. The illegal felon went to court and was convicted of the charges and he was sentenced to three years-suspended sentence, followed by three years probation. For those of you not in the criminal justice field, I'll explain. HE WAS NOT GOING TO SERVE ANY JAIL TIME. The officer again contacted INS and guess what? Believe it or not, INS did not respond. A previously deported felon, with a loaded gun, is arrested by the police and neither the federal or local government seem to care."

"Houston, we've got a problem," Hamilton said.

How can you expect police officers to do their jobs, if after making an excellent arrest, the response is to let the person go again? It demoralizes the cop and it encourages the illegal alien to continue breaking the law—knowing that there is no price to pay. If you wonder why there appears to be a breakdown of law and order, this is why.

This is an example of Third World Momentum accelerating into the United States. I've traveled in much of the Third World. Mail carriers only deliver mail when patrons pay bribes. You must have your postcards and letters canceled at the window or they will be stolen. You can not trust a single mailed package to make it to its destination from thievery. Entire police forces are on the take. Many help drug peddlers. You can not trust the food to be free from diseases such as hepatitis. Milk and meat are exposed to hot air and flies in the market place. Extortion and racketeering are the norm. Citizens run red lights as a matter of course. Litter is thrown with impunity on streets, country roads and major highways. Garbage and trash along with plastic are tossed into streams, lakes and into the oceans. There are no rules, or if there are rules, they are not enforced—therefore not obeyed.

For example, in Lima, Peru, the major river flowing out of the mountains meanders through the city. On each bank for 10 miles above the city are hundreds of millions of cans, bottles, junk, trash and filth. Additionally, the same trash floats down the river in a never-ending stream of pollution. Thousands of shantytown people live in the squalor and defecate/urinate and throw any amount of poisons into the water. The mouth of the river underwater and in the Pacific Ocean is a pile up of humanity's debris. It's beyond sickening and revolting.

This Third World Momentum manifests itself in Officer Hamilton's city.

"Illegal aliens in this country know that there is little chance they will be deported, so they keep sneaking in," he said. "While it is nice to see that we are deporting some of those that over stay Visas in the war on terrorism, we are not deporting the domestic terrorists that are slowly eroding our infrastructure. No one wants to disarm and remove the ticking bomb that is illegal immigration before it destroys our economy permanently. Instead, the government has proposed the novel solution of granting amnesty again, although that is not what they are calling it. It's a slap in the face to the thousands of Border Agents that risk their lives daily driving these immigrant invaders back across the border. For what purpose? If the police and border agents are not supported on the state and federal levels respectively, with aggressive prosecution of these criminals to include deportation, morale will continue to fall. What incentive does the front-line soldier have to stop the enemy, if his country refuses to admit there is a war?"

This crisis multiplies in every city in America. Cop by cop, city by city, the march of illegal aliens and loss of law and order proceeds steadily, methodically and perniciously. Thousands of examples manifest themselves daily in our land. It's like something or someone is planning the destruction of our country by applying an unknown force to crush law and order.

"This is the biggest obstacle officers face today, a lack of motivation and low morale because of our government's refusal to take action," Hamilton said. "You begin to develop an attitude of, "What is the point?" Why should I bother to do a good job, when ultimately it is for nothing?"

"We still end up making the requisite arrests, but there is little satisfaction at the end of the day. We constantly make arrests and advise the people in charge of the problem, but the politicians don't want to pass meaningful legislation. Instead they cater to these illegal aliens, hoping to win their votes and the support of the many Hispanic organizations popping up in this country. God forbid one of these elected officials takes a stand and demands that we stop trying to be empathic and start enforcing the laws of this country. He would be labeled racist, a political death sentence."

After the evening shift wove into a new day, Officer Hamilton returned to the station.

"As I enter the lobby of police headquarters to turn in my paperwork, I observe three Hispanics waiting for a Spanish interpreter so they can get some assistance," Hamilton said. "I can't help them because I speak English. I guess I should learn Spanish. I asked a buddy of mine in the locker room if he knew what the capital of Guatemala was."

He laughed and said, "Of course. We work in it."

PART III: WHEN LAW AND ORDER SLIP INTO THIRD WORLD MOMENTUM

This crisis already has more illegals and specific ethnic groups pandering even greater numbers of their passage into our country to the detriment of us all. It's now beyond dangerous for the continuation of this nation as a viable republic. Even more frightening, we are at risk as a sustainable society from the standpoint of clean air, energy, water and enough food—as we're pushed to add 200 million more people by mid-century.

Since the U.S. media will not broach it, much like the early history of our nation, patriots who live down in the streets of America—must awaken their fellow countrymen.

"Just so you know, these incidents that I relate are from personal experience, so they are accurate," he said. "I wish the public knew the massive problems these illegal aliens are creating."

What Hamilton's report brings to the surface is what the national media refuses to address. Somebody in power force-feeds us into criminal chaos. The national media winks at the existence of 10 to 13 million people who have illegally crossed our borders. Thus, the 'fluff stories' feature people who come here 'to work for a better life.' Today, it's not a few, it's millions, and now, millions of us are being affected—in every realm of American society.

"One area that is really frustrating is the lack of respect many of these illegal immigrants have for members of American society," Hamilton said. "As it is, they know there is actually very little to fear from law enforcement officers. Because of the political stigma attached to speaking out against the numerous crimes these people commit, most administrations turn a blind eye to the growing problem of the lawless behavior these people exhibit. Yet, over the last week, most of the calls I have responded to, and arrests I have made, have been of illegal or legal immigrants."

What officer Hamilton talks about is a general disregard for the rule of law. It is the same in the Third World. Laws are not obeyed as a natural aspect of a lack of respect for an ordered society. It's why so many societies do not function with any kind of standards. It's why chaos rules. It's why people starve. It's why for example, Mexico has no environmental laws. It's why drugs run easily through Columbia and Mexico. It's why so much of Mexico suffers human degradation. It's also why law enforcement in Mexico and Columbia is done without restraint or protocol. It's why gangs and lawlessness thrive.

"We have had two cases where officers were physically resisted and assaulted, forcing them to call for emergency assistance," Hamilton said. "The first case involved an illegal immigrant family from Peru. The three male cousins, all of whom had Virginia driver's licenses, were wanted for an assault they had committed earlier. Once the responding officers attempted to make the arrest, they were fought and the sister and mother also assaulted officers. All five were arrested. One of the men stated, "You can't arrest me. This is my house." What is interesting about this statement, is that a similar version was spoken to officers several weeks ago, on a call involving a family of illegal Colombian immigrants. Initially they would not open the door, but finally complied with the request of the responding officer. Only to tell him words to the effect of, "Get off my property. You can't arrest me. Do you have a warrant?" Once the officers grabbed the man to arrest him, other family members, who then shut the door, pulled them into the house. Another emergency assistance was called for and four people were arrested. Two officers sustained injuries in the melee that ensued and pepper spray was required to subdue one illegal. Both families requested Spanish interpreters after being arrested."

Hamilton continued, "These incidents and statements are a cause for alarm because they are not isolated. They reflect the disdain for America and American citizens that these people have. These statements typify the feeling of entitlement that has been created because of our nation's non-existent immigration policy. An illegal immigrant has enough working knowledge of our legal system to demand a warrant, yet openly flaunts those same laws, knowing he will not be held accountable. If he is held accountable, he can claim that there was a language barrier or that the responding officers were racist. I find it interesting that we, as law enforcement officers, must obey every rule and are held accountable for every action we take, yet there is no effort to hold these criminals accountable for their actions."

The only reason law enforcement is effective is that law-abiding citizens respect the laws of their community or fear being arrested for doing something illegal. They fear speeding tickets, because they may lose their license as a result. If their licenses are suspended, most of these people will refrain from driving or at least be overly cautious if they decide to again break the law.

"This is not the way illegal immigrants react to an arrest," Hamilton said. "In fact, many of these illegals go out of their way to draw attention to themselves. Speeding, running red lights, adorning your car with illegal lights, and blasting loud music are not the actions you would expect a person that has no license to take, but it is common."

This lawless behavior also extends to areas such as littering, noise ordinances, and being drunk in public. Yet, they have come here to work for the American Dream.

Hamilton added, "In my experience, this has not been the case. These are people that are becoming an increasing burden on the criminal justice system and costing taxpayers billions of dollars. In other states where I have friends that are police officers, they report the same thing. Ultimately, because we refuse to enforce the laws of our borders, the laws of the individual states are laughed at as well. This makes the job of law enforcement officers impossible. When faced with an impossible task, many people give up. Police officers are no different. Many have already thrown the towel in when it comes to dealing with these people because nothing ever happens after the arrest is made. The problem is only going to get worse."

Officer Hamilton and hundreds of thousands of other police officers nationwide face a mounting crisis in the 'Thin Blue Line.' At what point do illegal alien numbers become bigger than the number of police officers? What happens as the criminal element of these illegals 'enclave' themselves in cities across this nation like the 20,000-member '18th Street Gang' has done in Los Angeles? How about the growing Honduran Gangs in Washington, DC? At what point does lawlessness overwhelm the rule-of-law? With an average of nearly a million illegals crossing US borders annually, that equals 10 more million in a decade. What happens as these gangs spread? Who will check their progress? Will it lead to a mass flight by American citizens? Why should Americans be forced to flee from their own cities and states because their own congressmen and senators won't enforce immigration laws? How can police officers be called 'racists' when they are doing their jobs?

What's going to happen to us as more and more illegal aliens do not subscribe to the rule-of-law? Third World Momentum rolls into America on our freeways without so much as a warning ticket from Congress.

CHAPTER 15—

ILLEGAL IMMIGRATION COMES TO SMALL TOWN AMERICA

"A really efficient totalitarian state would be one in which the all-powerful executive of political bosses and their army of managers control a population of slaves who do not have to be coerced, because they love their servitude."

Aldous Huxley

The above quote hits, like a head-on collusion, concerning illegal alien labor used by companies and corporations across America. It's a formidable aspect of indentured servitude or some kind of modern-day slavery not yet defined. It applies to what is happening in Austin, Minnesota.

As stated before, illegal aliens continue crossing at 2,200 per day and 800,000 annually. They form an endless line injecting themselves into the Golden Goose and the Land of Milk and Honey—America.

They break into our country because their wages, living standards, diseases and personal lives in Mexico and hundreds of other countries reflect the misery, suffering, corruption and hopelessness of the Third World. They are SO desperate; they fling themselves into the mercy of summer desert heat at over 110 degrees F., while walking through hostile and unknown danger. Hundreds smuggle across border checkpoints with their kids placed in plastic pods on the sides of engines and under the hoods of cars. Others pay for tunnels dug from one side of the Mexican border to our side. Untold thousands ride in 18-wheeler freight boxes and some have died from suffocation. Others pay their life savings to have 'coyotes' lead them into America. It was estimated that Mexican coyotes in 2002 rang up their personal cash registers in billions of dollars in smuggling fees. That's how fast they invade our country.

Once they arrive, a well-oiled underground illegal alien railroad network transports them to every state in our nation. It forges documents and secures them jobs by companies who love cheap, compliant, uneducated labor that will not whimper under the worst of circumstances. Why? Anything in America is better than back in their home country. Once here, they live in a permanent underground and underclass of society. It could be called 'indentured servitude' which is a kind of modern day slavery.

Who are those employers? Some of the biggest, most time-honored companies in America participate in working illegal aliens. Tyson Chicken was caught. Contracting firms working at the Air Force Academy have been caught hiring illegal aliens. Huge construction firms, paving firms and Wal-Mart hire illegal aliens. Once caught, their official media staff responds, "We didn't know they were illegal aliens. They were independent contractors." Illegals work in our most famous fast food stores. They not only hire them, some, assist in hauling them up from the Border States in vans and busses.

In 22 years, meatpacking plants have turned the tiny town of, Austin, Minnesota into a quagmire of corruption, disease, drugs, gangs, school chaos and civic crisis. Town folks fight what they call a nightmare as it undermines American workers, undercuts their wages, fires them—knowing they have illegal alien replacements and subverts OSHA regulations at every juncture.

Austin with 27,000 residents is like any other middle-class, blue-collar town in America. Soccer moms cheer from the sidelines, bake sales abound, folks play bingo on Wednesday nights, paperboys throw papers, cheerleaders practice after school and dads take their kids to the old fishing hole.

It's also home of meat packing plants where generations of citizens worked at and supported the meat processing industry. They earned living wages with health benefits and made them the most trusted names in America.

Affectionately known as "Spamtown USA," Austin suffered 3,477 minor crimes in 1982. In 2002, that number jumped to 8006 small crimes. In 1982 Spamtown tallied 160 major crimes. By 2002, it jumped to 540 big crimes.

The illegal immigration into Austin has been estimated at 4,000 to 5,000 in 2003. No one knows for certain. But one point is clear: crime jumped 300 percent from the invasion of illegal aliens.

How did it come about? The strike in the mid-80s crushed the union and opened the door to cheap, illegal labor. The biggest lie is that Americans won't do that work. The facts show they won't do it for slave wages. They won't do it under unsafe working conditions. The key ingredient in meat packing plants' thrusts for higher profits was to replace an intelligent, dedicated American workforce for a Third World labor force that would never call for better wages, benefits or retirement. That uneducated labor force would also not question the breaking of Occupational Safety and Health Administration regulations.

A resident of over 50 years in Austin, Mark Jackson, (not his real name), said, "Illegal people hide in the shadows in fear. If they are made legal, they will want better wage and benefits packages. People who live in fear will do what they are told. The meat packing plants don't want legal citizens working for them.

"President Bush wants a guest worker force, so these people will never be legal," Jackson said. "The South wanted guest workers too, before the Civil War. They were called slaves. This slave labor supposedly bolstered the economy and helped the nation. After the war, the slave labor stopped and the country moved ahead. The economy returned without the need for slave labor. Is there a comparison here? You better believe it!"

In the following years after the strike, packing plants gradually replaced the entire workforce with illegal, Spanish speaking laborers. They colonized the jobs. The undertone of that is quite clear: an illegal, compliant workforce with an all white management hierarchy.

Jackson added, "If you dare to challenge this policy, you will be called a racist. In other words, in Spamtown, USA, if you point out a problem, you become the problem. Independent thinking is forbidden in Austin, Minnesota. Independent speech is a hanging offense. With all this in mind, you must now realize the need to acclimate the general public into accepting all the mechanisms of low wage slave labor. This sets the stage for corporate domination and brainwashing."

How is this accomplished? First, huge sums of money are used to source media tools that reach the most people. Then, you define the message.

"The packing plant," Jackson said, "slipped an intravenous needle into that vein and has been pumping messages into it on a daily basis with the help of immigration lawyers, the press and worst of all, the well meaning clergy.

"Communication of this mass immigration commercial is verbal. A language must be created to desensitize the brainwashing victim. Illegal alien sounds ominous. It must be palatable, hence the term 'undocumented worker' or 'guest worker.' It sounds sweet, helpful and innocent, when, in fact, it is a Federal crime.

What has this corporate greed for greater profits caused Austin's citizens?

The air around the plant is putrefied with the stench of burning feces, urine, hair and spam if one could consolidate the mix. That aroma wafts for almost a mile in every direction. Let it be noted that no executive lives anywhere near it, although 80 percent of its legal and illegal workforce does.

The sewer plant 1.5 miles to the south, also in a neighborhood, reeks 24 hours a day. Home values dropped and no one wants to play ball anymore in Prestigious Marcussen Park. Any team from out of town loathes the park. When a semi pro team located there a couple of years ago, no one attended.

Austin, once famous for having the highest home ownership in America, has now been recognized as the county seat for Minnesota's highest wage disparity. The local newspaper stated 46 percent of their school children qualify at poverty level and 20 percent of Austin High School seniors will not graduate and another 10 percent are borderline. In the 70s, that didn't happen. What's worse, there is now a daycare center for illegitimate children in Austin High School.

"ESL programs are a mask to dupe the public into believing immigrants are trying to become Americans as they did a hundred years ago," Jackson said. "This is not happening. For every success story, there are five failures. The fact is, illegals do not want to learn English." (refer to Lillian Gonzalez chapter)

Even worse, illegals skirt health screening as they break into America. In 2002, illegal alien arrests resulted in eight police personnel testing positive for tuberculosis. This is a frightening reality since 16,000 new cases of incurable multi-drug resistant tuberculosis migrated into the United States in the past six years inside the bodies of illegal alien immigrants.

Jackson recalls, "The worst of all the effects happening to us is the influx of unscreened (for any diseases), illegal aliens, six inches from your face. To start with, they are unknown persons. They have no identification and if they do, they carry forged documents. They have no criminal background check, no health exams and they are standing inches away from you in every Kwik Trip or Wal-Mart checkout line. The person 6" from your back may be fleeing from the law in his own country for wife beating, murder or child molesting. He may have leprosy, Chagas, hepatitis or TB.

"This is with the blessing of the Federal Government because somebody up there thinks it's good for the economy. When in fact, it only benefits a few millionaires."

Jackson continued, "In Austin, our crime has tripled since 1982, yet if you call the police chief, you will get a fuzzy math answer. He will tell you illegals cause no more problems than anyone else. Somehow he is unable to equate a tripling of crimes to illegal immigration.

"You can go to our hospital emergency room and find illegal aliens anytime day or night receiving free health care and even free kidney transplants brought to us by our County Commissioners. If you call St. Olaf Hospital and request a numerical total of illegal aliens on how much funding was spent on them, they won't tell you.

"But they had to report that eight of our police officers tested positive for tuberculosis last year," he said. "Our kids are at risk with all the illegal kids in our schools."

"What is left out of this is that all these services and criminal costs are in addition to crime and health problems we already have here. As our taxes rise every year in Austin, the services for illegals increases commensurately. Does it matter if the president says he won't raise taxes, yet you turn around to find the city and state can literally tax you out of your home?"

This lifelong Austin citizen added, "People never parked three cars in their front yards. Now it's common-place. Illegal immigration has changed the face of this once proud Scandinavian community forever. There is no generational recruitment for slaughterhouse labor which brings on the smuggling of illegal aliens forever."

Worse, almost every high school graduate leaves this town as soon as they can. Spamtown means mass illegal labor importation, rising crime and no opportunity.

He said, "America once needed manpower to build a nation, but now it imports labor for the wealth of a few."

Along with the illegal aliens came drugs, driving without driver's licenses, no car insurance, lack of health insurance, non-citizens using medical facilities on taxpayer's money, safe houses where illegals sleep 15 to 20 to a single-family house and growing tension in the community.

Finally, another upset citizen, Paul Roberts, not his real name, stood up at a local meeting, "Calling an illegal alien an undocumented worker is like calling a bank robber an 'unauthorized withdrawal' expert. Does anyone realize what a wonderful nation we created? We open our doors to the weak and downtrodden out of the goodness of our hearts. I don't think my grandparents expected existing Americans to pay for their babies or to celebrate Norwegian days or Viking celebrations. Immigrants wanted to learn English and become Americans. Not today! It's a huge problem for Austin because we speak English but we're forced to speak other languages in our own community. We're paying through the nose to educate another country's kids. When did law enforcement start looking the other way and why? Why to the detriment of American citizens in Austin?"

He continued, "If something is not done to stop illegal immigration soon, we will have a crisis in Austin that will force us into becoming another Third World town full of trash, drugs, gangs and worse. It's already happening. All this is done in the name of corporate greed at the meat packing plants."

"Excuse me," Roberts said, "But don't our elected officials and law enforcement officers take an oath of office to enforce the constitution and the laws of the land? I find it a little unsettling when officials do not prosecute laws. Why would our politicians wish to encourage illegal immigration when anyone with eyes can see what it has done to California?

"My advice to the leaders of America entrusted with the future of our nation is to stand up honestly and courageously for American workers, consumers, voters and investors. We're sick of their ignoring laws, putting corporations before people, and politicians from hell. I do not remember learning these tactics and methods in Social Studies or History while attending Austin High School."

Since in excess of 10,000,000 illegal aliens have invaded America, with 800,000 more annually, Austin's story is being played out in small towns across America. It's serious and spreading fast. It's like a cancer that is small at first, but if not treated or removed, spreads to all parts of the body. California is the first state in the union with 3,000,000 illegal aliens. By degree, those problems accelerate across America into towns like Austin, MN, Cadillac, MI, Delray Beach, FL, Jackson, MS, Midland, TX, Valdosta, GA, Barstow, CA, Portland, OR, Portland, ME and thousands more.

Small town America created this country. It gave up its sons and daughters in a war to overthrow colonialism. New leaders stepped forward. However, there was a moment at the birth of this country when George Washington could have quit and gone home. Thomas Jefferson could have enjoyed the safety of Monticello. Betsy Ross could have stopped stitching. Paul Revere might have decided to not take that fateful ride. But they stepped up for their country.

Today, we face an invasion of an 'unarmed army' of millions that can and will defeat this nation if we stand still—if we are afraid to act—if we stop stitching—if we don't make that ride.

Watching Jackson and Roberts at the town meeting was no different than the men at the Boston Tea Party. They stood up. Since our leaders won't lead, won't act, won't do what they were elected to do—it's time small town America or any town America—stands up for these United States—and takes action from every quarter, every household, every citizen.

President Lincoln, in his darkest hour, decided to make a stand for his country when he said, "It is rather for us to be here dedicated to the great task remaining before us—that from these honored dead we take increased devotion to that cause for which they gave the last full measure of devotion—that we here highly resolve that these dead shall not have died in vain, that this nation under God shall have a new birth of freedom, and that government of the people, by the people, for the people, shall not perish from this earth."

What Lincoln faced then, we face now. We face the destruction of everything our Founding Fathers bet on with their lives. We are in danger of losing everything that every man and woman, civilian and military, fought to preserve for posterity. Our children, language and functioning society are at extreme risk.

The worst decision that an American citizen can make today is to think that he or she can do so little that he or she does nothing at all. Because, if they do nothing, illegal immigration will expand past small town America and move into every community in our country. We'll all be reduced to subsistent wages as their numbers rise sharply throughout America. A look at California with three million illegal aliens, a bankrupted school system, major drug gangs and a $38 billion debt—illustrates what is in store for all of us when another 10, 20, 30, 40, 50 million people break into our country. When you add the ones that move in legally, the numbers stagger the mind.

It's a sure bet that President George Bush's 'guest worker/ amnesty plan' has inspired millions of desperate people to crash our borders and make our country like the one they left—an explosion of Third World Momentum.

CHAPTER 16—

WHOSE COUNTRY IS THIS, ANYWAY?

"Academic and aristocratic people live in such an uncommon atmosphere that common sense can rarely reach them."

Samuel Butler

In a British Broadcasting Company news release, dated, Friday, August 10, 2001, Colin Powell said, "We want to make sure that migration to the United States from Mexico is safe, legal, orderly and dignified."

In 2004, Bush offered a 'guest worker' program to match willing workers with willing employers.

Does that mean America is now the low-wage employment agency for the world? Come one, come all! While you're at it, drag down America's poorest workers into a spiraling wage depression like a Tarzan movie with quicksand sucking its victims into a death trap.

Powell said such a program would fulfill the needs of the American economy without putting American workers at a disadvantage. Powell did not mention the estimated 800,000 illegal aliens annually crossing our borders at the behest of Mexican President Vicente Fox. At that time, millions of Americans suffered losses from major corporations collapsing from corruption. Does the word Enron come to mind? How about a man named Ken Lay? Would you like to send him a bottle of champagne to celebrate his hard-earned fortune on his billion-dollar yacht named, "Sucker Born Every Minute?"

The outright greed of a few men in high places stood as a benchmark of loathsome human behavior. It staggered average citizens' sense of right and wrong. Further, insourcing, outsourcing and offshoring surged jobs out of the USA like a backward tidal wave—leaving millions in the unemployment lines.

All the while, a monster force of 9 to 13 million illegal aliens had marched into this country to undercut American workers. That mostly illiterate, uneducated human tidal wave splashed down on American families without mercy. Corporations demanding higher profits, transported those illegals from the Border States right into their processing plants, construction crews, fast food, hotel and paving jobs. They undercut wages, benefits and standards.

A quick look back shows Reagan 'solved' illegal immigration by giving a 'one-time' only amnesty. Bush I ignored illegal immigration. President Clinton, in between peccadilloes, winked at border security. Bush II, after him, nodded(s) at border control. The Congress, driven and paid for by big corporation money, which represented only greed and not American citizens—purposely fell asleep at the wheel concerning our national security.

Vicente Fox, shepherding his own corrupt government that has crushed that nation and its people for decades—like a second hand assisting the human tidal wave—offered every incentive to shepherd his excess human wave northward toward America. Why? His country benefited financially as millions of his 'worker bees' sent back in excess of $10 billion per year to the mother country, which in 2003, reached $14.5 billion annually. The 'aristocrats and academics' in Mexico laugh all the way to the bank with the money they rake in as well as the money they are not paying in taxes for the millions of people who escaped into the U.S. It also makes sure that Mexico has fewer voters to force change in their society. It will remain corrupt for as long as the United States keeps its borders open. Little wonder Fox had a hand in forcing his weaker counterpart, Bush, into submission with a guest worker amnesty.

In every realm of government from Bush down through the CIA, FBI, airport security and including Los Angeles Police Department's Special Order 40, which had been adopted by dozens of cities across the nation—our leaders walk around with their pants down around their ankles. In effect, the king's horses and all the king's men, along with the king, invited disaster.

Even Mayor Guiliani helped illegal aliens with his fierce promotion of Special Order 40 that ensured his police force could not bring illegal aliens to justice. Even after 9/11, millionaire Mayor Bloomberg who 'bought' his election, STILL protects illegal aliens with the 'sanctuary policy.' Governor Baldacci in Maine, March, 2004, signed a bill giving illegal aliens sanctuary. These are elected American leaders assisting illegal aliens. It's against federal law!

Senators such as Orrin Hatch and Representative Cannon of Utah promote increased illegal alien migration by supporting such bills as the Dream Act. This bill rewards illegal alien parents and their offspring with tuition breaks at the expense of American citizens' kids. For every illegal alien in college, an American student is left out. For every illegal alien admitted to a U.S. college, American citizens must pay a heavy portion of that student's tuition via state and federal taxes.

With hundreds of hospitals failing on the Border States because illegal aliens dump their sick and pregnant woman to the tune of 200,000 anchor babies annually, Senator John McCain of Arizona, instead of supporting immigration laws, supported billions of our dollars in a federal bailout via the Medicaid bill. Representative Nancy Pelosi thwarts border control agents at every turn. Dozens of senators and hundreds of congressmen do little or nothing to stem the tide of illegal immigration.

In Colorado, Representative Mark Udall supports continued 1.1 million legal immigration annually while ignoring millions illegally crossing over our borders each year. Ironically, he supports environmental causes, yet, with an estimated 200 million people being added to the U.S. population via immigration, he's like a man stepping out of a cellar into the teeth of a 120 mile per hour tornado to rescue someone out 'there.' The reality is, he'll be blown to his death and never be able to save the other victims. Udall becomes a victim. Unfortunately, we all become victims with him and his colleagues in Congress. They're forcing all of us to step out into a 120 mile per hour tornado. This illustrates self-inflicted national suicide.

Additionally, for anyone who knows about water and the West, there won't be any water to drink or grow crops as discussed in Chapter 29. Rain and snowfall remain constant. In Colorado alone, immigration population growth estimates exceed four million added people by mid-century. Some estimates total six million which accounts for millions that will escape California on the their way to Colorado's Western Slope. With California adding 20 million in the next 30 years, it's anyone's guess what kind of a train wreck will occur. It's not a question of if, but 'when.'

Those are a few examples of our leaders hoodwinking themselves and us in the process. Many more can be found in every state.

Samuel Butler's quote speaks to that group of men in high places who are so 'aristocratic and academic' that they can't see their shoelaces because their bellies and egos bulge beyond their belt lines inside the Washington Beltway.

What happened on September 11, 2001 trumpets the lack of common sense those men in power exhibit as their pants crumple around their ankles. By not doing their jobs to stop illegal immigration, they created an open invitation for terrorists. We were an easy mark. Why? When you practice sloppily and possess an arrogant attitude, any team can beat your pants off on any given night. Even with the dozens of warnings from our own agents and clues too numerous to ignore, 3,000 American citizens lost their lives at the World Trade Center towers.

For a moment, President Bush pulled up his pants. He hired Tom Ridge. He passed the Patriot Act. He bombed Afghanistan.

He declared war on Iraq but it's proving a Vietnam nightmare. Congress passed powerful acts to protect Americans.

With all their fiery speeches on protecting America, they failed and are still failing on the one invasion that will take this country down without firing a shot. What is it?

Immigration, both legal and illegal, invading our country by the millions. It is taking this country down linguistically, educationally, socially and environmentally. Immigration is taking this country from a sustainable society to an unsustainable society. It's taking it from a unified country to a Balkanized, fractious nation.

In a bluster of Homeland Security, Secretary Tom Ridge rushes from Red, Orange, Yellow and Green Alert warnings depending on the season. He's got 10,000 airport screeners patting down grandmothers before they jump on airplanes to see their loved ones. Yet, even in 2004, Special Order 40 continues its protection of illegal aliens across America. Any terrorist can walk across our border, hire a car with a friend, and set up shop like illegal alien Lee Malvo. Along with his father figure, John Mohammed, they shot up and terrorized Washington, DC—killing 14 American citizens. Any terrorist could walk to the end of an airport runway and fire a shoulder held rocket launcher into the engine of a 747 ANY day of the week. Another one could fly a single engine airplane loaded with C-4 plastic explosives into an NFL football game on any given Sunday from any one of thousands of unguarded private airports across our nation.

The lack of common sense of our Yale educated president and Congress falls below the common sense of the average American high school graduate.

However, slowly but surely, American citizens, in responsible positions, speak up. The National Association of Chiefs of Police, on January 27, 2004, claimed that national border security is a sham and the federal government is rewarding illegal alien criminals.

Jim Kouri, vice president of the 14,000 member organization said, "It's all smoke and mirrors in our border security strategy... even the president of the United States is prepared to reward lawbreakers."

Kouri abhors giving illegal aliens driver's licenses. He said, "Border security is the weakest link in our antiterrorism effort. It's our Achilles' Heel...billions of dollars are wasted on an immigration bureaucracy that does practically nothing to stop illegal alien traffic."

Kouri mentioned David Marsh, the Los Angeles police officer killed last year by an illegal Mexican alien. The alien fled back over the border and runs free today. Mexico won't arrest him or send him back because that country does not agree with the death penalty.

"If these killers aren't afraid to kill cops, then who in America is really safe from terrorists, murderers, rapists and other offenders?" he asked. "And anyone wishing to debate the problem is labeled a racist or xenophobe." (Refer to Lamm's speech in Chapter 3)

Looking back at Colorado Governor Lamm's speech warning that the 16th century word 'heretic' has been replaced with 'racist' and 'xenophobe'—it sobers any American citizen who formerly defined right from wrong in our constitutionally based rule-of-law. Plainly, our presidents and Congress refuse to enforce what we, the people voted into law.

To further unclothe our 'aristocrats and academics' inside the nation's Beltway, this is the story of a 27 year veteran U.S. Border Patrol Special Agent John W. Slagle. His story corroborates this crisis with facts, figures and experience. His is not video games and shoot 'em up, bang, bang. This man put his life on the line while our political leaders partied and still are partying in Washington, DC.

Slagle states:

"Perhaps living in a "High Intensity" illegal alien and narcotics smuggling region in Southern Arizona allows certain conclusions to be made by a 'citizen' regarding "Homeland Security" that are not seen or realized on the "Beltway" in Washington DC.

"Rural living in Southern Arizona from Cochise County to Pima County and areas west to Yuma along the Border is a unique way of life. It's far from the urban sprawl of large cities, remote areas are places of beauty with unrestricted views for miles that both ranchers and home owners appreciate for the solitude and the landscape, natural desert and dirt roads. People that chose to live in these areas are there by choice. Many owned land for generations, ranchers to people that are tired of city noise, crime and appreciate many acres between the nearest neighbor in a wilderness.

"From early 2002, after the declaration of War against Terrorist factions that attacked our nation, the Borders of Southern Arizona was a curious place to be. Despite the war, illegal immigration and narcotics smuggling seemed to escalate with major incidents border wide. Illegal aliens died in the deserts of the Tohono O'dham Indian Reservation to car crashes on 286 highway involving alien smugglers. From National Parks in Cochise County to the Organ Pipe in Lukville, narcotics and alien smugglers were a major threat and the situation was out of control.

"The U.S. Border Patrol was over-run throughout the sector, and similar to Park Rangers, had little support from Washington, DC. The alien and narcotics cadres were making massive amounts of money and politicians from both political parties generally ignored the very real problems in Southern Arizona. Illegal aliens crossed the Border by massive groups. The Tohono Nation was violated by both illegals and narcotics traffickers. The Native American Shadow Wolves, a U.S. Customs Patrol Unit composed of outstanding "desert trackers" were on the job and accomplishing narcotics interceptions on the Reservation lands as well as the B.I.A. police. The thousands on the reservation suffered tons of garbage left behind by the border crossers. Death on the reservation was commonplace for illegal entries in 2002 despite the best efforts of the U.S. Border Patrol Search and Rescue Medics and local police.

"Illegal Alien smuggling, human trafficking increased in 2002 from Texas to California. The average fees per illegal alien averaged $500 to $1,000 as a Mexican National. Central Americans could be charged from $4,000 up depending on the country of origin. Human traffickers that specialized in Mid-Easterners or Chinese could earn $20,000 to whatever could be extorted for illegal entry arrangements. The use of 18- wheeler tractor-trailer loads was common and for transportation of illegal aliens to interior cities net smugglers as much as $80,000 per human load.

"Stash houses, from Border areas to interior cities such as Phoenix were spreading like wildfire. Criminal operators openly extorted money from "human cargoes" or they were held for ransom prior to western union money grams sent by relatives in the States for their release. Kidnapping, rape, homicide were all a part of the never ending criminal conspiracies.

"Police Officers were killed by illegal aliens including Officer Zeppetella of Oceanside California, Officer Hernandez, Las Vegas, Nevada and U.S. Park Ranger Kris Eggle in Lukville, Arizona. U.S. Border Patrol Agents were fired upon by Mexican Military escorting narcotics shipments on the Tohono Nation and the news media and politicians were silent. Briefly, a news item appeared which involved the arrest of Iraqi National Tajirian who was arrested for smuggling over a thousand mid-eastern illegal aliens into the United States at $15,000 per alien. Politicians in Southern Arizona districts were very interested in Ranchers and property owners in rural Cochise Country and citizens watch groups such as American Patrol, or any person deemed to be a "Racist or Vigilante" for protection of home or property against a constant stream of "invaders" from the Border. Because of his stance, respect for Representative Tom Tancredo goes beyond politics.

"The oath of office for an elected official in Federal Government is similar to an oath taken by a commissioned U.S. Law Enforcement Agent. You swear to protect and defend the United States and its citizens. Perhaps politicians cannot or will not remember Article IV, section 4 of the U.S. Constitution.

"Evidentially, most political goals in Arizona in 2002 and 2003 involved drafting another blanket Amnesty for illegal aliens under a "guest worker plan.' HR 3142, HR 28999 and S. 1387 all provide no additional law enforcement measures to prevent further "illegal immigration" and are without numerical limits in the future.

"Politicians rarely remember previous disasters. However, most Federal Agents responsible for enforcement of failed policies remember quite well. In 1986, the first Amnesty fiasco, 2.7 million illegal aliens were made legal. Fraud was rampant throughout the admission process of IRCA. Special Agricultural Workers granted Amnesty were replaced by millions of other illegal aliens from Central America to fill the void. In truth, Amnesty has been on-going from 1986, a one time only political deal. Section 245 (i) in 1994 was a temporary rolling Amnesty for 578,000 more illegals. The extension of Amnesty continued through 1997, plus the Nicaraguan Adjustment and Central American Relief Act, NACARA Amnesty for one million illegals from Central America. The Haitian Refugee Immigration Fairness Act, HRIFA, 1998 allowed 125,000 illegal Haitians, Amnesty. By 2000, late Amnesty for 400,000 allowed Amnesty for those that claimed they should have been eligible under IRCA 1986. The Life Act 2000 was a re-instatement for another estimated 900,000 illegal aliens under Section 245 (i).

"With 13 million estimated illegal aliens in the United States now, a "job fair" to match workers with jobs is proposed by the President, guest workers to solve the problem. The illegal alien problem in the United States is created by Politicians. They "dangle" the carrot for Amnesty, free health care, education and social benefits for all illegal aliens that violate U.S. Law to be here. People from any country in the world would risk everything to get their foot in the door. Legal Immigrants that follow the rules, health standards to criminal records and integrity wait in the wings, as all lawbreakers are rewarded.

"Alien smuggling organizations love the system which will always make tax-free millions of dollars monthly with few problems with Courts or Law Enforcement. Police in most parts of the United States aren't allowed to inquire as to Immigration Status, Municipal Sanctuary statutes, and loads are released. Immigration Enforcement Agents cannot respond or are concerned with terrorist—only duties. USC 8, 1324 statutes for alien smuggling have always been a "slap" on the wrists in Federal Courts as opposed to narcotics Felony violations which per DEA, 80 percent of the Cocaine and most of the marijuana seized is smuggled from Mexico. The Phoenix Police Department reports that 60 percent of homicides involve Mexican Nationals that are involved in human trafficking and narcotics. In Tucson, Arizona the crime rate has grown 12 times the National Average. A vehicle is stolen in Arizona every ten minutes, most headed to Mexico. Street Gangs from Mexico and including the MS-13, El Salvadorian gangbangers has spread to over 30 states. In 2002, over 200,000 illegal aliens were arrested coming through the Organ Pipe National Park at Lukville, Arizona. More than 700,000 pounds of Narcotics were intercepted by Border Officials. Organ Pipe is still the most dangerous Park to visit in the United States as a tourist.

"In 2003, conditions are better in Southern Arizona. National Parks have a few additional armed Rangers and barricades are under construction at narcotics crossing areas for vehicle traffic. In Sasbe and Altar, Sonora, Mexico, potential border crossers arrive in large groups daily for illegal entries into the United States for connection to alien smugglers. The U.S. Border Patrol has established "High Intensity Enforcement" areas in the Southwest and accomplishes an "outstanding job " as manpower allows. The territory that has to be covered is immense from Nogales to Yuma Arizona. The Organ Pipe alone is 860,000 acres of desert, just a small area of coverage by a few Rangers and the Border Patrol. The Altar Valley, Sasabe, Arivaca and the Tohono Reservation Tucson Sector were dangerous and deadly in 1974 when ten Agents were on duty to cover all the Station needs with no political support from any quarter. Cocaine alley and the Reservation has for over thirty years been a place where death and violent confrontations was a normal tour of duty.

"Ten Agents in 1974 to hundreds for a station area now cannot control the Borders while politicians actively promote illegal immigration and reward all violators of law with amnesty. We are either a nation of laws, or the whole concept of laws is to be ignored, subject to political interpretation. If politicians' goals are a lawless society, instead of taxpayer moneys spent for Homeland Defense, they should abolish the U.S. Border Patrol, Park Service, U.S. Customs, DEA and just let nature take its course. Drug smugglers, criminals and human trafficking cadres can do whatever suits their goals.

"In a politically correct society, people should have a right to do whatever they please per the ninth circuit court in the United States. Don't offend any group or person, don't think or presume to have the right to think, don't love your country or cling to ideals which made this country great by citizens and legal immigrants through decades of working class people. Deaths and wars mean nothing as long as you are not the person killed or maimed in your comfort zone. Never get involved in any issue in life and never take a stand, which is contrary to the accepted standard of patriotism.

"Holidays, Christmas, the Flag of the United States and God should only be spoken of in private. The English language is not necessary in the United States, nor should it be the official language of this country despite most state constitutions. Fraud, deceit and dishonesty are traits to be admired and rewarded."

Is this still our country? The fact is, it's no longer your country being led by your leaders, and soon, it's going to be everybody's country. Those 'everybody's' include incompatible cultures that encourage suicidal martyrdom, violent religions that practice 'female genital mutilation' as well as abuse women and children, incurable diseases, multiple languages and worse.

Illegal aliens are being rewarded for their lawlessness. Thus, you can expect more and more of their numbers. That includes terrorists who don't belong here, those who didn't earn legal entrance, those who won't and can't sustain our country, and worse, they will not support it. Forget the word 'assimilation' into the American Dream.

This invasion creates the American Nightmare.

CHAPTER 17—

CORPORATE GREED SETS
NEW RECORDS

"Life would be so simple if the issue of free trade
was just about bags of sugar. However, free trade is
about far more than that."

Vicky L. Davis

One of the dirty little secrets concerning both legal and
illegal immigration is the power of corporations over common
sense, rational thinking and a sense of loyalty toward one's
country.   Think Ken Lay or his side kick Skilling. The word 'greed'
to CEO corporate America is like a clever man who attaches a 747
jet engine to a Power Vac. Let's say he wants to suck all the ants
out of an anthill. He sticks the vacuum hose onto the anthill. Not
only does he suck out all the ants, he sucks everything out of the
forest.

Now picture him sticking his jet-powered vacuum into your
checking account, savings account and your parent's accounts

along with all your friends. They're sucking money out of Americans from one end of our country to the other. Every time a Martha Stewart or Ken Lay of Enron manipulate, or, in some way alter the fair playing field, Americans not only get their entire life savings sucked out of their lives—they have to pay their tax dollars for bailouts like Neil Bush's Silverado debacle in Denver, Enron's collapse and a dozen others. And, like the next 747 coming in for a landing, you can bet more Enron's are coming into an airport near you.

In an interview with Vicky Davis who said, "I am nobody and I'm everybody, an unemployed computer systems analyst, an American citizen who cares about her country and the future of America's children." She brings rare insights into the depth and the width of this crisis.

She offered a word from Lori Wallach of the Public Citizen who wrote: "When most people think about trade, they conjure up images of ships ferrying steel beams and sacks of coffee between nations and of agreements about cutting tariffs and quotas on trade in goods. In reality however, today's "trade agreements," such as the 1994 North American Free Trade Agreement (NAFTA) and the 1995 World Trade Organization (WTO), have little to do with trade. Instead, they focus on granting foreign companies new rights and privileges within the boundaries of other countries. They attempt to constrain federal, state and local regulatory policies, and to commodify public services and common resources, such as water, into new tradable units for profit."

From that statement, Davis said, "What Lori Wallach didn't include in this paragraph was the fact that the WTO agreements include 'Services' as being tradable commodities on the world market. Simply stated, 'Services' means people and jobs. It means exporting jobs to cheap labor markets and importing cheap labor people. It means trading people for oil or other products to balance trade."

IMPORTING PEOPLE

"Setting aside the criticality of the types of jobs that are 'exported,' consider the implications of trade in services," she said. "It means turning immigration control over to corporations.

141

When fully implemented, corporations will be able to import foreigners to jobs in the U.S. without regard for the impact on our economy, our infrastructure, and our resources. George Bush's program of "any willing employer being able to hire any willing worker" is the implementation of free trade in labor. The massive illegal immigration that is occurring within the U.S. is the implementation of free trade with Mexico. That is why only lip service is being paid to solving the 'border problems.' It hasn't been announced formally for obvious reasons."

It means you are a puppet on a string and you do the dance according to corporations' choreography. If you don't like it, you starve. Even if you don't starve, your standard of living and your quality of life drops out of the sky like the Space Shuttle Challenger. It's ugly, horrifying, offensive and deadly.

If corporations are allowed to export service jobs and import people, consider what this means for the future of the United States. Basically free trade as it is being implemented will dissolve the United States as a nation-state. It means the elimination of borders and corporate control of the labor market. It allows corporations to decide who lives here. It is a race to the bottom in terms of wages and living standards. It gives foreigners all the rights and benefits of citizens. It makes American Citizenship meaningless. That is why President Vicente Fox is getting so bold and demanding and getting so much from the United States taxpayers.

"All of the above concerns the issue of globalization as it pertains to Mexico but this is not the only country to which our borders will be opened," Davis said. "India has a population of 1.1 billion people. They are now being imported by corporations and 'our' government to take American jobs under the agreement for trade in services."

EXPORTING JOBS

In spite of what the corporate propaganda would have you believe, it is not just call center jobs that are exported. In fact, calling them 'service' jobs deliberately masks the nature of exported jobs.

"It is primarily the high dollar jobs because there is the biggest payback for exporting them," Davis said. "They include engineering, computer programming, telecommunications networking, maintenance and development of critical computer systems like banking back office operations, financial analysis, scientific research and development, radiology, accounting and legal services."

The above represents just the tip of the iceberg of exported jobs. Our country and our economy is so dependent on technology that exporting it to a foreign country leaves us stripped bare and vulnerable.

"Another issue that this writer has yet to see addressed is those losing jobs have invested tens of thousands of dollars in their education," Davis said. "They have built their lives around careers that were high paying. Their investments in knowledge are no less important than a person who invests their money in a small business, yet there is no consideration for the losses being suffered by them. The exportation of high value jobs tells them and our young people who are now in college is that an investment in knowledge will have no value in the 'new economy.' The American Dream to work hard, play by the rules, get an education and aspire to great heights is being exported."

Free trade in services does in fact, work the same way as free trade in products. What Americans have to decide is if we want to export our high value knowledge jobs and import cheap labor, which includes the poor and uneducated as well as the more educated.

"Do we wish to consider that the high cost American Worker/Citizen is the equivalent of the proverbial buggy whip—an obsolete entity that is no longer required because we can import cheaper versions or simply export their life to a foreigner in a foreign country," she said. "Do we want to race to the bottom so we can compete on a wage scale equivalent to China and India— keeping in mind that we can't maintain a first world infrastructure with a Third World economy. Is this the future you want for American children? Do we want to reduce people to a commodity on the global market? These are the real issues surrounding the outsourcing of jobs."

Globalization is the utopian dream of a group of central planners. Free trade is the tool that is used to implement it. Simply stated, globalization is the elimination of nation-states.

"The United States is used as the test case in this grand experiment of social engineering," Davis said. "Corporate targeted marketing is used to sell the different factions within our country on the concept of globalization without ever discussing what it really means to our future. On the left globalization is sold in the form of multiculturalism, the nation of immigrants message, and the dream of a 'global village.' Globalization is sold on the basis of greed and self-interest, i.e., the stock market is soaring, that's all that matters, as long as I'm making money, I don't care what happens to my fellow Americans. They are lazy bums that don't want to work anyway. The targeted marketing pits left against the right, middle-class against the poor, the poor against each other in a struggle to survive, citizens against non-citizens, farmers against steel producers, religion against atheism, morality against immorality and the wealthy laugh all the way to the bank. In other words, globalization is tearing us apart as it must in order to implement the utopian vision. So if you love your country, next time you fly your flag, fly it upside down because the union is in trouble."

Instead of rolling over and playing dead, Vicky Davis took action.

"In a Thoreau moment of quiet desperation and inspired by the case of Clarence Earl Gideon versus Wainwright in which a convict wrote and submitted his own Supreme Court appeal of his conviction," she said, "I decided to submit my own appeal to the Supreme Court to stop the cannibalization of our country bythe corporate forces that are destroying it."

"I have vivid memories of touring the Supreme Court building. The brochure said that the building was designed with all white marble to inspire awe at the magnificence of it and to serve as a reminder of the solemn purpose and responsibility that the Justices have to keep our nation on course within the framework that our Founders gave us," Davis said. "It certainly filled me with awe at the magnificence and I thought of it constantly as I was preparing my Petition. The Petition was my version of a Hail Mary Pass. I hoped and prayed that the Supreme Court would catch it. In my wildest dreams, they would read it, assign me an attorney and a proper case would be filed. Not surprisingly, they threw it back at me. I didn't dot an 'i' or cross a 't.'"

"I didn't bother to resubmit my case because I knew that if they read it and rejected it, that it wouldn't matter what changes I made," she said. "It was not to be. As fate would have it, I'm now presented with an opportunity to resubmit my case. This time though, I'm presenting it to the ultimate authorities in our Democratic Republic."

IN THE
SUPREME COURT OF THE UNITED STATES

IN RE Vicky L. Davis - PETITIONER PRO SE
VS
The United States Government, RESPONDENT

PETITION FOR EXTRAORDINARY WRIT OF CERTIORARI

Vicky L. Davis
July 7, 2003
QUESTIONS PRESENTED

1. Does the Constitution of the United States of America enumerate a power of the government to bestow the fictional designation of "Person" on a collective unit of persons organized for commercial purposes (herein called "Corporations")?
2. Does the fictional designation of "Person" for Corporations diminish the status of natural Persons thereby denying them their constitutional rights to equality under the law?
3. Can this government be a government Of the People, in view of the Court's creation of a fictitious class of persons with rights and privileges exceeding those of natural persons?

Frosty Wooldridge

PARTIES TO THE PROCEEDING

Solicitor General, Attorney for the United States Government

RULE 14.4 (c) CERTIFICATION

Petitioner certifies that a copy of this petition has been served upon the Solicitor General, Attorney for the United States of America.

RULE 14.1 (e) JURISDICTION

The Supreme Court is the court of original jurisdiction for constitutional issues ARTICLE III Section 2 of the Constitution of the United States.

STATEMENT OF THE CASE

1. The Petitioner contends that the Court exceeded its authority under the Constitution when it bestowed the title of "Person" on a Corporation. By so doing, the Court gave these collective units of commerce all of the rights and privileges reserved for the People in the Bill of Rights[1]. These rights and privileges are in addition to the rights and privileges granted to Corporations by Charter.

It is indisputable that collectively, 10 people are more powerful than one person. The power of a collective unit of commerce, in the form of a Corporation, grows exponentially with the number of persons involved in the unit. By bestowing the designation of "person" on Corporations, the Court has effectively created a class of "super-persons" thereby relegating natural persons to the role of 2nd class citizens, unequal in every respect.

---

[1] Freedom of the Press is the only commercial activity singled out for specific enumerated rights under the First Amendment of the Constitution and therefore is not considered an issue in this petition.

The supremacy of fictional Persons over natural Persons subverts the democratic process causing the people to lose control of the government, threatening the very sovereignty of our nation.

2. A Corporation is a collective unit of people joined together by charter for the sole purpose of engaging in commerce and generating profits for the many stakeholders involved. A Person on the other hand, even the least among us is a multi-dimensional being. People have a vast array of concerns and interests including but not limited to: the health and well being of their relatives, friends, neighbors, their city, their state, and their country. They care about having clean air, pure water, animals, trees, parks and schools. They can appreciate sunshine and a blue sky. They care about having time to spend with family and friends and they care about making money. Simply stated, Corporations are single dimensional, People are multi-dimensional. When people join together to form a corporation for commercial purpose, their multi-dimensional natures do not transfer to the Corporation. No matter how many people are involved in a Corporation, the Corporation remains single dimensional: to make money.

3. As Persons by decree, Corporations have claimed the right to participate in our political process under the First Amendment Right of Free Speech. Since a Person in the form of a corporation is a fiction, the only way for a Corporation to express its will is with money. The fact that most Corporations contribute to both parties proves that they have no value system and no loyalties. Corporations exist for the sole purpose of making money; their only purpose for involvement in our political process is to buy legislation that furthers the goal of making money.

Corporations reward or punish our Representatives using money. If the Representative votes on legislation favorable to the Corporation, the Representative is rewarded with extra contributions to his party. Those contributions filter to him at election time. If the Representative opposes legislation, he loses contributions. The bidding war for campaign contributions has locked our Representatives into a system in which they must support legislation favorable to Corporations over the interests of the People.

Direct Corporate campaign contributions represent only a percentage of the money flowing into our political system. Corporate sponsored Political Action Committees (PACS) are front organizations to funnel even more money into the political arena. Our Corporations both collectively and individually, have a virtually infinite capacity to spawn PACS through which to funnel money.

Corporate money has even become a family affair. Far too many of our Representatives have family members who are employed by or own lobbying firms. Hundreds of millions of corporate dollars flow through lobbying firms with a significant percentage going to the family members of our Representatives. A family member is a branch of the same tree.

The voices of the People are muffled by the torrential flow of corporate money and influence into our political system. Our Representatives, by necessity of political survival must consider the interests of the fictional Corporate "super-people" first; the needs and general welfare of the real People second.

REASONS FOR GRANTING THE WRIT

1. The Court erred when it bestowed the designation of "Person" on corporations. Corporations are engines of commerce and should therefore be governed under Article 1, Section 8 of the Constitution and by state charter.

2. The American people have suffered grievous and incalculable harms to themselves and their democratic institutions as a result of the Court's error.

3. Chipping away at the power of Corporations to influence our

political process has been ineffective. The Court should address the issue head on and make right the wrongs that have been done to the American people.

CONCLUSION

Petitioner requests that an Extraordinary Writ of Certiorari be granted for the stated reasons. Respectfully submitted, Vicky L. Davis

CHAPTER 18—

IMMIGRATION AND THE DOOM OF AMERICA

"It is dangerous to be right when your government is wrong."

Voltaire

Seldom do little people speak up. They send their kids off to school, work their jobs, pay their taxes, attend church and coach little league. Wives sponsor bake sales and car washes to pay for cheerleading outfits. Often, when the big, crazy things happen, they shake their heads in disbelief. However, most have a belief in America—that it will continue on its daring path of freedom for all and justice for the common man. They believe in life, liberty and the pursuit of happiness guaranteed by the Constitution.

Unfortunately, President Bush and Congress aren't acting on those basic guarantees. These men are sworn to 'defend and protect' this country from all enemies both 'foreign and domestic.'

Each state in our Union is guaranteed safety from invasion. Each citizen votes for men who are sworn to uphold Article IV, Section 4 of the U.S. Constitution: "The United States shall guarantee to every State in this Union a Republican Form of Government, and shall protect each of them against invasion; and on Application of the Legislature, or of the Executive (when the Legislature cannot be convened) against domestic Violence."

It is evident that the past several presidents have not upheld what Dwight D. Eisenhower found very easy to uphold—our borders. He was a president who stood for our country and defended it as a General of the Army and, as president of the United States. He knew his duties and he performed them. That has not been the case with Reagan, Bush I, Clinton and Bush II. Each of those presidents allowed the constant flow of illegal aliens into our country even as the consequences escalated. They were/are supposed to serve this country. They failed in their duties. They made excuses. They did little in stopping the erosion of the sanctity of our sovereign nation.

Presently, President Bush II manifests the least proficient of these presidents because he panders to Mexico's Fox in the deliberate dismantling of our borders. But he is not alone. More senators and congressmen aid and abet this invasion into our country. Nancy Pelosi of California openly chastises the Bureau of Immigration, Customs and Enforcement agents for DOING their jobs. "They're harassing immigrants," she said after dozens of illegal aliens were arrested in Chicago. Throughout Congress, men and women voted to represent American citizens are not doing their jobs. If they were, we wouldn't be in this crisis.

When the Democratic candidates debated during the primaries, none of them took a stand on the massive invasion of immigration. Instead, they wanted to help them become legalized. None of the press asked hard questions as to the costs, diseases, job losses, wage suppression, language chaos and schools being over run.

Therefore, whether you vote for Bush or Kerry, you're completely unrepresented as a citizen in your own country. They both pander to illegal aliens. Why? Because millions of illegal aliens are illegally registered to vote. Again, it's another aspect of corruption as we sink further into Third World Momentum.

Readers often write to me about their despair, frustration and anger. It's like American citizens have been tied to a flagpole in the middle of a football field by their own leaders and left screaming at the moon while standing powerless under Old Glory. Yet, they are encouraged to vote for the next candidate who will change, but as all indicators demonstrate, we're damned if we do and we're damned if we don't.

That's the feeling across the country by the little people. One of them wrote me concerning how bad it is.

"If something drastic isn't done soon this country is going to collapse like a cheap card table," Paula Jackson said. (not her real name) "Illegal immigration is taxing this country beyond repair. Not to mention the handouts our Congress gives legal and illegal immigrants!"

She relates what is happening to her town like it is happening to thousands of towns across America.

"My local courthouse used to be a ghost town, they rolled up the halls by 3:00 PM, judges just went home, there was nothing to do," she said. "Now the courtrooms are overflowing, the staff is overworked. Everyday there are illegals standing in long lines to get free shots for their babies, free diapers and formulas. Is it little wonder they are risking their lives to sneak into a country like this? The illegal Mexicans hate America and hate Americans but they come to take whatever they can for free. They fly their Mexican flags on their businesses, on their cars, on their apartment and house windows. They refuse to assimilate. My town's police force had to take a Spanish course so they could communicate with the Mexican criminals because there are so many of them. They go to court; no driver's licenses, no insurance and the judges tap them on the wrist. One judge is telling them to go to Wisconsin to get one of those ID cards because we don't have them yet in Illinois.

"We have the corrupt Richie Daley in Chicago who will not allow the Chicago police to even question immigration status. Chicago is one of the safe havens for them. Since I fled Chicago years ago, I wouldn't mind but now they are pouring into the suburbs of Chicago at record pace. The Chicago suburbs kowtow to them, having Hispanic appreciation days, etc.

"If somebody wants to come into this country through the proper channels, I have no problem, but to break the law and then the government rewards them, is treason at the least. For what the politicians are doing, they should be dragged through the streets and publicly stoned for destroying America. Despite what the liberal fools in this country say about a "Melting Pot," the truth is this country is turning into a Third World cesspool. I feel like a second class citizen in my own country. I have no voice. Everybody saw what happened to Howard Dean when he tried to embrace the "Confederate Flag" crowd. To speak of American rights in this country is forbidden. A real travesty. Enough is enough, I want the country my grandparents enjoyed with people who came here to become Americans!

"The sad thing is that it is not just happening here, Europe also has an immigration problem, instituted by the same people who brought us our problem.

"I will never cast a vote for either major party, democrat or republican because neither party speaks for Americans. They have taken Americans' votes for granted for too long so let them fight it out for the ethnic votes.

"When I wrote to my senator, Peter Fitzgerald about this illegal alien problem, he wrote back that he was sorry but he couldn't address my concerns at this time. I am glad he is not running for reelection because he wasn't going to get another vote out of me. This is the attitude of all politicians; they don't care what the majority thinks. And when I saw a gentleman on Bill O'Reilly's show who said politicians are signing up illegal aliens as voters, it explained what's going on because I was wondering why they pandered to illegals when they can't vote. Guess they can vote after all.

"Thank you for trying to address this serious issue and let's hope we can turn this government around and replace it with patriots instead of the dead weight darkening the halls of the Senate, Congress and White House."

You can multiply this letter millions of times to get a feel for what Americans are saying, thinking and writing.

Nonetheless, our leaders continue on a disconnected, out of touch and insulated march toward America's demise.

CHAPTER 19—

A LETTER TO THE COMMANDER IN CHIEF OF THE UNITED STATES

This is a letter written to our president by an extremely frustrated American citizen. It caught my eyes in bold colorful letters as it landed in my email 'In Box.' It depicted a Mexican flag. I debated showing it in this book, but then realized it speaks volumes for average citizens across America. It reflects much of what millions of Americans feel, think and say. He allowed me to share it with you.

"They only come here to work and make a better life for themselves."

Frequent quote read in politically correct newspapers

TO GEORGE BUSH...OUR 43RD PRESIDENT'E...MR. PRESIDENT'E, I DROVE BY THE WHITE HOUSE TODAY AND SAW OUR NEW FLAG. IT'S RED, WHITE AND GREEN.

SO WHEN DO YOU OFFICIALLY ANNOUNCE WE ARE NOW THE UNITED STATES OF MEXICO?

Mr. President'e Bush...I tried to find work today...but every company I applied at...I was asked if I would accept minimum wage...I said I could not because I have a family to raise and that accepting minimum wage would put me in the poverty income level and my family would starve...most of the employers told me that they were sorry ...and that they understood...but since you started your <u>GUEST WORKER POLICY</u> they all pretty much had an abundance of <u>GUEST WORKERS</u> all too <u>WILLING TO WORK FOR MINIMUM WAGES!</u>

<u>A</u>ND THE COMPANIES THAT USED TO PAY WELL...THEY DO NOT HAVE TO NOW BECAUSE OF THE DANGEROUS CONTINUING FLOW OF MILLIONS AND MILLIONS OF AVAILABLE ILLEGAL ALIENS WHO CONTINUE BREAKING OUR LAWS AND ENTERING OUR COUNTRY ILLEGALLY!

NOW WE HAVE A PRESIDENT WHO ENCOURAGES EVEN MORE ILLEGAL ALIENS TO POUR ACROSS OUR BORDERS...BY REWARDING THEM FOR THEIR CRIMINAL BEHAVIOR.

EMPLOYERS CAN NOW DRAW FROM THE MILLIONS OF ILLEGALS WHO ARE WILLING TO WORK FOR MINIMUM WAGE...WITHOUT ANY FEARS OF PROSECUTION OR PENALTIES...EMPLOYERS HAVE HIT THE JACKPOT...ALL AT THE EXPENSE OF THE DISPLACED AMERICAN WORKER.

WHAT EMPLOYER CAN RESIST THAT?!

MY WIFE AND MY TWO YOUNG DAUGHTERS THANK YOU!

IT IS VERY CLEAR NOW THAT WE MADE A MISTAKE ...WHEN MY WIFE AND I VOTED FOR YOU IN 2000

I CAN ASSURE YOU WE WILL NOT MAKE THAT SAME MISTAKE AGAIN!

MR. BUSH, I AM JOINING WITH MILLIONS OF OTHERS ACROSS THIS

NATION WHO ARE OUTRAGED BY YOUR DANGEROUS IMMIGRATION
PROPOSAL
I AM SENDING MY MESSAGE TO THE MEMBERS OF CONGRESS AND
TO ALL MAJOR TELEVISION…RADIO AND CABLE NEWS NETWORKS

MR. PRESIDENT, THE VAST MAJORITY OF AMERICANS WANT OUR
BORDERS AND IMMIGRATION LAWS STRONGLY ENFORCED

AND YOU <u>DO NOT</u> ENFORCE OUR IMMIGRATION LAWS

AND THOSE WHO BREAK OUR LAWS AND CROSS
OUR BORDERS ILLEGALLY …YOU WANT TO REWARD THEM… AND
THUS ENCOURAGE MILLIONS UPON MILLIONS MORE TO ILLEGALLY
POUR ACROSS THOSE BORDERS…AND SOME OF THEM WANT TO
DO US HARM AND TO EVEN KILL US AND OUR CHILDREN!

AND AS THE MAJORITY OF AMERICANS SPEAK OUT
YOU CONTINUE TO DENY THE WILL OF THE PEOPLE
<u>Sincerely The</u>
Carey Family

CHAPTER 20—

AN EDUCATION CRISIS VIA IMMIGRATION ACROSS AMERICA

"Education is learning to use the tools which the race has found indispensable."

Inscribed over the Royce Hall stage at UCLA

Educators from elementary schools to the college levels in the United States today suffer an unending crisis in personal integrity while at the mercy of political correctness. They must give bogus grades to students who have not finished or can not complete their academic work. As an educator in the early 70's, I remember being forced to 'pass' failing students from my classrooms in Colorado. The reason given was, "We don't want their emotional development impaired by being held back a grade."

The problem accelerated as students discovered they could continue through school without doing their assignments. Many parents that did not value academic achievement allowed their kids television viewing as a major form of homework. Much like their parents, the children became functionally illiterate as they passed through each grade without performing minimum academic standards.

Back then, as well as today, a large percentage of those children drop out on their 16th birthday. They entered our society without necessary skills needed for a First World country.

Additionally, in America today, we have 'installed' graduate assistants, who cannot speak adequate English, into college classrooms across the nation. American students cannot understand the instruction. There is a kind of 'pretending to educate' forced down America's throat.

This crisis continues today throughout America. Critics might come to believe that someone at the higher levels of control in the United States wants to 'dumb down' America's middle class. Do they want an intellectual vacuum in our country? Will it be easier controlling a populace composed of television-watching 'couch potatoes' who vote the name seen most often on the screen? Is this dumbing down system a method to drive this country further toward Third World morass?

SYSTEMIZED CHEATING AT THE COLLEGE LEVEL TO ACCOMMODATE IMMIGRANT STUDENTS

A veteran college professor expresses her frustrations as this educational crisis has escalated into the college ranks. I asked her what she felt was going on in her neighborhood and at her college? She wrote the following response:

"As a life-long resident of the Los Angeles area," Mary Breckner (not her real name) said. "You can imagine the frustration that I feel as I watch the cities and neighborhoods in this area be completely altered. I've turned to tears many a time as I watch the decay before my eyes. However, instead of "escaping Southern California" like so many have done, we will take a stand to defend our "hometowns," which, in the end, will be defending the way of life in the United States.

"I could focus on the visible changes that are all around us, like the signage in foreign languages, the additional graffiti, lots more litter, filthier public rest rooms, and altered behaviors in public places. I could focus on the failing social institutions, like schools, hospitals, and prisons. However, I will tell you about the specific experiences I had as an instructor at the college level for thirteen years.

"At the local community college, the student population is composed of many foreign students, predominately Asian and some Hispanic. I was an instructor of Freshman English, the course that requires the reading of non-fiction articles, the discussion and analysis of content, and the writing of research papers.

"On the first day of class, I gathered writing samples from my students, one-page essays on a simple topic. One-third of the students could not write a grammatically correct sentence. Now, remember that this course was NOT a remedial course. This was the composition course given college credit at four-year colleges. So, I attached notes to each of the unqualified essays: "You need much more practice with English before attempting this course."

"I was called into the dean's office and told that I could not place these notes on the students' papers because it discouraged them. I responded that it seemed unfair to ask these students, who could not write a sentence, to take a course in the writing of the argumentative research paper. It dramatically slowed down the level at which I could teach the course, thus affecting qualified students. I explained, also, that these unqualified students were paying huge fees as foreign students, and it seemed like theft for the college to accept fees for a course the students could not pass. Nevertheless, I was told that my notes must be eliminated. "After all, the teacher before you thought they were qualified to be passed on to the next level." The following paragraphs explain why those teachers might have thought these students were qualified.

"The students stayed in the class; some dropped out long after the time when they could receive a refund, and others passed the course in this way. They used several options, all of which were a form of systematized cheating, not to be blamed on the student but to be blamed on the department. First, another course was offered to ESL students to help them write their papers for English 1A. That course discusses how the students should organize the arguments for their papers. As a result, everyone taking this assistance course writes his or her essay with the same thesis and the same points of argument. They do no thinking or organizing on their own. Next, they go to the writing lab, required for one hour a week, and they have a tutor go over the papers to edit any errors. The tutors are told to just offer suggestions and not to edit the papers, but I have seen their editing marks all over the students' papers. Then, the students go home and make all the corrections and, eventually, turn in their completed essays to me. They, of course, might receive a "B" on this paper because I must grade what is presented to me, even though I know that a "team" has written the paper. The students believe that they are using the facilities offered by the college, so they do not even realize that they are participants in systematized cheating.

"Recognizing that students could pass the college-level course for composition and the research paper while not being able to write a sentence, I tried to develop a method that would test the students' real writing levels. For every out-of-class essay, I assigned an in-class essay, one written by the students before my eyes. Naturally, these essays often resulted in failing grades. Again, I was called in by the head of the department and told that I could not have a balance of in-class and out-of-class essays because this was unfair to the students. "After all, your objective," the dean said, "should be to get your students to pass the class not to fail the class." It, obviously, did not matter how that objective was achieved.

"After eleven years of growing frustration, I resigned from teaching English and went to a four-year university to teach cultural geography. Now, you would think that conditions would be better at a four-year college, but they were not. They were just changed. Now, instead of Asian students, the student population was ninety percent Hispanic. As many professors will agree, fifty percent of the students at this college are not prepared for college. They cannot write, read, or think on the college level. To compensate, I saw professors drop the number of books required for their courses, distribute all the questions for the exams the day before the exam, and lower their grading curves so that the majority of students would pass. The students were "nursed" through the system, leaving the college with little more skill than when they entered.

"Why does all of this matter? Because U.S. citizens are paying to operate these colleges, filled primarily by foreign students, while American-born students are forced to head elsewhere to get an education. To not go to colleges where the majority of students are English-speaking and college-ready would be to minimize one's chances of getting an adequate education. Many parents are not only paying the taxes to educate these foreign students but must pay high tuition fees to send their own children to private colleges.

"I share these observations because many persons outside of academia do not know to what lengths our schools are going to get students passed through the system. People should know these tactics are diminishing the value of a college degree for everyone. Yes, we need to educate our foreign-born students, but they must be proficient in English and have earned the privilege of entering college. They cannot be "given" the opportunity without earning it, just as native-born students must earn the right to enter college as well.

Otherwise, all of our college degrees become worthless!"

One of the aspects of a functioning society is the power of an educated citizen. That person thinks intelligently, works intelligently and operates as a contributing member of society at a higher level. The reason Third World societies do not function at higher levels stems from the fact that an uneducated or unenlightened citizenry is at the mercy of corrupt public officials. What is happening in the United States with this dumbing down of our educational system—is a loss of standards that have supported our society throughout our history. The more we incorporate Third World Momentum, the faster we sink into the same crises of many of the nations on this planet.

Most Americans have heard about football players who spent four years in college, but were functionally illiterate upon graduation. The athletes felt they would make the NFL with riches beyond belief. They 'pretended' to be college students. However, when they didn't make the big time in football, they were relegated to menial tasks. Without a legitimate education, they lost out and the society lost out on their individual potential as well.

Another aspect of academic 'affirmative action' is a trail of literate incompetence that must be 'covered' by others on the job. In the end, much of the graduation class is composed of uneducated people pretending to be qualified for the job market.

Recognizing the low competence of college graduates, Breckner writes further on education's accommodation of immigrants:

"As an employer of a small business or a huge corporation, you are often placed in the position of seeking college graduates to fill vacant employment positions. You believe that a college degree assures that the applicant can read, write, and think at the college level or beyond. Your assumption, however, is mistaken.

"During the past thirteen years as an instructor at the college level in Southern California, I have observed the many methods used to pass students through the college system, allowing them to earn degrees without ever having had their abilities tested. Most of these methods have been applied to accommodate immigrants, who have difficulties with the English language and who may not, yet, have the skills necessary for success at the college level. Let us examine these methods that result in incompetent students earning college degrees. You, the employer, and you, the client or customer, must be concerned about these methods because business will inherit these graduates.

"How can students graduate from college without being able to write the grammatically correct sentence? Several methods contribute to this possibility. First, some colleges offer courses that help ESL (English as a Second Language) students prepare and organize their essays. Second, writing laboratories, provided by the college, assist the student in editing their papers, allowing for rewriting and reorganization before the paper is turned in for a grade. These two methods result in a team effort for writing the paper, so if any member of the team is proficient, the student may receive a passing grade.

"While I attended UCLA in the late 1960s, students were given very few out-of-class assignments. Instead, course grades were taken solely from the midterm and final exams; these essay exams were written by each individual student in front of an instructor or teaching assistant. These in-class writings were the only method used to test the student's mastery of content and the student's ability to think and write. No team effort went into these papers. The individual student earned the grade that he or she deserved.

"Colleges, today, however, feel that having immigrants write in-class essays when they are not native speakers places too much pressure on the students. The stress disables the students from being able to express themselves clearly and to demonstrate their knowledge of the subject matter. So, the colleges have turned to out-of-class essays, resulting in team efforts, described above, that allow unqualified students to turn in passing papers.

"Another method used by colleges to accommodate immigrant students is "group work." This approach is promoted by academia as providing practice for individuals to learn the skills of teamwork needed in the work place. However, the minimal producing student earns the grade of the group. Consider this example. The teacher places two native English-speaking students with one who might act as a translator and two limited English speakers. The project is divided among the group members, with any part requiring language skills assigned to the native speakers and with other portions assigned to the limited English speakers. When the project is completed and presented to the class (by the native English speakers, of course), the "group" is assigned a grade. Thus, the minimal contributors receive the same grade as the maximum producers. In this way, students without skills are passed through various classes. Academia defends this approach as being the compassionate approach for the immigrant, but the reality is that students without skills are passed through the system. This only delays the trauma for the immigrant, who believes he has earned a college degree but who finds himself failing in the work place. The graduate is frustrated, and the employer is frustrated.

"To further accommodate immigrants, content in the courses has also been altered. Teachers have found that non-native speakers, who may have difficulty reading academic texts, select courses that have the least number of recommended texts. If a teacher required three texts for a class, then students would not enroll in the course. Without the required twelve students to carry-on the course, the course would be dropped by the department, and the instructor would not have a complete teaching load. So, instructors have learned to limit the amount of required readings. This naturally impacts native and immigrant students who are being exposed to less material by which to develop reading and analytical skills. Also, because complex texts are extremely difficult for non-native English speakers, texts are selected on the basis of readability for immigrant students, since in Southern California, the majority of students in the classrooms are immigrants. Without gearing the texts to the student population, class discussions would be severely limited because students did not understand the content of the texts. Again, we see the dumbing down process at work.

"Most colleges, today, are requiring every course to have one out-of-class essay assignment, intended to give students practice in writing. Physical education courses as well as other non-academic courses must meet this requirement. To be of value, these assignments must require students to analyze material, to consider micro- and macro- ramifications, and to write the organized report. Some topics, however, are too simplistic to meet any of these requirements. During a recent observation, I was present to hear the instructor give this essay assignment in order to meet the writing requirement for the college. It was to be a two-page paper on some place that the student had visited and what he liked or disliked about the place. Does this sound like college-level work? It reminds me of elementary school when the teacher would begin each new year with the assignment, "What did you do for your summer vacation?" Yes, the student will be writing, and any writing is valuable experience, but the level of thinking required for such an assignment is too simplistic. Was this assignment geared down to accommodate immigrant students or does it reflect the lack of creativity on the instructor's part? If this is gearing down, then all students, native speakers and ESL students, are suffering from having too little required of them.

"Still, other accommodations of immigrants are affecting our education system. Consider the impact of immigrant teachers, who often have a thick accent but who are hired for diversity on the staff. Recently, I was observing a series of lectures given by a personable and knowledgeable professor in physical geography. The course material was quite complex for students, even for those who were native speakers. Imagine the extreme difficulty that was experienced as students struggled to understand this professor, whose accent was so thick that words were unrecognizable. The professor spoke with a heavy Chinese accent to a classroom of predominately Hispanic immigrants. The task of understanding was nearly impossible for the students as it was for me, a native English speaker with three college degrees. When I mentioned this problem to the head of the department, he just shrugged his shoulders because he, too, was Chinese and, apparently, did not want to face the teacher about the problem. To accommodate diversity, immigrant instructors are hired, but immigrant students and native students suffer enormously if the instructor is unable to be understood due to a heavy accent. This story is repeated over and over again in Southern California universities. Many students have had to repeat courses that they did not pass or had to drop due to their inability to understand the immigrant professor.

"This brief paper does not intend to discuss the economic ramifications resulting from education's accommodation of immigrants. The purpose here is to offer some explanations as to why employers are receiving college graduates into their work places, graduates who can neither read, write, nor think at the college level. In Southern California where I have taught for the past thirteen years, I have witnessed a "dumbing us down" system that has been created to accommodate immigrant students. The result is that all students, native and foreign born, are suffering from an inadequate college education. This inadequacy is then carried out into society and into the work place."

When asked whether education's accommodations of immigrants is affecting the quality of education for native-born Americans, Breckner wrote these comments:

"Across Southern California, the demographics have changed dramatically, resulting in a complete alteration of student populations at community colleges and state universities. To accommodate the changing population, systems have been modified to assist limited English speaking students so that they might earn a college degree. "After all," the administration would claim, "the campus is in the business of educating students." Changes in demographics have resulted in changes in the way teachers conduct their classes, in the textbooks required for various courses, in the coursework assigned each semester, in the testing processes, and in the remedial programs available to assist students with their work. The administration would never admit to having lowered their standards for earning a college degree; yet, employers from around the United States would stand up and shout that the college graduates coming to them today do not know how to read, write, or think on the college level.

"Let us return to the administration's claim that the role of the college is to educate students. This is absolutely true! The local colleges where I have worked during the past thirteen years, however, have not focused on educating their students; they have focused, instead, on <u>graduating</u> their students. There is a great difference between the two. Educating students involves a step-by-step approach to acquiring skills that will lead to proficiency in reading, writing, and thinking. Students should not progress to a higher level until they have mastered the present level. Graduating students, on the other hand, focuses on the end product—the accumulation of a certain number of class credits, by whatever means, to receive a diploma, ignoring the process of learning.

"We can certainly agree that when it comes to graduating students, the end does not justify the means. Graduation must come only after students have successfully passed through various levels of competency. I have spoken with several teachers who do not believe in giving students a grade lower than a "C" because the students have tried hard to gain knowledge in spite of the terrific handicap of limited English skills. These teachers are focused on the "end" and not on the means; this supposed compassion can only come back to haunt the students when they realize they have passed through the system without mastering the skills necessary for success in the business world.

"If we continue handing out college diplomas that do not represent the acquisition of vital skills, we diminish the value of the college degree for all students, for immigrants and for native-born students. Businesses will come to distrust degrees granted from various institutions, the ones noted for their "awarding of diplomas" rather than for their "educating of students." All students, regardless of their skills and achievements, graduating from particular colleges, will be disregarded in the job market because of the poor reputations of their educational institutions.

I asked Breckner if she had any suggestions for accommodating immigrant students at local colleges. She responded, "Certainly, as a result of changing demographics, local colleges in California have an immigrant student population which needs to be educated, but the requirements for the college degree must not be altered or else the earning of a diploma will be worthless. Instead of granting diplomas to unqualified students, the system needs to offer another program that focuses solely on mastering English before beginning the academic subjects for the degree. Successfully completing this English acquisition program might earn the students certifications in English, certifications that could be recognized by businesses.

"The ESL program at the two colleges where I taught allowed students to take other classes while enrolled in ESL classes. This slowed down the progress of native-speaking students and frustrated teachers as they tried to educate limited English students who did not comprehend lectures or textbooks in subject-matter courses. Subject matter courses should not be opened to students until they complete an English-certification program. Also, more stringent tests must be given for passing out of the ESL programs and into English only courses. Everyone suffers when these students are passed along too soon. On campuses composed of primarily immigrant students, subject-matter departments might need to shrink while English acquisition departments increase in order to meet the needs of the local population. This certainly seems a far better way to use tax or tuition money than to artificially push students through the academic curriculum.

"Consider, also, the time it took for our forefathers to make their ways from manual laborers to college graduates. This took, perhaps, three or more generations. They did not arrive on America's soil, not knowing English, and expect to learn English and graduate from college within a four or five year period. It takes time to learn a new culture, to learn a new language, and to learn the skills necessary to pass from the manual labor role to the professional role. It seems, today, that colleges are rushing this process, resulting in many gaps. The administration would defend their position using arguments about student rights, compassion, and equality, but in the end, giving out college diplomas that do not represent the gathering of reading, writing, and thinking skills can only lead to future frustration.

"In dumbing down the educational process to accommodate immigrant students, we see that all students suffer. In the end, businesses suffer and the community as a whole suffers," Breckner said.

Breckner gives us first hand knowledge concerning the calamity of unrestricted immigration that is forced on our educational system before spilling out into the society as a whole. The accommodation of immigrant students is not only felt at the college level.

Consider these written comments from Sarah Lansing (not her real name), an elementary school teacher for twenty years in Southern California.

"To those who live in Southern California, having more immigrants in the classroom than native-born students has become a way of life. The immigrants struggle to learn subject matter as well as English while the native-born students amuse themselves with wandering minds, doodling, or teacher-assigned busy work. Why are they bored? Because the teacher's pace has been slowed down to accommodate those students who are lagging behind. Since the majority of students fall into this category due to limited language skills, the teacher has no choice but to accommodate them.

"One year, while teaching sixth grade in Southern California, I had forty-one students in my class; thirty-two of the students were Armenian, five were of Hispanic descent, and four were native-born, English-speaking students. The class did not start out with these statistics; to begin, we had twenty-eight students.

However, approximately every other week throughout the year, a new student was added, one who, generally, had just immigrated and who knew no English. This means the apple cart of students was upset thirteen times during the year.

"How does a teacher handle a wide range of English-speaking abilities within the same classroom? She forms groups, based on the student's level of English. She not only has different reading groups, as we have always done in elementary education, but she has different language acquisition groups, which must meet daily as well. While the teacher works directly with one group, the other students are essentially doing busy work, desk-work, and individual assignments. If the teacher is lucky, she has paid and/or parental aides, who can assist the individual students at their desks; otherwise, the independently working students must wait until the teacher has completed the reading group and the linguistic group before asking for guidance.

"How does the teacher go about teaching the other subjects? The teacher cannot have separate history, math, and science groups, based on language levels, because there are not enough hours in the school day. The teacher must present these subjects to the class as a whole. What about those who do not understand English or who have only a minimal understanding of the language? They receive their information from students slightly more fluent, who are able to translate as the lesson goes along. This means that there is a constant din of conversation going on at all times while students translate and explain the teacher's comments to others. Along with the distraction of the constant mumbling, the teacher must also move at a very slow pace so that the translations can be taking place.

"Who suffers in this arrangement? The teacher herself might become frustrated, but she is an adult and must learn to cope. She is paid to do so. Of real concern is the frustration felt by the native English-speaking students. They grow bored with the slow pace; they become irritated with the constant talking among their fellow students; they suffer from not being exposed to stimulating classroom discussions; they feel isolated in a room full of non-English speaking students; they miss out on all the material not covered due to the slow pace of instruction.

"The lesson I have learned as a teacher is that parents should never let their native English-speaking children be in a classroom that is filled predominately with limited English-speaking students. In those conditions, the parents can be sure that the native speakers are not getting a full education. Everyone's education suffers in such an environment.

"What are the options in Southern California? Sadly, for the parent, they all lead to private schools. Those who cannot afford to send their child to a private school must face the reality of a sub-par education. Tragic! These parents have paid taxes for years, but the system is not educating their child. Instead, it is educating an immigrant's child, even though that immigrant has just arrived and has not been paying taxes.

"The schools have some options, however. For example, like colleges, students should be admitted into already operating classrooms only at semester breaks. In the mean time, schools should be providing full-immersion English programs for the immigrant students who arrive during the school term. Also, schools might hold non-English or limited-English speaking students in ESL classes, learning English throughout the day, until they have mastered the language enough to enter an all-English speaking classroom. In this way, the immigrants receive the intensive English instruction they need while the native English-speaking students receive the instruction in subject matter that they require. It appears that such a system would be a win-win situation.

"Currently, our taxes are paying to educate immigrant students, but they are not being used in the most efficient way to benefit immigrant students and native students. The system in elementary education needs to be redesigned so that "no student is left behind."

At all levels of education, from elementary school to the college level, American students suffer in classes that do not address their best educational interests when professors are forced to teach to the lowest common denominator. Tax dollars are wasted in an effort at 'pretending' to educate both legal and illegal aliens who are incompetent in the English language. Additionally, they may not have the learning skills and intellectual abilities necessary for success at a particular level; yet, they are being carried by an incompetent system that pretends to educate.

Once an immigrant or native-born American student 'graduates' with a degree from college, he or she is expected to sustain a certain 'degree' of excellence on the job and within society. They are expected to perform at above minimum levels since they are college graduates. In the work place, when they cannot function adequately, they force all other employees to cover their unacceptable performance. In this way, society as a whole suffers from an educational system that practices 'graduating' students rather than 'educating' them.

CHAPTER 21—

CALIFORNIA: THE LEADING EDGE OF THE UNITED STATES OF TITANIC

"Too late gringo. Your country and your government are under our control as is the boarder. America knows it, Mexico knows it, the whole world knows it and all your ranting and raving just makes us happy. We laugh at your sissy impotence at defending america, which is no longer a sovern nation. A country without boarders, what is that? Nothing! Stupid! Weakness in its highest form! But this will change soon because when Mexico takes it back through America's own laws and lack of will to enforce its laws, Mexico will have the strongest most enforced boarders in the world and Americans will beg on their knees to come to it. Mexico has won, and spits in your face."

Anonymous email to my office

The quotation above arrived a day after the following column was published across the United States. The writer shows brashness, certitude and audacity. He maligns the greatest super power in the world. He demeans the greatest army in the world. He laughs at our loss of the rule-of-law. He's beaten us with sheer numbers invading our country from Mexico.

All the while, President Bush and Congress keep dancing and partying as if all is well on the southern border. All is NOT well on our southern border. Ranchers fight for their lives in shoot-outs with drug smugglers and 'coyotes' carrying illegals across.

What was once a proud ship, the United States of America, suffers from a form of hemorrhaging that threatens to sink it in the not too distant future.

Much like the Titanic that sank on April 15, 1912, the United States stands at a critical juncture in the history of our nation. Few realize it, but, like the Titanic, this nation smashed into a piece of legislation in 1965 that was never asked for or approved by the American public. Our 'Captain' Lyndon B. Johnson along with helmsman Senator Teddy Kennedy drove America into an 'iceberg' of massive, unrestricted immigration that opened the flood gates with the 'IMMIGRATION REFORM ACT.' At first, the flow of one million immigrants annually wasn't noticed. We were benevolent. Our country was big. There was plenty of room and resources.

However, the massive flow of humanity from that 'hit' still pours into our country 39 years later in 2004 and few seem to notice— much like the party-goers and dancing on the Titanic continued for hours after hitting the North Atlantic iceberg. However, even the invincible Titanic could not survive the onslaught from the constant flow of incoming water—slowly, methodically stealing its ability to stay afloat.

Today in the United States, 60 million immigrants later and pouring in at 2.3 million annually—both legal at 1.5 million and illegal at 800,000—our nation shudders from San Francisco to New York and from Chicago to Miami. They forced us from a stable 200 million people in 1965 to 300 million by the end of this decade. What was once a benefit to our country is now a full-scale overpopulation and societal crisis. From stem to stern, our

English language is under assault and our schools are drowning in ethnic violence, rapes, drugs and gang warfare.

Much like the Titanic, our standard of living drops and our quality of life sinks with the influx of unrestricted immigration. Soon, we too, will become like the countries of Bangladesh, India and China.

Our leaders are standing in the wheel-house totally insulated and isolated from those of us who shovel the coal, build houses, repair cars, teach our kids, drive school busses and plow roads.

We can not save the world, but we can destroy our country by failing to act.

Like the Titanic that cracked in half before plunging to the depths because no one stopped the incoming water, the United States could sink. If you look about you, we're shuddering from stem to stern—from the stacks to the rudder.

Since California is the bow of the Titanic, I present two major concerns and five 'slices of life' presented by college English professor Mary Breckner. Americans in every corner of our country could add their own slices of life.

MICRO VS. MACRO REGARDING IMMIGRATION

If we look at the issue of immigration from the perspective of the individual, we all, whether conservatives or liberals, will get caught up in the desire to be compassionate, to let just one more person into this country, to let his family into the country, to give him and his family a free education and medical services, and to support him while he gets started in our generous country of the United States.

Jose wants to enter from Mexico, Juan wants to come from El Salvador, Sako wants to enter from Armenia, Dat wants to enter from Vietnam, Mohammad wants to enter from Iraq, and Hwang wants to enter from Korea, to name a few of the people from all around the world who want to come for a better life in America. If we meet them face to face, get to know their names, and listen to their stories, we will find it very difficult to deny them entry into a better life in the United States. An endless line gathers. The length of the line forces us to step back from

175

observing immigration from the micro perspective, from that of the individual, in order to focus on the macro perspective, that is, on the consequences from excessive immigration to the country as a whole.

Looking closely at California, we can see the effects of massive immigration. Until now, our state has taken the liberal view, the micro perspective, that of the individual. We have been soft hearted to those unfortunate people from other countries that have come here for economic or political reasons. We have not enforced immigration laws. We have let millions enter our state illegally, and when added to those who have entered legally, California has been assaulted by excessive immigration.

Now, the dire conditions in California require that we look at the macro perspective, at the effects to the state as a whole as a result of our being too lenient on immigration.

➤The line of immigrants wanting to enter our country is endless, while our funds to support them are limited.

➤Many immigrants are unskilled and many are illiterate.

➤The number of those desiring to enter far exceeds the number of unskilled laborers needed in the U.S.

➤Immigrants tend to have large families, placing further demands on our social services.

➤Although only one worker may be admitted, 'chain migration' policies allow him to bring in parents, children, siblings, parents-in-laws, and on and on. These numbers dramatically strain the social services.

➤Immigrants from Mexico often see the U.S. as a temporary stop over and do not desire to assimilate.

➤Large numbers of immigrants from any particular country settle together forming ethnic enclaves, which lead to the Balkanization of the state.

➤The economic costs of excessive immigration far exceeds the economic advantages because of our generous policies in regards to social services and our maintenance of the infrastructure to accommodate the new numbers.

➤Lack of monitoring of immigration increases the possibility of terrorism.

➤Excessive numbers of unskilled and illiterate immigrants

increases poverty and the crime associated with poverty.

➢Poverty also seems to foster 'victimization,' which completely contradicts the American values of self-sufficiency and hard work.

➢Multiculturalism in place of Americanization results in the loss of the values that hold America together.

➢A huge influx of immigrants from any particular country increases the possibility of those immigrants never having to learn English, thus dividing the country.

➢Excessive immigration leads to increased density in our inner cities, leading, eventually, to slums.

➢Excessive immigration leads to increased sprawl spreading across the countryside.

➢Excessive immigration allows for undesired behaviors practiced in other countries to enter our culture, behaviors like littering and graffiti.

➢Excessive immigration increases our concerns, especially in the West, about water availability.

➢Continuous immigration does not allow the system to keep up with the demand for services.

➢Continuous immigration does not encourage dispersion and assimilation.

We seem to make two errors in our perspectives on immigration: first, we tend to focus solely on the micro perspective, which encourages us to assist individuals; second, we tend to forget that the ideal that looks good on paper often does not work so well in reality. We must stop looking at the wishes of individual immigrants, who by themselves would pose no threat, but who in excessive numbers completely drain our country of resources. We must also step out into reality, leaving our compassionate theories behind. We must pay attention to the "real" consequences that are resulting as we let excessive numbers of people into our country.

If quality of life for us and our children and grandchildren matters, then we must look at the macro perspective rather than the micro perspective in regards to immigration policy.

OPEN YOUR WALLETS! THIS IS A STICK UP!

Back in the days of the Pony Express and stagecoach rides, roadside hold-ups were common place. Just a few years ago, in Southern California, car-jackings were occurring with too great a frequency. While bank hold-ups and sidewalk robberies are less frequent in today's California, the residents of this state feel they are in the midst of a "never-ending stick-up." Why? The legislature keeps passing liberal bills that tax Californians more and more. In addition, the cost of existing legislation keeps growing to cover the growing numbers of low wage, low-taxpaying immigrants. The state has run up an enormous debt, in spite of increased taxes. Recently, Californians voted to pass a one-time bond for $15 billion to try to rescue California from its financial nightmare, but it is doubtful that the state can be saved. Too many people are entering our state, and too many special interest groups are fighting for privileges for those people. Eventually, voters will refuse to pay another cent, and the state will reach rock bottom: a total collapse due to financial crisis.

What has contributed to this financial crisis? The state has been the victim of excessive immigration, so much so that we cannot pay the bills to keep the state running. Here are some of the costs related to accommodating immigrants:

- Additional school hours for courses in English.
- Additional teachers for ESL classes.
- Increased number of teachers and classrooms for increased enrollment.
- Increased number of administrative personnel to handle immigrant population.
- Increased uses of free breakfast and lunch programs, provided by schools.
- Increased use of day care facilities at schools, resulting in the hiring of more personnel.
- Increased police officers to handle the rise in crime associated with the increase in immigrants.
- Increased legal fees in cases dealing with immigrants.
- Increased penal facilities to handle the increase in crime associated with immigrants.

- Increased personnel in hospitals because emergency rooms are used by immigrants as medical clinics—at taxpayers' expense.
- The hiring of crews to clean up graffiti associated with the increase of immigrants.
- The hiring of crews to clean up the increase of litter associated with the increase of immigrants.
- The hiring of additional truant officers to stem the rise in truancy associated with immigrants.
- An increase in welfare programs and food stamps for immigrants.
- Increased funds for road maintenance resulting from increased usage.
- Increased funds for additional water and utility usage as population increases.
- Additional funds to print voter's pamphlets, driver's manuals, etc. in another language.
- Additional funds for translators at schools, hospitals, and government offices.

Some argue that immigrants are paying taxes in this country and are, therefore, paying their fair share for the services they receive. This assertion is highly exaggerated, however, for several reasons. First, many immigrants are paid in "cash," leaving no paper trail; therefore, they do not pay income taxes. Others spend very little of their earned money in this country but, instead, send much of their money to their families in Mexico. Also, many earn too little to qualify for paying income taxes. In addition, with low incomes, their spending habits must also be curtailed, so they contribute little to sales tax revenue. Also, they rent their living quarters so are not paying property taxes. Thus, American citizens are footing the bill for immigrants to receive social services and to use our infrastructure.

American citizens are being robbed, not by immigrants, but by the systems that allow the immigrants so many advantages. The immigrants arrive with their hands wide open, ready to take whatever the system so generously offers. However, just as in the case of highway robbery back on the stagecoach, the taxpayers have handed over their wallets, and they are now empty. As a result, the taxpayers are on a mission, now, to find the bandits, the government systems that are robbing them of their money to support the needs of immigrants. Some generosity is always the American way, but when the generosity is taken advantage of by government legislation that can no longer be afforded, then the givers must stop giving. Besides, the citizens cannot give what they do not have. Their purses are empty.

California is billions of dollars in debt. That means that the government gave out services for which it could not pay. 800,000 Californians left the state last year, many to avoid the robbery taking place as the legislative bandits placed the state in so much debt that it, most likely, will never recover. Certainly, it cannot recover if the programs and benefits offered to immigrants continue. Why? Because the line of immigrants is never-ending, and taxpayer purses are empty.

Anti American Behavior in Public Places in America

In the process of growing up, we learn from our parents and from observing those around us just how we are to behave in public places. A list of unwritten rules makes us civilized, allows us to be tolerated by others, and results in pleasant surroundings in public places. We learn, for example, to refrain from being loud and annoying others, to pick up our trash, and to walk on the right-hand side of aisles, stairways, and walkways. Generally, these behaviors are absorbed from the culture around us, and these homogeneous values contribute to the harmony that is possible in public places. Today, however, thanks to the influx of so many immigrants in such a short period of time, Californians are finding that they must be ever so tolerant of behaviors that go against the cultural norm of the native population. Respect for public places and for the people occupying those places has been replaced by free-for-all behaviors.

A few months ago, I took my car to the car wash to be hand waxed. The job takes a couple of hours, so I took a handful of essays to grade. I sat at one of three tables inside the car wash to do my work. I had graded papers for about thirty minutes when an Hispanic gentleman sat at an adjacent table so that he could watch the news on CNN. I inserted a couple of earplugs so I could continue working through the television noise. In another thirty minutes, a Chinese woman came to the third table and sat down to make a cell phone call. She spoke very loudly, so my earplugs were no longer effective; she spoke in Chinese. Her phone call went on and on. Eventually, the gentleman watching the news grew frustrated, gave a frown to the lady, and walked out. I kept my head down, trying to focus on my work, but the loud distraction was extremely annoying. This woman's behavior demonstrated her lack of awareness of the people around her. When she completed her call, I looked up and said quietly, "That was very rude." She immediately screamed at me: "How dare you say that the Chinese are rude!" Note: I had never mentioned her ethnicity. She continued yelling for a couple of minutes, but I put my head down and made no further comments. She concluded by ranting, "This is a public place, and I can do whatever I want to do." Her statement showed that she did not understand the expectations of people in "public places."

We are not free to do whatever we want in public places. The word "public" suggests that others will be present; we are obligated to keep a perspective on how our behaviors are impacting others. Each culture has a particular set of accepted behaviors, and the native population must educate immigrants about behavioral expectations in particular social environments. Immigrants have the responsibility of adapting to new social environments.

The problem we face, today, in California is one of assimilation. It reminds us of an experiment we did in our high school chemistry classes. If one sprinkles a teaspoon of sugar into boiling water, the sugar will dissolve and blend into the water. If, however, we dump a cupful of sugar into the boiling water, the sugar will form a lump and will sink to the bottom of the container. Today, we have let so many immigrants into California in such a short period of time that the immigrants are not blending in with the native population. Instead, they are living in neighborhoods, surrounded by their own people practicing the language and customs of their places of origin. They are seldom exposed to the traditions and expectations of the native population, so assimilation is not taking place. Local schools have not taken it upon themselves to teach the ways of the native population; instead, they have adjusted to the ways of the immigrant population. These accommodations have resulted in the Balkanization of California.

How would you have responded in the following situation? On the Fourth of July at Shoreline Park in Long Beach, many families of various cultures came to watch the fireworks. As the fireworks were displayed, a brass band was playing "God Bless America" and other patriotic songs. Blasting loudly, in order to drown out the patriotic music, boom boxes played Mexican music. This behavior demonstrated disrespect for the band, for the patriotic music, and for the celebration of America. The native-born Americans were disgusted by the disrespectful behavior, but did not confront the offenders. In remaining silent, they seemingly accepted the inappropriate behavior in this public place.

The same groups that played the loud music during the band's performance left the park grounds filled with litter, including beer bottles (law prohibits the drinking of alcohol in a public park), paper plates, food wrappers of all kinds, and dirty diapers. Their behavior, once again, showed disrespect: disrespect for laws, the park, the maintenance crews, the event performers, and the other attendees. With no show of respect, public places become spaces to be avoided. Empty public spaces, eventually, become locations open to crime. In avoiding public spaces, native-born citizens are turning over their favorite places and favorite traditions to immigrants. Instead of giving up the places and customs that we hold dear, we must train people to ask themselves, "How is my behavior impacting others?" It seems such an easy rule, but it requires individuals to be "other-oriented" rather than "self-oriented." Without this perspective, the pleasure of our public places will be lost to all.

The Changing Face of the Urban Environment, Thanks to Immigration

The face of Southern California is dramatically changing as a result of incoming immigrants. For the immigrants, these changes are positive as they see their new destinations take on the characteristics of the countries they left behind. For native-born Americans, however, the changes to the urban environment are symbolic of the loss of culture that is rapidly sweeping across our nation.

Let me offer the changes that occurred when a Korean market opened in the strip mall at the bottom of our street, replacing a pharmacy that had been in business for thirty-five years. First, a huge sign has gone up in a language that is not English. Next, the windows of the business, which once held nice displays, are covered with advertisements in Korean. Now, in front of the shopping center, along the street where people were accustomed to seeing green trees and plantings, a huge truck is parked with advertising placed all over the truck. This is, in reality, a movable billboard. In addition, along the front of the store which serves as a walkway for many businesses, several newspaper stands are lined up, all selling Korean newspapers. Also, blocking the walkway, the store owners have placed several shopping carts, no longer hidden from public view by a short wall. A card table is set up at the door where merchants sell even more Korean products. Then, to further contribute to the deterioration of the shopping center, the store managers have placed stacked boxes of merchandise along the walkway. Does this sound like a store you might see in downtown Seoul? Perhaps. It is not what one expects to see in America.

This description may not seem so shocking to you unless you know what it replaced. The pharmacy had large glass windows artfully displaying merchandise. The walkway was kept cleared for customers, allowing people to easily pass from one business to another in the shopping center. Bordering the street was a green belt of grass and trees, which are still there, but which are, now, covered from view by the billboard truck. In other words, the aesthetic qualities of the shopping center have been replaced with the clutter and signs of a single business, greatly upsetting the other entrepreneurs in the center and the residents who have long frequented this shopping center.

This single example has been repeated hundreds of times all over Southern California. The business signs may appear in Korean, Vietnamese, Chinese, or Spanish, but the rest of the description is seen over and over again.

Let me invite you to take a drive down the ugliest street in metropolitan Los Angeles, Valley Boulevard in the City of San Gabriel. You will believe that you have arrived in downtown Hong Kong. The signs alone has absolutely destroyed any aesthetic quality of the street. Hundreds and hundreds of signs, mostly in foreign symbols, fill every corner of space. The signs no longer have any significance because there are so many. Driving by the stores, one cannot possibly read all the signs because to do so would result in a car accident.

Not only is the signage a negative impact on this urban environment, but the density has greatly increased. The sense of any open space has been erased by the closeness of many small businesses. Parking lots are enormous and are filled to capacity. No green space is apparent from any perspective. A visitor to the area, one who has grown up in the open spaces of the Los Angeles area, feels penned in when going into these foreign enclaves.

You noticed, undoubtedly, that the immigrant is no longer the visitor here; in the example above, the native-born American is the visitor. Huge areas of Southern California have been converted to foreign enclaves, so that the native-born American feels uncomfortable to enter these areas. He is a visitor in his own country.

The visual aspects of the urban environment have changed in other ways as well. Graffiti has become the norm whenever a large wall is available, whether that wall is along the side of private businesses, freeways, or churches. Graffiti artists are not discretionary in their choices about where to place their identifying marks. The cities in conjunction with Cal-Trans must send crews out regularly to cover up the graffiti markings. Their efforts are commendable, but the blocks of paint left in place of the graffiti also present an eyesore. These clean-up efforts are also expensive to the taxpayer.

Litter has greatly increased in urban areas, especially in areas where immigrants live or work. Fast food wrappers, empty beer bottles, and dirty diapers are among the usual items discarded along the streets and in the parks. This is a dramatic change over the litter-free areas, which were the norm in the past.

Billboards, in any language, have always been an eyesore and should be removed from every urban landscape. However, they are even more annoying when they are in a language one cannot understand or in symbols that are unrecognizable by the native-born American. These 'foreign language' billboards are becoming more and more frequent in the Los Angeles area.

Consider, too, the changes in residential architecture that are taking place in various neighborhoods. Take a tract of homes that has been done in California ranch style architecture. The homes are all one story and spread out across the property, blending in with the trees and landscaping because of their single story. Now, bring in an immigrant with lots of money, one who decides that he wants his home to be like those in his home country. He may build a two-story home, one that covers as much of the property as possible under the city code. This home no longer blends in with the landscaping, but dominates the whole street with its size. As if the size were not enough to attract attention, this person may cover the front of the home in marble slabs and may place lion statues in front of the house. Now, the homogeneity of the neighborhood with its subdued architecture and the predominance of landscaping has been completely destroyed by the newly built fortress. Certainly, the new homeowner has the 'right' to build what he wants within the city codes, but the immigrant often does not give attention to the homogeneous styles that have contributed to making the neighborhood harmonious.

This same disruption can occur when the immigrant moves into a neighborhood and decides to paint his house the color that is popular in his country, but which does not fit well into the already established neighborhood. His choice, although his 'right,' disrupts the continuity that had been present in the neighborhood before his arrival.

To immigrate to a new country is no easy task. Besides learning the language and the customs, one must be sensitive to the existing landscape, whether rural or urban. If the numbers of immigrants entering an area are low and stretched out over time, they adapt to their new surroundings. If, however, the immigrants come in as large groups, as occurs in Southern California, then they do not feel the pressure to adapt. Assimilation capacity has been exceeded. They feel supported in their efforts to create a new environment, one which approaches the characteristics of the country they left behind. For native-born residents, however, changes to the physical environment greatly increase the tension between the various groups. When the physical environment changes so dramatically, the sense of "home sweet home" is lost forever.

Barber Shop Chatter

Not so long ago, one would have entered a barber shop and heard conversation centered around fishing holes, skeet shooting, basketball, football, Angelina Jolie, race cars, V-8 engines, and the World Series. The voices might have been saying lines like these:
"How about them Lakers?"
"I can't believe the Lakers traded Robert Horry to San Antonio!"
"Have you tried fishing the north edge around the protruding rocks at Lake Casitas?
"Do you think those Chargers are going all the way to the Super Bowl this year?"
Today, however, guy talk has turned to politics, and, in Southern California, all political talk eventually leads to a discussion of immigration. Why? Because no matter where you are standing in Southern California—in the market, at the mall, on the street, in the post office, at the bank, or on the beach—you are surrounded by immigrants. On the freeways, in the restaurants, and in the parks, immigrants abound.

Californians are feeling the crunch, big time! They have reached their limits of generosity, patience, and tolerance. They are demonstrating their frustrations at finding their hospitals, classrooms, and prisons bursting at the seams with immigrants. To show their desire to stem the tide, Californians voted by a large margin in 1994 to discontinue social services to illegal aliens. Citizens believed that by reducing these free social services, they might discourage illegals from entering the state. Their votes were of no use, however, for liberal judges of California declared

Proposition 187 to be illegal. So, Californians are still paying and suffering the consequences of excessive immigration.

Not so long ago, one would have entered a beauty salon and heard conversation centered on movie star gossip, the latest anti-aging cream, the newest shade in hair color, the benefits of Weight Watchers, and Catherine Zeta Jones. The voices might have been saying lines like these:

"Did you hear that Ben Afleck and Jennifer Lopez broke up?"

"Do you think Lucy looks good with her new hair color? I think it's too red."

"Sarah is sure looking better now that she has lost weight and joined Curves."

Today, however, girl talk has turned to politics, and in Southern California, female political talk eventually leads to name calling as one party blames the other for California's immigration problems. The liberals are blamed for their giving away of the state and its revenues by easing laws on welfare, making social services available to illegals, and being weak on internal immigrant enforcement. The liberals are labeled, 'compassionate FOOLS.' In contrast, the conservatives are seen as cruel, cold-hearted individualists, who care for no one but themselves, who do not want to share their hard-earned wealth with the world, and who demand personal responsibility from all people, including immigrants. The conservatives are labeled, 'drill sergeants.' Liberals do not understand the conservative's view that instead of giving fish to these immigrants, as the liberals would do, the conservatives would rather teach the immigrants how to fish.

Beauty shop conversation, just like that of the barbershop, is reflecting a growing frustration among Californians. The immigration issue is dividing the state's populace, making the passing of any legislation almost impossible. No agreement is ever reached by the warring parties, even on issues that would improve the quality of life for everyone, issues like education reform, power plant construction, or freeway planning. Each side refuses to budge because so much anger exists over the conditions in the state, conditions greatly magnified by excess immigration.

One response is to return to the barber shop chatter or the beauty salon girl talk of the past, leaving politicians to deal with the irregularities in the state. However, the adage, 'Ignorance is bliss," does not work in California because the taxes will be due, and taxpayers will soon realize that they are paying the financial, emotional, and social costs of excessive immigration.

Believing that it is not too late to fix California's immigrant problems, native-born Americans must take action to begin Americanizing the newcomers, to limit legal immigration quotas, to enforce internal illegal immigration laws, to demand self-sufficiency and personal responsibility, and to come down hard on those who break our laws, even those seemingly minor offenses of littering and graffiti. Not knowing the laws is no excuse; the immigrant must take it upon himself to learn the laws of this country.

In the past, residents met around the cracker barrel of the general store and talked up the issues of the day. Eventually, their concerns spilled out into streets and town squares, where they joined together to form grass roots organizations that could make a difference. Today, as we leave our barber shops and beauty shops, having expressed our concerns about the damaging consequences of excessive immigration, let us join together to form grass roots organizations that can abate this problem and return our towns to those representing American qualities.

The Psychological Effects to Native-Born Residents Resulting from Mass Immigration

I was born and raised in Southern California. I am a daughter of a veteran of World War II, and my ancestry goes back to the 17th century in Jamestown. I do not hesitate to call myself an "American." I have grown up in the midst of American culture and have learned the importance of individual responsibility, a strong work ethic, self-sufficiency, and the well-being of society as a whole. I have learned to respect public property, diversity, and the public forum. I have learned that adhering to a strict moral and ethical code is vital to an organized society. These are just some of the American values that I have absorbed as a life-long resident of the United States.

During the past two decades, however, my home state of California has been taken over by hordes of immigrants from Mexico, Latin America, Armenia, the Middle East, and Asia. When I open the windows of my house, I hear Armenian being spoken by the neighbors on one side and Korean being spoken on the other. I see the signs of businesses being changed to symbols I do not recognize or foreign words I do not know. I see the American values of "respect for public property" being ravaged by graffiti, litter, and increased density. After 56 years in the same location, I have come to feel a stranger in my own home state. Today, I am the visitor.

Much has been written about the impact of immigration on the schools, hospitals, and prisons of California; they are unable to withstand the sudden surge of immigrants. Much has been written, as well, about the economic costs to the state, the local government, and the taxpayers. These are all vital observations. My purpose in this article, however, is to write about the psychological effects to native-born residents as they encounter the tidal wave of immigrants into their neighborhoods, towns, and state. These effects are more subtle and, certainly, more personal than the observations made above. Nevertheless, the mindset of the native-born residents is being dramatically altered, and the change is unhealthy to themselves and to social relationships in their communities.

When I asked my college students to describe life in Southern California, two words dominated their lists: diverse and lonely. The diversity cannot be doubted as one sees faces from all over the world along all sidewalks in Southern California. You may wonder, however, why loneliness is so prevalent in a state that is bursting at its seams with people. This unhealthy frame of mind is certainly worthy of study. Consider the examples below that might illuminate the reasons why loneliness is so pervasive in Southern California.

My husband and I love to go to ball games: baseball, basketball, or football. It is fun to watch the games and to interact with the crowds. In the past, people cracked jokes and shared a common passion for the teams. This sharing with the crowd has been altered over recent years, however, because very often the people around you do not speak your language. You may crack a joke, but no one around you understands what you said, so what is the fun in that? Again, in the midst of a crowd, people can easily feel lonely in Southern California.

I do not doubt that when many immigrants come to this country, they intend to become Americanized; they intend to adapt American customs and values. However, they feel comfortable with their own people and language, and since there are so many of their kind here, they are able to join in with their ethnic group and continue the same customs they had in their countries of origin. This has many complications, but one is that the choices people make can either bring people together or can further separate them. Immigrants of the same ethnicity make similar choices, so their identities and bonds are strengthened. Native-borns continue to be comfortable with their set of choices. Without encouraging immigrants to gradually adapt to the choices of their new country, the divisions among the groups continue to exist. When individuals of the different groups are brought together, they find that they have little in common. Their choices are, most likely, completely different. They choose different food, different music, different books, and different clothing styles. They may choose different political perspectives and different sources of allegiances. With little in common, bonds between the different groups are unlikely to form. Thus, although surrounded by people, native-born Americans, who are finding themselves to be in the minority in Southern California are experiencing increased loneliness.

Going to the market used to be a social event as well as a practical errand. One talked to the people in the aisles, sharing friendly chatter. Then, waiting in line for the cashier, people often interacted, making the waiting time more pleasant. This friendly interaction has been replaced with silence, however, because sharing a common language has become more rare in Southern California. Also, sadly, the growing diversity has resulted in a growing mistrust of others. People around the community just are not the open, friendly, easy-going people that used to occupy my town. The result is that a sense of community is lost, resulting, again, in a sense of loneliness.

You must understand that the great increase in immigration in our state has not only resulted in diversity. Diversity, alone, is not the cause of tension. A much larger contributor to tension results from the great increase in the numbers of people that an individual must deal with day in and day out. The large numbers require immense patience as one waits in lines along the freeway, in the market, at the bank, and in front of theaters.

Numbers. . .lines. . .numbers. . .lines. . .People are reaching their breaking points of tolerance, not tolerance of diversity, but tolerance of hordes of people. Southern California is a highly stressful environment in which to live and has become so over the past two decades with the giant increase in immigration.

Another major change in the psychological health of long-time residents of our state is the growing mistrust of others. Increased numbers of people and increased diversity has resulted in a more closed society, with individuals remaining more to themselves than being open and friendly. This is a major alteration of the real-life image of the sunny, friendly, relaxed, and out-going Southern California where I grew up. You may say that I am seeking "the good old days." Well, yes, I am because they were a wholesome environment in which to raise kids and to make friends.

Change is always difficult for people to accept in their own hometowns. If you have been fortunate enough to live in one place for most of your life, then you have a real place to call 'home.' You know the good feelings of a comfort zone, of living in a place you know like the palm of your hand, of sharing relationships with people over decades of time. It is these long-time residents who are suffering the most as California is being converted from a place of familiarity to a seemingly foreign space. Many of these long-time residents feel a strong sense of depression and talk, regularly, of escaping this space that they once called 'home.' How tragic!

Definitely, the rapid influx of immigrants in such a short period of time has had major psychological ramifications in Southern California. It is no longer a psychologically healthy environment in which to live. The geography may be the same, but the people, the buildings, the density, the physical landscape,

191

the values, and the relationships have changed dramatically, approaching the characteristics of a Third World country. In the name of generosity, we have given the 'house' away!

California: The Living Liberal Experiment Gone Astray

Wake up, America! Turn your binoculars on California and study the effects of thirty-five years of liberal practices. Our open-door policy, generous welfare programs, generous public facilities, promotion of multiculturalism rather than Americanism, and liberal interpretations of laws have resulted in third-world conditions: our schools rank among the lowest in the country, our hospitals are closing down, emergency rooms require hours of waiting, and our prisons are full. The population is not united; instead, ethnic neighborhoods are flourishing, and the native-born American feels himself to be a visitor in his own state. If you do not want your state to follow in the footsteps of California, then you must act now before it is too late. The following ideas are not popular because they appear to be non-compassionate; however, they are protecting native-born Americans and those who have entered your state by legal means.

You must stem the flow of illegal immigration into your state. This can, most effectively, be accomplished by denying social services, like free education and free medical assistance, to illegals. Also, you can enforce internal immigration laws that fine those who hire illegals, that require police officers to turn illegals over to the INS, and that deport those who have entered the country illegally. Since police officers are busy responding to the increase in crime that has coincided with the increase of immigrants, then, the INS must greatly increase its numbers, placing INS officers on the streets, just like truant officers. The second offender, who has entered the country illegally, might be placed in jail for a period of time in order to discourage his future attempts to enter your state. Also, you might set limits to the number of students who can attend a particular school, requiring the remainder to move to other areas where schools are less crowded. Today, schools keep placing more students into classrooms, no matter that they are overflowing. Limits also might apply to patients desiring medical services. Finally, you might enforce housing codes that limit the number of persons per room in a dwelling. Each of these steps might discourage illegal immigration into your state.

To work with legal immigration, other processes must be used. We need an immigration moratorium in order to regain ourselves as a nation.

Thereafter, the government must set quotas that are far below the numbers allowed to enter the country today. Chain migration must be limited to parents and children only. All others must go through the legal immigration process on their own, filling out their own applications. Next, the country should set some standards that will be used for entry into the country; those standards might include English speaking ability, literacy, particular job skills, the possession of money to support the immigrant and his family for a given period of time, and the meeting of health requirements. Also, imported workers should not be brought into the country on a temporary basis for employment unless those positions absolutely cannot be filled by the country's current residents. This will mean that we must greatly improve our education process so that we turn out qualified workers. To improve the education process will require a temporary halt, say for ten years, of immigrants into our states so that our education system can catch up with those non-English speaking students it already has in its classes. Standards must be raised, and immigrants must be educated to pass those standards, rather than our current method of accommodating immigrant levels and bringing the expectations of all students, including native-born students, down. In addition, allowing people to enter under refugee status must be used discriminately; the reasons accepted for entering as a refugee, today, are far too lenient.

In addition, you must change the out-dated law that allows any child born in the United States to be a citizen. This was an important law when our country was in its growing stages; however, we are about to burst our seams, so this law must be changed to accommodate the current population conditions. A child born in the United States of parents who are illegal is not to be granted citizenship. One parent must be a citizen for the child to receive this privilege.

Finally, the concept of multiculturalism must be examined for it is not resulting in a unified country. Everyone can benefit from learning about other people's backgrounds and cultures; this makes us more understanding of each other. Also, as we learn about French art, Spanish customs, English literature, or Italian design, we gain depth of character while expanding our knowledge of cultures from around the world. However, to encourage multiculturalism as a way of life within a country is to be on a path of doom. In California, we have done a poor job of Americanizing immigrants; instead, we have promoted multiculturalism, claiming that all cultures are equal and worthy of being maintained. This may be a grand ideal, on paper, but in reality, the promotion of multiculturalism leads to the Balkanization of the state.

We must assume that people entering our country with plans of living here are choosing this location above others because they like the way of life in the United States. Their reasons may be for a better standard of living, a more peaceful and secure environment, or the freedom that allows them to reach their full potentials. They chose the United States for personal reasons; otherwise, they would have chosen to stay where they were or to go elsewhere. Why, then, would they want to change the United States to make it more like the place they just left behind? It makes no sense. So, I am going to make the assertion that most legal immigrants want to assimilate and to become Americanized.

However, humans, very often, take the road of least resistance, and in this case, immigrants often choose to live in neighborhoods with people of the same culture. Thus, they are not required to learn English immediately, if at all, and they do not have to learn the customs of their newly-adopted country. Still, even then, I want to be optimistic here and claim that the ultimate desire is still to become "American."

The next step in the formula is our responsibility. Is there a method by which immigrants can become Americanized? Are we in California giving the immigrants opportunities to learn our culture and traditions and, especially, our language? In this area of Americanization, I believe, California is failing.

The public schools, I give them credit, are making every effort to give students opportunities to learn English. English as a Second Language (ESL) courses are offered for all grade levels and into college. The testing, however, to pass each level must be more stringent if individuals are really to learn our language. While children are encouraged to learn English at school, their parents must also be motivated to learn the new language. We must offer free courses, morning and evening, for parents to develop English skills. Testing and certification should accompany the completion of these courses.

In the Americanization process, we are failing when it comes to teaching about American culture and traditions. Most every immigrant defines American culture as "freedom." That is the extent of their knowledge of what America stands for. That response demonstrates a definite weakness in our system. If we can not define American culture and TEACH it to immigrants, then we can not blame them for not assimilating. We must give a book in the necessary native language to every legal immigrant, a book detailing the customs, traditions, and ideals of this country and, especially, the expectations of behavior for each individual. Then, with that information made available to everyone, we must expect adherence to the American code of ethics and values.

Just what does America represent? Just how do we define its basic principles? We cannot expect immigrants to pour through the Constitution and to understand what America is all about. Even native-born citizens, except those studying law or political science, have not done so. We must present the ideals and philosophies of our country in an easy format, one that is readily understood by the majority of people. These ideals must then be taught throughout the education process to native-born students and immigrants. What might be included in that book of American principles?

> ➢ Personal responsibility: Personal responsibility must precede the American ideal of freedom. We have the freedom to develop our potentials, but we do not have the freedom to do whatever we please, whenever we please. The words 'freedom' and 'personal responsibility' should rarely be separated, just as salt and pepper are most commonly associated. Individuals are to be held accountable for their behaviors. No

195

excuses! No exceptions! Period.

➢ Respect of other people and places: Respect is to be shown to other people by the use of appropriate behavior in public places. Manners and politeness must become second nature to people. Places, themselves, are to be fully respected and unmarred; litter, graffiti, and destruction of public places should be punishable by law. Also, respect is to be given to laws and to the authority figures enforcing those laws, like police officers, teachers, and parents.

➢ Cleanliness: Cleanliness is a way of life in America, requiring individuals to pick up after themselves, in fact, to leave each place a little better than they found it. People must be physically clean so that they are not carriers of disease. Home places must be kept clean and orderly for a stress-free environment in which to raise children and for the aesthetic appreciation of neighbors.

➢ Respect of American traditions and institutions: Respect must be shown to American traditions and institutions. Schools must teach about American heroes and the forefathers who built this country in which we live. American history must be taught so as to foster pride in native-born people and in immigrants who have chosen to make this country their home. Our forefathers demonstrated individual determination, team effort, hard work, courage, and patriotism, qualities to which we should aspire.

➢ Self-sufficiency: Self-sufficiency is vital to the well-being of this country. Each individual has the responsibility to provide for his own maintenance, his home, food, clothing, insurance, and other necessities. Parents are responsible to train their children with the skills necessary to be self-sufficient. Parents are responsible to pay the costs of raising their children. Period.

➢ Community participation: Individuals must contribute to the well-being of their communities. They might do this by participating in youth groups, neighborhood clean-up groups, or community planning. They should also participate in community functions: clubs, picnics, parades, bands, sport groups, bowling leagues, and other such activities that encourage interaction with their neighbors. They should be involved in schools, churches, service organizations, and YMCAs in order to interact regularly with their fellow community members.

➢ Education and being informed: Individuals are responsible to get a good education and to learn skills that are usable in the work place. People must also be informed so that they can vote intelligently.

➢ Honesty: People must believe in each other, and for a democracy to be successful, people must trust that all individuals are held up to the same ideals. People, whatever their level in society, must be honest in their relationships and on the job. Without mutual trust, democracy fails.

These are some of the values of American culture that, if practiced by all, could turn the state of California, as well as the nation, into a positive living experience for immigrants and native-born residents as well. These values need to be taught, however, which means that parents, schools, churches, and the media must join together to be the educators of American values. Whether you are born in this country or not, whether you attend church or not, whether you speak English well or not, you must learn the values important to the American way of life. Otherwise, America will turn into another Third World country, just like those from which immigrants escaped. There is no logic in devolving from a top-rate, industrialized country to a Third World country. We must demand that those entering our states understand that we intend to keep our country a desirable place, so they can enter ONLY if they choose to follow our American values. Perhaps, they should be required to sign a pledge of allegiance to learn and pass on American values. It is everyone's responsibility.

Now, that you have used your binoculars to see the lessons to be learned from California's downward spiral as a result of massive, uncontrolled, and unmanaged immigration, you might turn those same binoculars on your own state to determine where in this cycle you find the conditions of your state. Unlike California, you may still have opportunities to make a difference in your state. If ever you are in doubt that actions must be taken, just cast your glance once again to our West Coast, and you will be quickly reminded of the dire need you have to act now to MANAGE immigration with COMMON SENSE. As a frustrated native-born Californian of fifty-six years, I can only wish you luck!

IT'S THE NUMBERS, STUPID

Disneyland was built to handle a particular sized crowd. When the crowd is held to the appropriate level, individuals enjoy themselves. They feel the excitement of several rides, enjoy food and drink in various locations, attend the various shows, and shop as they please. Twenty years ago, Disneyland always promised to be an enjoyable experience for everyone.

Let me, however, take you for a trip to Disneyland today. First, you wait in a long line to buy your $75.00 a person ticket. Once you enter, you search out the lockers where you can store your jackets and gear. If you are early enough, you might be lucky and find an available locker; otherwise, you will carry your gear for the eight or more hours of your visit. You head for your favorite rides, only to find that you have to wait in line for an hour or longer to get on the two-minute adventure ride. So, instead of standing in line, which you mistakenly imagine will be shorter later, you head for the shops. Along the pathways to the shops, you become quite frustrated because the walkways are so crowded that you have to dodge strollers, bump shoulders, and change direction several times. This is no exaggeration! Now, you finally make it to the shop of your choice. You barely make it inside the door because of the crowd, and when you do, you find it difficult to get close enough to the merchandise to see what is offered. After several frustrating minutes, you find something you want to buy. You search for the checkout line and find that fifteen people are ahead of you, waiting for the one cashier. So, you set the product of interest down on a display that is close by, and you exit the store. Feeling more frustrated, now, and hungry, you head for the food stand, perhaps in Tomorrowland, where the band is playing. You cannot believe the lines ahead of you. It is highly likely that thirty minutes will pass before you reach the window where you can buy that expensive hot dog and soda. Now, to find a table. There are none available because of the crowd, so you stand in the corner, leaning, if you are lucky, against a railing, where you eat your meal. So, half of the day has passed, and you are exhausted, having enjoyed no moment of your Disneyland experience. You need to use the restroom and upon arriving to your destination, you see another line has formed. As you stand in yet another line, you start thinking about that $75.00 ticket, the one you bought that essentially allowed you to stand in line throughout the day. You start thinking seriously about leaving now before you spend any more money or experience any more frustration.

You see, the reason that Disneyland has become such a miserable experience for so many people is because of the NUMBERS. The "population" of Disneyland has far exceeded its plan and its infrastructure. People are paying lots of money for the privilege of entering Disneyland, but the park is far too crowded to accommodate the people. Everyone loses in this arrangement, except, of course, the Disney stockholders. If, however, the crowd had been limited to a size that fits the infrastructure, then many people could enjoy the park as it was meant to be. Who gets in and who does not should depend on a first-come, first-served basis. When the park is full; it is full, and no one else should be allowed to enter. Otherwise, everyone suffers.

The same reality applies to the population levels that our cities can handle while still providing a healthy and pleasant life for the residents. The service industries, highways, utilities, water supply, and social institutions, like schools, hospitals, and prisons, were all designed to handle a certain number of people. These systems function well when carrying a particular load. However, when that load is exceeded, just as in the Disneyland experience, everyone suffers the consequences.

In Southern California, thanks to excessive immigration, the population load greatly exceeds the numbers that can be accommodated. The systems have begun to fail: schools rank among the lowest in the country, freeways are jammed during most hours of the day, medical clinics are closing, emergency rooms in hospitals require hours of waiting, and prisons are full. Just like that expensive Disneyland ticket, the taxpayers continue to pay higher and higher taxes, but the quality of life within their city environments continues to deteriorate.

Residents of Southern California stand in lines far more often than they did in the past. Let me take you through a routine day to show you the amount of time you will waste in lines. You leave your house and head for the freeway ramp closest to your home. You miss two or three green lights on the way, so you wait patiently for the lights to turn green. Perhaps, five minutes are wasted of your ten-minute trip. You arrive at the freeway ramp and join the line of cars waiting for the green light that allows you to enter the flow of traffic. More time is lost. You arrive at the bank and wait, either in the walk-up line or the drive-through ATM line. A few more minutes are spent. You head to the store and find that you have to wait in line to receive the butcher's assistance, for slow customers to move their carts down the aisle, and for the cashier to check you out. Another ten minutes are wasted in lines. So far, you have wasted nearly thirty minutes waiting in lines, and your day is less than two hours old. Waiting in line has become a way of life in Southern California because the NUMBERS of people have increased so dramatically.

Also, because a tidal wave of immigration has engulfed our cities, we have had to change the ways we plan and carry out events. For example, if we are planning on going to a 5:00 p.m. movie, we must make a special trip to the theater to buy our tickets at noon because we know if we wait until just before 5:00, the movie will be sold out. We also must call for dinner reservations a week ahead of time so that we can be sure of getting a table in the restaurant of our choice. We avoid the many restaurants that do not take reservations because, thanks to too many people in the city, we may have to wait hours before we get in. In addition, we must plan all of our cross-town trips during particular hours of the day so that we encounter slow, but moving freeway traffic, rather than sitting still in a traffic jam. Californians must plan their days around the traffic; the frustration mounts as they are forced to encounter lines and delays throughout the day.

All of this frustration results from too many people in the city. We have exceeded the planned limits that can be accommodated by our infrastructure, institutions, utilities, and social services. Daily life has become stressful for everyone because population limits were not set and maintained.

Some people call those of us against further immigration 'racists' or worse; we are nothing of the kind. We are simply 'realists' complaining about the excessive immigration that has bombarded our cities in such a short period of time, making it impossible for social services and the infrastructure to keep up with the growth. The problem comes down simply to excess. Just as we observed from our experience with Disneyland's crowds and from our routine day in the city, "It's the NUMBERS, stupid!"

CHAPTER 22—

AMERICA'S PROMISE IS LIFE, LIBERTY AND THE PURSUIT OF HAPPINESS

"Whatever anguish of spirit it may cost, I am willing to know the whole truth; to know the worst, and to provide for it."

Patrick Henry

My dad spent hours on the baseball diamond with my brothers and me. My mother cheered from the stands for baseball, football and basketball games. She cooked dinners, washed clothes, and helped with homework while providing for her children. My father and mother did what millions of parents do across this country. They support their children for 18 years in every way they can—to launch their offspring into the world with every advantage possible to live the American Dream.

Parents encourage their kids to become everything they can become—to realize their highest potential. Some go to college. Others go to vocational technical school. Still others serve their country in the Marines, Army, Navy and Air Force.

Each kid follows a dream. What's more, each parent has a dream for that kid. The unique aspect of America is that any kid from any walk of life can make his or her life whatever he or she chooses.

In 1776, Thomas Jefferson, in his profound brilliance, faced treason and death to bring our Constitution into being. He wrote, "We the people...blessings of life, liberty and the pursuit of happiness." Jefferson, along with all who signed that document pledged "our lives and fortunes" in order to bring this nation into being. If you look back into history, many of our founding fathers were killed and lost fortunes bringing this nation into a reality.

Today, we see elected men and women walking the halls of Congress and our own president doing everything they can to assist illegal immigration into our society. We see top corporations facilitating illegal immigration for the express purpose of maximizing profits to the detriment of American citizens. Most of them live immune to the realities of their decisions. Because they allow and encourage massive, unrestricted illegal and legal immigration, they are destroying the ability of this nation to function.

Any day of the week, you can pick up a paper and see the 'fruits' of their 'labor' in helping illegal aliens. After NOT doing anything to stop illegal immigration for the past 20 years, politicians vote for driver's licenses for illegals. They give away taxpayer money for 'anchor babies.' They vote to give illegals free medical care while our own citizens suffer. They vote for free schooling from K-12 for illegal alien kids on the backs of American taxpayers. They vote for in-state college tuition for illegals. Politicians allow illegal immigrants to bring in diseases that cause our kids horrible consequences. Our elected officials facilitate depressing our wages while corporations outsource and offshore our jobs to foreign countries. Congressional officials assist drug smugglers to bring drugs across our southern borders by not doing anything to stop them. They do nothing to stop crime via such insane policies as 'Special Order 40' that allows illegals to NOT be deported or detained by our police departments. With those cities that have adopted 'Special Order 40,' they provide sanctuaries for illegal immigrants.

But what they don't appreciate or understand is that American citizens pay a price for this anarchy. This growing lawlessness finds new Honduran, El Salvadoran, Chinese and Mexican gangs running drugs like billion dollar corporations. Sometimes, it's only money or new diseases, but at its extreme, it's deadly.

Two years ago in 2002, National Park Ranger Kris Eggle at Organ Pipe National Monument on the Mexican border—was a 28-year-old, handsome and enthusiastic young man. Kris stood out as the valedictorian of his high school class. He graduated from college with multiple honors in sports at the University of Michigan. His parents Bob and Bonnie Eggle had raised what could easily be said was an ALL-AMERICAN BOY.

His passion? Kris loved people. He became a park ranger. He wore his Smoky Bear hat with pride. He gave ranger talks to park visitors. He served at Sleeping Bear Dunes National Park, Great Smoky Mountains and Canyonlands National Park before serving at Organ Pipe Cactus National Monument. He adored the desert. He loved fishing, camping, hiking and adventure. He rode his motorcycle to be as free as a bird. This young man would make any parent proud.

But, instead of enjoying his job as a park ranger, he contended with an average of 400,000 illegal aliens crossing over the border annually at Organ Pipe. Because our U.S. Congress refused to stop illegal immigration, drug smugglers became emboldened.

On August 9, 2002, an illegal alien gunned down Kris Eggle. The alien and his partner had committed four brutal killings the night before in Sonoyta. The two killers stole a vehicle, but got stuck in the desert and fled on foot. Kris' murderer hid in the thick shrubbery laying in wait with his AK-47. As Kris neared the area, the alien gunned him down. The alien was a hired assassin for a drug cartel as well as a drug trafficker.

What is so disgusting is the fact that it happened in the first place. It was a direct result of our past and present president(s) and Congress doing virtually nothing to stop this invasion.

How would you like to be a visitor at any of your national parks and become involved in a shoot-out? How would you like to be hiking in the wilderness when somebody starts shooting at you simply because you came up on their drug route? What if it was your son assassinated by smugglers' bullets? How would you feel about what your president and Congress are doing concerning the security of our southern borders? They were doing nothing before 9/11 and two years later, they're still allowing massive drugs and illegal aliens over our borders?

The following first hand story is written by Bonnie Eggle, the mother of National Parks Ranger Kris Eggle, who was shot to death by illegal alien drug smugglers on August 9, 2002. You could as easily be the parents of this fine young man. If this invasion continues, at some point, you or a loved one will be affected by this crisis.

Life Without Kris...

August 2002 came so quickly. Summer was almost over and the time to head back to school loomed closely. Kris and Jennifer were both at different National Parks, one in Arizona and the other in Wyoming. Because I spent almost two weeks with Kris the summer before, I decided to head toward Wyoming for a short week of hiking, watching the geysers, and enjoying the beauties of nature at Yellowstone with my daughter Jennifer.

Thursday, August 8th was a day filled with exploring the mud pots, the hot springs, the geysers and watching the temperatures drop from the mid-50s to the mid-20s, accompanied by rain, sleet, and snow! Jennifer and I laughed about these drastic changes, knowing that Kris was enduring the heat of the summer in southern Arizona. After we ate our dinner that evening, we drank some hot chocolate and made a call to Kris. He laughed as we chattered about the weird, cold weather—-it was 95 degrees at Organ Pipe that day! After visiting a short while, we said goodnight and sent our love and hugs to each other. Kris' last words to me were "Goodnight, Mom I love you and I'll see you later."(Kris never said goodbye—from the time he was little, he heard his dad say, "See you later," and so it stuck with him. He didn't like good-byes.)

Friday morning the sun was out. We decided to go gaze at the bison and look for any sign of wolves. We sat in a field around noon eating our lunch and watching the beautiful and majestic animals. Jen and I talked about how we wished Kris were with us because he so loved this place and the abundant wildlife. We headed back to her home around 2:30 p.m. to do some letter writing and computer work.

At 4:00 p.m. MT, there was a knock at Jennifer's door. It was one of her Law Enforcement Ranger friends, Mike Harding. Jennifer introduced us and told me that Mike and Kris knew each other through a Special Operations Training Course they had taken together. I said "Hi," shook his hand, and wanted to visit more, but he was very nervous and ashen-faced. He asked us to sit down, and my immediate reaction was that one of their friends from Yellowstone had had an accident. Jen kept saying, "What is it, Mike? What is wrong?" He finally blurted out, "Kris has been shot. He was ambushed and it is really bad."

Both Jen and I reacted by yelling, "No. What? Not Kris! No! No! No!" Then she started asking what happened and if he were okay. I kept saying, "I must get to him. Where is he? Where is he? I need to go now." Mike just kept repeating that Kris was really hurt badly.

Then the phone rang. It was my husband calling from home in Cadillac, Michigan. Jennifer answered the phone and all I could hear was Bob yelling and Jennifer saying, "No, Dad! No, Dad! No, Dad!" When I got to the phone, Bob kept yelling, "HE'S GONE! KRIS IS GONE! KRIS IS DEAD. HE WAS MURDERED!" I know I kept saying, "NO, NO, NO, NO! I want to go to him. I want him back."

Next I remember many Law Enforcement Rangers coming in and out of Jennifer's house, comforting us, talking to us, asking what they could do to help. The only thing we wanted was to leave and go to Kris in southern Arizona. There were no planes out of the area that evening and I cried, "We have to get out of here! We have to get to Kris! We have to get to Kris! We have to take him home."

By pulling strings, District Ranger Lane arranged for us to fly from Bozeman, Montana on the earliest flight the next morning. They escorted us to a motel near the airport Friday evening. Jennifer and I felt so alone, but we knew we had to keep moving to be joined with family and Kris. For three hours we laid in bed sobbing, then got up, dressed and headed for the airport for that early Saturday flight.

Because we had only emergency verbal reservations, we were totally searched. I sobbed through it all while Jennifer tried to explain to the security guards what had happened. I couldn't think it through without sobbing, so she ended up making all the flight arrangements, taking care of me, and protecting me like I was her child. She pushed through crowds of stranded travelers in Salt Lake City when all flights were canceled going into Phoenix and where everyone else also had to rebook flights. She made her way to the front desk, gave the attendants the notarized letter detailing Kris' murder as a Federal Law Enforcement Ranger. We finally were detoured to Tucson, and were able to meet up with some family members who had landed shortly before we did.

Upon arrival at the Tucson Airport, a contingent of military and NPS officers were there to whisk us away to a private area. That is where we were informed of more details of the shooting. We also learned that Kris' body could not be taken home at that time, due to the fact it was a Federal criminal investigation and it warranted an autopsy. All I wanted was to get my Kris and go home, but that was not meant to be.

At this time we were told that hundreds of people from the community of Ajo and the surrounding areas were requesting a memorial service to pay their final respects for our son/brother Kris. We agreed, knowing how much he loved the community, the people, and Organ Pipe. We felt it was the only fair thing to do for them and for Kris' memory.

A National Park Service Incident Command Team was established to be with us at all times and to help with any plans needing to be made. Our team helped us think through every single detail and they made every arrangement. They "lifted us, carried us", listened to us, and grieved with us. They truly were a team of angels sent to minister in a very special way.

Monday, August 12, 2002 blazed hot with the intensity of a funeral and crowds to meet. Were we going to be able to manage our emotions? Would we hold up through all of the stresses and the trauma? As we were ushered to our vehicle, we looked behind us and for as far as our eyes could see, there were Law Enforcement vehicles—-178 vehicles from all over the region and from surrounding states. We followed behind the hearse, with miles and miles of cars trailing behind. As we approached the town of Ajo, a Blackhawk helicopter escorted Kris from above. The shadow followed the hearse all the way to the church, with the rotors kicking up sand and dirt to acknowledge that one of their own was being protected on his final mission.

Kris' first funeral was held in the tiny town of Ajo, Arizona, population of around 750-800. The attendance at the service was well over 700. People from the community came bringing food from their kitchens; the restaurants supplied special pans of entrees and desserts for all those in attendance. People from the National Park Service and other branches of Law Enforcement came by the hundreds to say goodbye to one of their fallen comrades. Washington DC sent the National Park Service Director, the Border Patrol sent their Chief, and many other dignitaries came. The two people who touched our hearts were Representative Tom Tancredo of Colorado and U.S. Attorney Paul Charlton, from the District of Arizona. They both vowed that Kris' murder would not be in vain and that his sacrifice would be remembered forever. Their words helped guide us through that day and consequently, through many days and weeks that followed.

After the funeral we went outside for the helicopter fly-over, and the lost man formation. It was heart wrenching, but what really made the tears flow was when the dispatcher called, "1207, 1207, 1207. Come in, 1207." After a couple more attempts she said, "1207 over and out...and goodnight."

After the exhausting funeral and the hours of meeting and greeting the people who came out of the goodness of their hearts, we finally went to the crime scene to visit the place where an evil and cowardly person hid under the brushy vegetation for camouflage, and then methodically "mowed down" my beautiful son. From the prone position, he could see Kris' feet and realized he was walking near his hiding area. With that, he opened-fire with his AK-47 and blew my Kris away. One bullet hit his radio and deflected under his bulletproof vest, cutting his femoral and aortal arteries. My beautiful son lay dying in that dirty, desolate desert. However because of drills and practice, he tried to save his own life. He unbuckled his belt, loosened his shirt, undid his vest and tried to put pressure on his wounds to stop the flow of blood. His injuries were too devastating, and his efforts were to no avail. His friends found him shortly, and tried to do CPR and to work on his injuries as quickly as possible. They carried him to a Border Patrol vehicle and charged out of the desert, meeting the ambulance about halfway.

The EMS team, some Border Patrol Agents, and Rangers worked on him while heading north to meet the Life Flight helicopter. However, when it finally arrived, the decision was made that nothing more could be done...he was dead. They telephonically made the call with the time of death for Kristopher William Eggle charted at 2:40 PM. Just two hours before, Kris had been vibrant and full of life, ready to take on another mission... which ultimately turned out to be his very last.

At the crime scene that afternoon we were "walked through" what the possible scenario would have been. The agents had people in positions where the killers and the Border Patrol agents were, as well as where our swift-footed son was when he cautiously moved along the outside of the wash, past the area where his murderer lay in wait. Each step of the possible scenario was explained to us and we were given ample time to ask any questions. The FBI and the Special Agents in charge of the investigation were with us because they insisted correct information be given to us. As we reached the actual place where Kris was shot and where he fell, we got on our knees, touched the ground and cried buckets of tears for our horrifying loss. Our thoughts ran the gambit of grief—did he suffer long...how much was he aware of what had happened....did he realize he was injured badly....did he think about us....did he speak at all....did he see angels as his body and soul separated from this earth. As we pondered all these questions, with no real answers, Bob made a statement that we will always remember. "Are we going to let evil win?" We all gathered around, prayed, and vowed that evil was not going to win.

Our Kris was dead and we were not going to let his murder be in vain. We would go on fighting for his causes— a safer border environment, continued protections for the visitors and the resources of the parks, and work toward better follow-through of laws concerning immigration, legal and illegal. We knew we were going to write a newsletter and contact members of Congress. That was the first revelation of our mission/crusade. Little did we know that on that hot afternoon in the Sonoran Desert near the Mexican border, that those words would prove so powerful to help turn our heart-wrenching grief into an action that continues through today.

The next afternoon our family group was able to bring Kris home to Cadillac, Michigan. The National Park Service arranged a charter flight to transport the eight of us home because we refused to be separated from him. As we gathered around the plane and watched some members of the Air Force, some Rangers, his Uncles, and his Dad load his body onto the plane, disbelief still reigned in all our hearts and minds. It just couldn't be...it just couldn't be...it must be a nightmare that we would awaken from. However it was real and our flight home was soon to begin.

We arrived in Traverse City, Michigan with the airfield lined with Law Enforcement vehicles, officers, and some family and friends. It was a very emotional time because we knew we were getting closer to home and to his final destination. All the Law Enforcement vehicles led us or followed us the entire trip. They stopped traffic and cleared the way for the whole cortège to stay together. When we arrived in Cadillac, the same thing was evident. Roads were closed off, policemen and firemen were everywhere, and people were flying flags and standing at attention as the hearse drove though the town and to the funeral home. Kris was ushered out of the hearse by many of these Law Enforcement men and women, firemen, deputies, and others who knew and loved him. His body was handled beautifully and respectfully every step of the way.... and now we were home.

Home...our little bundle of joy, Kristopher William Eggle— born August 15, 1973. He was the most alert baby ever. He moved his eyes and his head, while listening to the crickets and to my voice. The true feeling of happiness was now complete with this addition to our lives.

As he grew into a young boy, the characteristics of kindness and caring showed through everyday. He loved his little sister Jennifer. They were best friends. They played with the kittens, played baseball, climbed trees, made forts, took hikes and played army. They both loved Star Wars, Superman, Batman and Robin, and fishing. They were a "pair and a spare"—you hardly ever saw one without the other. Many cousins were also part of this friendship core and they stayed that way through life.

School years arrived before we knew it. Kris enjoyed each day and the adventures that went with them. He always excelled in academics, athletics, and was what many of his teachers said, "The student that every teacher dreams about." His elementary years were filled with much fun, many new friends, and exploring new dimensions into music, acting, and leadership. Kris documented his weeks/years by journaling and by filling his many photo albums.

As he moved into Junior High School and then into High School, the leadership abilities were ever more obvious. He maintained the rank of #1 in academics, he became an Eagle Scout, he was Captain for both his Cross-Country and Track teams for 3 years, he was a class officer, and he served on different community committees, such as Junior Rotarian, Co-President of a Community Foundation, and a volunteer for the recycling center. Kris' days and evenings were filled with activities, but he always managed to take time for family and friends. He also was involved with his church group, spent a lot of time at the library studying and tutoring others, spent many weekends camping, hiking, backpacking, and hunting in glorious places with his dad, scouting groups, and with friends. He also had devoted himself to working with his dad at the family farm where he learned a lot of lessons about nature, wildlife, and the land.

College years came way too quickly. His decision to decline the West Point nomination and acceptance came with some sadness, mixed with relief. The choice of finally attending the University of Michigan and running with their glorious teams was one of the best decisions ever. He admired his new teammates and coaches and quickly became known for his leadership, kindness, caring, integrity, and thoughtfulness. Pre-med was the future for Kris, until I became sick and was treated at the University of Michigan Hospital. Because of my cancer diagnosis, treatment, and return to health, Kris wanted to say thank you. He did this by volunteering many hours throughout the next year at the hospital. He loved helping people, but because of this time in the hospital, he made the final decision that he could not work inside of a building for his life. Therefore, he began searching for another choice, which would fulfill his hopes and aspirations.

This is when he decided to pursue a career in the National Park Service. Finally, Kris felt as though his dreams were really going to come true. He would be working for our country in a service-oriented position, protecting the beautiful treasures of our land, working with the visitors, and ultimately, helping to protect and defend the Constitution of the United States of America as a Federal Law Enforcement Officer. He took the Oath of Office and respected those honored words, " I will support and defend the Constitution of the United States of America against all enemies, foreign and domestic...So help me God."

In 1995 Kris accepted a position at the Great Smoky Mountains National Park in North Carolina tracking wild boar and bears. He served as an NPS Law Enforcement Ranger at South Manitou Island, Sleeping Bear Dunes National Lakeshore in Michigan, and at Canyonlands National Park in Utah before arriving at Organ Pipe Cactus National Monument on the Arizona/Mexico border in 2000. During the Spring/Summer of 2002, Kris attended the Federal Law Enforcement Training Center in Georgia where he was elected president by the members of his class. He graduated at the top of his class and was awarded the FLETC Director's Award for outstanding achievement. Upon graduation from this Academy, he went back to Organ Pipe to continue with his mission of protecting the resources and visitors, and to continue with the drug tracking and interdiction, which had become such a key to the job of the Law Enforcement Ranger on the border. While serving as a Ranger, he also performed as an Emergency Medical

Technician, a Wildland and Structural Fire Fighter, and a Search and Rescue Team member.

Three weeks before his murder, Kris came home for a short visit to see family and friends. He packed every minute with doing activities and seeing people he had not seen for a while. He was very concerned about the continued incursions of smuggled drugs, humans, and weapons and knew in his heart there was so much more that needed to be done at the border, even though he realized the ever- present dangers. While home, we visited about his future with the Park Service and plans for a possible life with a wife and children of his own. He confided in me that one of his desires would be to have a family and train up his children as he had also been raised. He wanted to share the beauties of our land and all God had so richly provided for us. He would have been such a wonderful husband and daddy! These are the future memories that have been robbed from me and for that I weep every single day.

Thoughts abound as to why he had to die. He was such a beacon of light, and to have this brilliance extinguished just doesn't seem right. We continue to grieve and feel the loneliness of the separation from our beloved child. However, Kris would not want us to go on grieving forever. He would want us to refocus our lives into doing good works for others. That was his mission as well and therefore we will try to follow in his footsteps until the end of our lives, when at last, we will be reunited with Kris. My vision of our reunion is that he will run toward us with his arms wide open, smiling, and saying, "I have been waiting for you. This is a beautiful place and I have so much to show you. Come on, Mom. There are no more tears here. You can now be at peace forever. We are together again." Home...really, really home this time.

We are so grateful for all the kindness and caring that has been directed toward our family since Kris' murder. He truly loved others and was loved and respected in return.

As a final note from this writer, I suspect you cried while reading this chapter. I did. It is a profoundly touching story from a mother who lost her son. Heaven knows the pain Kris' dad suffers or Jennifer, Kris' sister. What about his friends and fellow rangers? What about America's loss?

Is there anything about it that angers you? I'm angry because this chapter never should have been written. It shouldn't have happened. Kris Eggle should be out there in the park today giving visitors an orientation course on desert beauty or a campfire talk about the Great Horned Owl. He should be riding his motorcycle into the wind on a summer's night. He should be dancing on the dance floor with his girlfriend. He should be laughing and cheering his Michigan Wolverines to beat the Michigan State Spartans every autumn. He should be looking forward to what Thomas Jefferson wrote about in the Constitution, "Life, liberty and the pursuit of happiness."

But he isn't because our Congress and the past and present presidents have not and are not doing the job they took upon themselves when they placed their hand on the Bible for their oath of office. They swore to protect this country from "enemies both foreign and domestic." Instead, they have facilitated this illegal alien invasion by doing mostly nothing.

If you want to dig further into this crisis, consider this: BECAUSE Congress and the president weren't doing their jobs, BECAUSE they have not upheld our immigration laws for 20 years, BECAUSE corporations have been facilitating illegal immigration for cheap labor, BECAUSE this invasion is about money and power for politicians and corporations, BECAUSE it's gone on for so long and BECAUSE terrorist groups discovered how easy it was to gain entrance into the United States— 3,000 people died in the World Trade Center on 9/11.

That means 3,000 people and their families suffer as much as Bonnie, Bob and Jennifer Eggle. When you note that 29 percent of our prisons are filled with legal and illegal immigrants, it means hundreds of thousands of Americans have been affected. They were raped, robbed, shoplifted, vandalized, and maimed or killed in traffic accidents. When you look at the unemployment rolls, more facts bear out this crisis. If you look at our schools overrun with dozens of languages that dilute our childrens' education, you see how much it is affecting you. California's crisis is your crisis. As this book points out in the realm of our medical services, highway safety, infrastructure, overpopulation, advancing diseases, clashing cultures and worse, all of us are affected. If you don't think this invasion will touch you because it's 'out there' somewhere, you've got another think coming and it's only a matter of time.

CHAPTER 23—

AMERICANS OUTRAGED AT ILLEGAL IMMIGRATION

"Beware the leader who bangs the drums of war in order to whip the citizenry into patriotic fervor, for patriotism is indeed a double edged sword. It both emboldens the blood, just as it narrows the mind...and when the drums of war have reached a fever pitch and the blood boils with hate and the mind closes, the leader will have no need in seizing the rights of the citizenry. Rather the citizenry, infused with fear and blinded with patriotism, will offer up all their rightsunto the leader, and gladly so. How do I know? For this is what I have done. I am Caesar."

Julius Caesar, 44 BC

Does that quote chill you to the bone? How about the Patriot Act? How about the reasons our leaders used to provoke a war with Iraq? Why didn't Bush attack North Korea or a dozen other dictators who brutalize their populations? How about 13 million illegal aliens invading our country while our president sends troops 10,000 miles away? Why does Bush ignore our borders? How about the fear perpetrated by the media daily in Iraq while we're being overrun in our own country? How smart and cunning was Julius Caesar? How clever is Bush to follow suit? How fast are we being sacrificed in this deadly global chess game?

"We are fast approaching the stage of the ultimate inversion: the stage where the government is free to do anything it pleases, while the citizens may act only by permission; which is the stage of the darkest periods of human history, the stage of rule by brute force." Ayn Rand, The Nature of Government

Below is a section of immigration law that is not being enforced in the United States of America.

"A person (including a group of persons, business, organization, or local government) commits a federal felony when she or he: assists an illegal alien s/he should reasonably know is illegally in the U.S. or who lacks employment authorization, by transporting, sheltering, or assisting him or her to obtain employment, or encourages that illegal alien to remain in the U.S. by referring him or her to an employer or by acting as employer or agent for an employer in any way, or knowingly assists illegal aliens due to personal convictions." Section 8 USC 1324(a)(1)(A)(iv)(b)(iii)

Because these laws are not being enforced by President Bush and our Congress, American citizens by the millions write their frustrations daily in newspapers. The editorial page marks the pulse of their communities. It's where they can read nationally syndicated columnists spout their brilliance. Liberal and conservative columnists jabber from one end of the page to the other.

However, readers zero in on 'letters to the editor.' Those letters speak about their communities. That's what's happening at the ground level of America. People vent their spleens in the 'Letters' section. It's the one place where they tell it like it is. They express their anger, frustrations and sense of futility at politicians, neighbors, government policies, wars and national problems.

Major polling companies track the 'LTE' pages for the latest 'feelings' of the American public. With the immigration invasion growing by the thousands daily, the letters fly thick and fast at congressional members, governors, local officials and anyone who is aiding both legal and illegal immigration.

As can be read in these letters, this invasion is not about race, creed or color. These writers include democrats, republicans, libertarians, independents, Hispanics, Blacks, Whites and all other American citizens.

Below are a few of those letters sent to me:

Dear Editor: Immigration is the most formidable weapon of mass destruction threatening America today. Ironically, invaders have put our country at risk without firing a shot. The White House, the heavies in Congress and the smaller fish in state legislatures do not seem to have the collective intellectual depth or common sense to see what is upon us and how rampant immigration will degrade the lives and opportunities of our progeny. Every day forces America closer to irreversible chaos. Behind this issue are blind forces to reckon with. No politician, political party, corporation, religious fervor, investment, pop morality or individual aspiration should come before country. Ever! The brokers who recklessly advocate or condone pervasive immigration are steersmen with Titanic-like wheelhouse credentials.

Dear Editor: I spent the first 18 years of my life in a Latin American country. Mexico's economic structure is no different from other Latin countries, with the only difference that Mexico is a very rich nation in natural resources. In Mexico, like other Latin countries, the middle class is almost non-existing. The wealthy few rule the masses of extremely poor people. That is the reason why Mexico's wealthy will NEVER tax themselves for the good of their country. They prefer to send their poor people to the U.S. to avoid political unrest. Trying to fix Mexico's problems is like trying to make the sun rise in the West. Why should wealthy Mexicans fix their country when Uncle Sam is there to send billions of US taxpayer's money every year and at the same time take millions of poor Mexicans in?

Dear Editor: True to form, party officials are out of touch with the bone and marrow of the Republican Party. My sons, who have been master carpenters for 25 years, are seeing the field of work that they were proud to enter be "colonized" by illegal alien labor. Because of harassment, vandalized work, tools, and vehicles, reduced wages, etc, younger men are not entering the construction trades, which are quickly becoming "work that Americans won't do." These are the willing Workers who President Bush wants to protect, instead of my sons. For that reason our 4-generation Republican family will not vote again for George "Willing Workers" Bush. Party officials who acknowledge "some grumbling" among rank-and-file members, but don't think it will hurt the President, are whistling past the graveyard with that hopeful spin. You have in effect discarded the states with heavy concentrations of illegal immigrants, such as California. No respect, no protection, no vote, Mr. President.

Dear Editor: Hallow sees little chance of a significant grass-roots revolt of our President giving away American jobs to illegal aliens and Mexican Nationals that openly wish to control the policies of our country? I am Hispanic and a loyal American and I have left the Republican Party and will vote Democrat next year! That is how angry the Presidents proposal has made me! American jobs belong to the American people!

Dear Editor: As a Hispanic/American and native Californian, I would like to say that Tom Tancredo is one of the few leaders today that has retained our forefathers' principles. President Eisenhower and most American leaders always placed the American citizens first. Very few political leaders today are working for us citizens today. California is in dire problems due to illegal immigration. Congressman Tancredo's initiative will help stop illegal immigration. Why we must educate illegal foreign children and not dedicate our educational system to our American children alone is beyond me?

Dear Editor: We have NEVER needed illegal aliens and we don't need them now! Has anyone noticed that jobs for Farm Workers and custodial workers are never published in the "work wanted" section of the classified? If these jobs were posted for Americans, the jobs would be taken, probably by the unemployed and those on welfare. But of course employers want cheap labor instead of hiring Americans. I also think that criminals like the Enron executives and their kind would do Americans good by being made to do this type of work in exchange for restitution.

Dear Editor: The Bush administration somehow feels that we can provide adequate security by checking the front door, while it leaves the back door wide open.   We should utilize our military troops to assist the beleaguered Border Patrol, with high-tech detection equipment. This egregious dereliction of the duty to protect our borders fringes on treason!

Dear Editor: It is remarkable that President Bush spends millions of American tax dollars to guard borders in other parts of the world in his quest to fight terrorism. Yet the President will not guard our own borders with the strength the American people deserve.

Dear Editor: Allowing illegal aliens into the U.S. without deporting them is the biggest mistake in the history of this Country! That is, next to the disastrous Immigration act of 1965, when Democrats sneaked this anti-Western law on the American people without asking if anyone wanted it? Isn't it ironic that Mexican students can have an anti-American "MECHA" meeting in peace? We must enforce our immigration laws or we will no longer have a United States!

Dear editor: I personally believe that this current rate of mass immigration (legal and illegal) is going to destroy the way of life we were accustomed to. With illegal immigration not being enforced, we don't know who is entering our communities nor do we know what crimes many of these people have committed in their own country? Also the population growth has me extremely worried about the future of my children and grandchildren.

CHAPTER 24—

STORIES FROM THE TRENCHES OF AMERICA

"The liberties of our country, the freedom of our civil constitution, are worth defending at all hazards; and it is our duty to defend them against all attacks. We have received them as a fair inheritance from our worthy ancestors: they purchased them for us with toil and danger and expense of treasure and blood, and transmitted to us with care and diligence. It will bring an everlasting mark of infamy on the present generation, enlightened as it is, if we should suffer them to be wrested from us by violence without a struggle, or be cheated out of them by the artifices of false and designing men."

Samuel Adams, 1771

With between 10 to 13 million illegal aliens roaming our country, millions of Americans suffer from the continuing invasion.

Below are stories from individual Americans from all sections of our country. The sad aspect of these cases is the fact that they happened to your neighbors and, given time, you too, will have a story. Why? Because our president and Congress refuse to serve American citizens and stop this immigration invasion.

THIS IS GOING ON ALL OVER THE COUNTRY

"After retiring from the Army I went back to college to continue my education. When I graduated I took a job in the aircraft industry. My first posting was in the Middle East and I was there for a few years and then returned to the States. I was working in Southern California when the Berlin wall came down and within months everyone in the Defense industry was looking for another job. My wife was from Utah so we decided it was cheaper to be broke there that in Orange County California. I took a few months off to spend time figuring out what I wanted to do with the rest of my life.

"My wife said one night, "'You have changed so very much since retiring from the Army you should do something to help people. It will make you feel good.'" I took her up on this and got a job working for the state welfare department. I got my first dose of reality in the first week of training where I learned how much the state was spending on illegal aliens. I asked the instructor why we were spending anything at all since they were here illegally. I was told that attitude would not be permitted in our department as it bordered on racist. Well, not being the sort who is intimidated I shot back, "Do you mean that by breaking federal law and enabling illegal aliens to remain here and continue to break our laws is considered racist." The matter was dropped and after class I was called into the office of the only other man in the department. What an eye opener that was!

"I was told that I better not ever talk like that again if I wanted a career in Human Services. I tried to explain that I had only brought up the point that our department was breaking the spirit of the law by not reporting illegal aliens to the INS. That's when I learned that even if we wanted to we couldn't as there is an overriding law that bars the identification of people on any type of public assistance. So I asked why the government would make laws that overrode other laws. The answer really shocked me. I was told that in the not too distant future the Mexican vote would be the largest right next to the white vote and I had better just get used to it. Well, my first thought is why is this happening? I don't remember having a national referendum on turning our country into a Third World country.

"This was back in 1990 so the astute among us were able to determine what was going on way back then. I couldn't believe it. I just assumed that the guy who told me this was just burned out and waiting to retire. Why else would he have such a defeatist attitude? Within six months two things made me leave the Welfare department. First, I was sued by La Raza for suggesting that an illegal alien might consider getting a job to feed his family, and stop using drugs and alcohol. They said I "IMPUGNED" his manhood. The hearing officer dismissed his charge but cautioned me to be more racially sensitive to our new citizens. I reminded the hearing officer that this person was a citizen of Mexico and not America. BIG MISTAKE! In the office that I worked in there was only one other person who was not a Socialist/Liberal and this person warned me that they were trying to figure out a way to get rid of me despite having the best team stats in the department and the best attendance record.

"I started looking for a new job right then and there. I had one more memorable run in before I left the Welfare department. It was on payday for the recipients. In our parking lot the pimps and whores and drug dealers were waiting to get their share. A woman came up to me and reported that a woman was shooting up in the ladies room with her newly bought drugs, and had passed out. I got a woman employee to go in there and we called 911. Since I had been a "Grunt," I was well-versed in first aid and after determining that she was unconscious I went in and started giving her CPR. I really did not want to do this as She looked really bad and I was worried for my own safety what with AIDS and such. Well, after she threw up on me I got her back on her feet and helped her to wash up a little. The medics finally got there and so did the police. I had put her "works" in a bag to use as evidence if it was necessary.

"The next day she came back and went up to see the Assistant Director. Well, I thought I would be getting a "attaboy" for helping her and what happened was she was complaining that I stolen her "kit." The Asst. director said I should have given her drug parafinallia back to her. I said that I thought our job was the welfare of children and why in the hell would we give a drug addict her kit back so that she could further neglect her children by continuing to take more illegal drugs. She explained to me that what the clients did was not our concern as long as no laws were broken in our building. Well, I mentioned that doing drugs was illegal in or out of our building. I mentioned that being in this country illegally was breaking the law. I mentioned that putting her children at risk by her neglecting them was illegal behavior. At that point the Assistant Director told me off the record that I had better find a new position. I told her I would be happy to and within a week or two I took a job at the state child support agency. I thought the worse was behind me. It was only starting."

THOUGHT I COULD TELL YOU MY STORY

"I have a son who was in an auto accident who lost his right arm and left leg. Now, my son lives in California where all his Doctors are. I am a senior citizen and need to help him as much as I can, but, when I call agencies in California for assistance, I get the run-around. The Housing Authority has shut down, so I am told when I called them. Several other Government Social Programs are out of funds (they say temporarily, and also tell me there are thousands of other people ahead of my son) so there is not the help and assistance I need to help support my son's rent payment. I am frustrated and totally at a loss.

"THEN, I learned from one of my friends, who works with the Hispanics, that there is a Hispanic illegal from Mexico who is currently getting assistance from our Government to pay for HIS rent. This Hispanic pays only around $230 per month and has re-rented his place for $1,000 per month (illegally making money off our Government Program). I am so angry, it has affected my health.

"THEN, my neighbor, who works for a Dentist in Nevada tells me: An illegal comes into her office and when she asked for

ID, he gave her 6 different ID's, one at a time because none of them would clear her computer system. These ID's were all in his name. Then, he complained about having to pay $1.00 for his visit. Yes, that was (one dollar). I almost feel like breaking the law just to survive just like our friends from south of the border."

MEDICAL NIGHTMARE VIA ILLEGAL IMMIGRANTS

"My name is Paul and I live in a small town situated on the US/Mexico Border approximately 120 miles southeast of Tucson. I am a retired USAF veteran, and at the time of this incident, owned and operated an Archery Pro Shop complete with indoor shooting lanes inside the city limits. I also was a Private Contractor for the State of Arizona, monitoring and maintaining Air Quality Monitoring Systems. It was in March of 1996, while I was performing my duties on this job that the incident occurred; I was 56 years old at the time.

"I usually started on the most distant filter systems located about twelve miles out of town and the Paul Spur Lime Plant, notorious for the powdered gypsum in the air. I was driving my 1976 Chevrolet van and had noticed a small car approaching me from behind at a high speed as I approached the Paul Spur turnoff. With its speed in mind, I turned on my turn signal early, since this particular portion of highway 80 narrows rapidly and at the same time has a sudden "No Passing" zone.

"Reaching the turn off, I made my turn and proceeded onto Paul Spur Road. I was more than thirty feet off of the highway and had slowed down to cross the cattle guard when I was struck in the left front corner of my van. Anyone who has never been in an accident simply cannot understand the forces involved. Since I had been in the process of accelerating, my vehicle moved forward as the sideways impact turned me to the right as my body was twisted around inside of it as I fought to re-gain control. When I finally managed to stop it, I had gone through a fence and was facing south, with the car that had hit me, its front end shortened by at least three feet.

"As I sat there making sure I had actually stopped, the doors flew open on the car and six people jumped out, five adults and a little girl. They didn't stop, but ran north along the railroad tracks as the driver began kicking at his door in an attempt to get out. I managed to get out of the van before he got the door open and when I pointed my finger at him and shook my head, he got the message and stopped.

"Ironically, a Highway Patrol Officer, taking a new vehicle to have its equipment installed had been passing at the time of the accident and had returned. I told him I felt that the occupants were illegal aliens and he requested that the Border Patrol be notified which he did. The Border Patrol arrived and found the other six people hiding under a bridge less than a hundred feet away, and after about ten minutes of inspecting the vehicle, took them away to be extradited.

"Normally this is where you'd expect the story to end. However, for me, it was just beginning. At the advice of the DPS officer, I went to Ft Huachuca in Sierra Vista, AZ and had x-rays taken which showed nothing out of the ordinary. The doctor diagnosed me with bruises and contusions and I was given a prescription for Ibuprofen and a muscle relaxant and sent on my way. A week or so later I still felt that things weren't right, and returned to Fort Huachuca where I was told by the doctor to quit wasting their time and sent away; at no time was an MRI suggested.

"Over the next eighteen months I saw a Chiropractor and was able to get some relief for my back, but I still had periods of extreme pain in my left shoulder and I began to drop items when I tried to hold them in my left hand. In October of 1997 I was in the local Wal-Mart when my left hand began to feel as if it was asleep. By the time I got home the tingling sensation had reached my elbow; I couldn't feel anything in my left hand and could barely hold anything in it. In less than two days my entire left side had gone completely numb and my vision was affected to the point that I was afraid to drive.

"The chiropractor referred me to a neurosurgeon who requested an MRI since I was required by the military version of an HMO (Champus/TriCare) I had to get permission before it could be performed. The MRI showed what the x-rays couldn't: a small crack at the base of the brainstem inside my spine has begun secreting spinal fluid in an attempt to heal the injury. Instead, the excess fluid began a hydraulic action, and was literally forcing my spine apart, destroying the surrounding nerves as it expanded.

"The neurosurgeon wanted to operate immediately, but again was required to get permission from TriCare, which took another two weeks. Finally, on December 31, 1997 the operation was performed. When I woke up in my room in the hospital I felt so good I told my wife I could probably chase the nurses! I was released on January 1, 1998 to recuperate at home. On January 2, 1998 I passed out and was air-evacuated back to Tucson where I spent the next ten days in a coma.

"To sum it up, the results of my personal encounter with this one group of illegal aliens resulted in permanent partial paralysis of my left side. This in turn resulted in my having to close my business and made it necessary to reduce the extent of my Contractor's agreement with the State of Arizona. In addition my medical bills amounted to over $117,000.00.

"I am now 65 years old and draw Social Security and am on Medicare. I am considered "un-hireable" due to my disabilities but draw no compensation for them. But I was lucky. I didn't lose an arm or leg, and I'm still alive and able to speak up for the rights of my fellow Americans who are being constantly forced to bend over for the benefits of 8 - 10 million criminals who seem to be the favored ones."

WHAT IS NEXT FOR AMERICANS?

"My name is of no importance, but I feel my story is. I'm a white female in my mid 30's. I live in a border town only a few miles from the Mexico border. I've lived in the area for 3 years, and am appalled at what is going on here!

"The Government has made it mandatory for our local ambulance service to go and pick up illegals from across the border, and transport them to a US hospital over 30 miles from the border for medical treatment ranging from stomach cramps, injuries, child birth, etc. Many of them refuse treatment when they arrive at the hospital, and can legally just walk off into the sunset. Other illegals have gone into labor. They have their child in the US, and then their children, when old enough are picked up and shuttled to the elementary school in the very small town where I live. A large percentage of the children in our school live in Mexico whose parents are Mexican, but they were born in the US, thanks to our government. How do I know this? I know this because my best friend and friends are the EMT's that go on the ambulance runs. It seems to me, that all are border patrol are good for is to hassle us locals. I get harassed constantly. I have long light blonde hair, blue eyes, and very fair skin. I don't look Mexican by any stretch of the imagination, but still I'm harassed. They ask you all kind of personal questions like: What is your citizenship? Where do you live? Where are you going? What kind of work do you do? How long will you be gone? Is that your dog? Is your dog an American?

"Where does the border patrol get off asking such personal questions? So much for protecting the freedoms of the US citizens! Here is the irony in it all. Guess what nationality the majority of the border patrol is...YOU GUESSED IT, MEXICAN. It's like letting the rooster guard the hen house...The rooster got out of the coupe, and wants to sneak all his cronies out. One of the top-level men at the border patrol on the American side was busted for letting illegals bring drugs across the border. Why would he do that you ask...? THE MONEY IS GOOOOOD!"

AN ENDEMIC INVASION REACHING INTO OUR DEEPEST AGENCIES

"I am a retired child support agent for the state of Utah. Let me tell you another dirty little secret about illegal immigration. When I started working for the state after I retired from the Army, the portion of my caseload consisting of Illegal Aliens was not worth mentioning. When I could not stand another day of working for Mexico and its citizens and quit in disgust, my caseload was over 25 percent illegal aliens. Here's the rub. Most of these guys have real families in Mexico so most are bigamists also. Since we have so many polygamists living in Utah no one makes a stink about it for fear of retribution from the Mormon Church. More than 50 percent of the murders here in Utah are by Mexicans. The paper stopped mentioning the legal status of them so as not to cause a popular uprising. My wife and I are moving to northern Nevada next year. We have had enough diversity."

OMINOUS FUTURE

"After reading your column today about the ominous implications unchecked immigration holds for America, I must agree! Illegal immigrant labor has virtually WRECKED our once-proud and self-sufficient economy. My mother was born of Ukrainian-speaking Russian refugees from Communism in Jersey City, NJ, during the Great Depression.

"When she was nine, Mom was sent to school to learn English. There were no Ukrainian radio stations, newspapers, magazines, or other such media outlets when Mom was growing up. She and her family had to learn English—indeed, in those days, immigrants were EXPECTED to learn English! Today, my mother still uses Ukrainian in family talk, but otherwise is UNRESERVEDLY ENGLISH in her spoken and written communications. I was born in Endicott, NY, in 1955. When I was eight, my family moved to Miami, FL, and there I grew up learning Spanish and Portuguese from Latino immigrants (and at my father's request, I studied both languages in school through college). And, like immigrants of my parents' generation, the Latino immigrants I grew up with in Miami WANTED to learn English.

"Today, however, immigrants seem to think they have every right to the best this country has to offer WITHOUT having to learn English. I hate to say it, but today immigrants are SPOILED! There are TV and radio stations, newspapers, books, magazines, and all sorts of other media outlets in so many foreign languages that why should the immigrants even BOTHER to learn English? It seems they want the good things of life in America, but want to replicate their OWN nations in OUR country! I have resided in Dallas, Texas for the past ten years, but have been unable to find gainful employment involving bilingualism because greedy employers are seeking far cheaper illegal labor.

"These employers SAY they want bilingual help, but, although, as previously mentioned, I know three languages, these employers prefer to hire illegal foreigners, even if they don't know a word of English!

"Isn't that TWO-FACED? While employers I have confronted over this issue either dodge my inquiries or remain silent, I strongly suspect the REAL reason they refuse to hire me is because I am a NATIVE-BORN AMERICAN CITIZEN and Americans DEMAND FAIR PLAY and WON'T TAKE ANY NONSENSE! I continually hear these hypocrites complain that Americans don't want to work or won't take the jobs the illegals are shunted into. The REAL truth, of course, is NOT that Americans are lazy or unmotivated, but that these employers are GREEDY exploiters who REFUSE to pay FAIR WAGES to American workers. They prefer illegal aliens, because they can RUTHLESSLY EXPLOIT these hapless folks to NO END!"

IN THE HEARTLAND

"I am a 40-something American married to a Dutch national; a linguist who specializes in French, Spanish and Dutch in addition to my native English; an ESL volunteer, teaching English to Mexicans in my Illinois hometown; and a translator who does business internationally via the Internet. Yet, having said all that, I have to add that the flood tide of Mexican immigrants scares the pants off me. If I remember right, Phyllis Schlafley has written that there is a definite plan on the part of some in Mexico to retake good portions of the U.S. At first I was skeptical about that, but now I can see this as a real possibility, especially when I hear from one of my ESL students that her friends aren't at all interested in learning English.

"In my opinion, this particular effort to weaken the foundation of our country is but one of many that are being enacted simultaneously—others including the business-education merger, with its socialistic roots and its attempts to dumb down the populace and give away all the job opportunities except for low-paying service jobs; the efforts to take away property rights (sustainable development, biospheres, etc.); the one-world government that is coming as surely as the dawn."

FROM THE STREETS OF BROOKLYN, NEW YORK

"My mother died last February after a three years battle with dementia, broken hip and cancer which necessitated me quitting my job and foregoing health insurance. While home with my mother my eyes were opened to the drastic change Third World immigration has brought to Bay Ridge. The filth, the garbage, disposable diapers and half-eaten food thrown into the streets. I never leave the house without a garbage bag to clean up my neck of the woods.

"I was horrified at the local hospital I was forced to bring my elderly mother to realizing that the majority of the staff and the patients were crude, noisy, unruly Third World immigrants. I saw the fear and disorientation in my mother's eyes.

"Even the last few months of my cancer-ridden, demented mother's life turned into a "immigration issue" as the home hospice tried to foster a rude, surly RN from the "Islands." I objected and had the good fortune to get an RN of Irish/German extraction who grew up in the neighborhood. And through good neighbors I managed to obtain a Norwegian-American practical nurse who made my mother's last days very happy and comfortable.

"Both the Irish/German RN and the Nowegian-American practical nurse verified my fears regarding the state of health care and the problem of the large number of non-European, non-white health care workers and the sub-standard level of care they afford. The Norwegian Lutheran Home in Bay Ridge was always a model nursing home. The Norwegian-American practical nurse told me that under new management the Norwegian-American staff of RNs and practical nurses has been replaced with non-white non-European immigrants because it is "cheaper."

"I felt lucky that I was able to protect my mother from Third World health care providers even if it was the cost of quitting my job and going without health insurance."

THIRD WORLD MOMENTUM IN ANIMAL SACRIFICE

"Santeria is the practice of "black magic" or "witchcraft" to bring evil or good to their subject. There are 120,000 Cuban exiles in Miami, Florida practicing this type pagan witchcraft and about 150 plus Botanica shops selling rituals used such as powdered egg shells, red cloth, copper and iron objects, urns to offer food to the evil spirit to enable them to bring bad luck upon their enemy. The Santeria witchcraft stems from African rituals 400 plus years ago and brought by slaves from Nigeria, Africa to Cuba and practiced there and intertwined with Catholicism.

"The more radical type witchcraft stems from the Congo region of Africa, which practices "human sacrifice!" I witnessed the Santeria practice whereby the Chief Santero cuts the throat of a goat or white pigeons and blood splatters all over the Santero's white ritual gown and cap. The subjects wanting to get rid of evil spirits have the white bird rubbed across the subject's body and is believed to cleanse the evil spirits by doing this and the pigeon is thrown into the river.

"My wife and I saw Santeria ritual remains at the Miami City Cemetery at a recently covered grave. There was an aluminum pie pan with small rocks and red pieces of cloth placed around the periphery of the plate having a dogs head and flowers and an urn of water to feed the various gods and make them happy to carry out this witchcraft ritual. The practice of human sacrifice from the Congo is called Payolo Mayombe. Ernesto Pichardo, a Cuban exile high Santeria priest (Santero) spoke at the City of Hialeah on June 9, 1987 requesting a permit to operate his Babalu Aye Santeria Church.

"We spoke against this type witchcraft black magic because the Santero gives subjects concoctions of roots and herbs that create toxic hallucinogenic drugs that put the subject into a catatonic trance like a zombie. VooDoo is practiced by Miami exiled Haitians brought to Haiti by African slaves. I argued that only Medical Doctors could dispense hallucinogenic drugs and Santero priests were not MD's. We also argued that diseases could be obtained from drinking blood from these animals during rituals. The Hialeah City Council loaded with Cuban exiles voted it down. Santeria rituals grow as the number of immigrants continues arriving in Miami."

CHAPTER 25—

CHILLING FACTS ON IMMIGRATION

"The only difference I ever found between the Democratic leadership and the Republican leadership is that one of them is skinning you from the ankle up and the other, from the neck down."

Huey P. Long

The price tag of this invasion defies one's imagination. It reaches into every area of your pocket book. While the public sleeps in its trust of politicians—the costs of immigration both legal and illegal grow beyond reason. Paul Craig Roberts, an economist said, "Will America become a Third World country in 20 years?" All indicators say there's a really good chance of it happening.

In this chapter, the problems areas are broken down in categories of costs, crime, diseases, population, education and miscellaneous.

POPULATION

- The needy poor greatly out-number the charitable rich, and the poor breed faster. Africa's numbers are increasing ten times faster than Europe's. Garret Hardin
- The United States receives more immigrants annually than all other countries combined. US Census Bureau 2000
- Illegal aliens number between 10 to 13 million. www. numbersusa.com
- Immigration, both legal and illegal, accounted for nearly 80% of the US population growth in the last decade. US Census Bureau 2000
- 1.1. to 1.3 million legal and one million illegal aliens come to the USA annually. Over the last century of the U.S., we invited two immigrants per day. We now receive more than two per minute. www.stoptheinvasion.com
- At the current rate of 2.0 to 2.3 million legal and illegal immigrants along with 1 million added American births, which equals 3.3 million annually, the USA will add 200 million people or reach 500,000,000 people by 2060. That is well on the way to one billion by the beginning of the 22nd century. Carrying Capacity Network
- At current fertility levels worldwide, the human population would reach 296 billion in 150-years. Even if it dropped to 2.5 children per woman, the population would still reach 28 billion. "A Special Moment in History" by Bill McKibben May 1998 Atlantic Monthly
- The world is adding a city the size of Los Angeles every two weeks. CCN
- Every 20 minutes, the world adds 3,000 human beings but loses one or more species to extinction of animal or plant— 27,000 species annually. www.populationconnection.org
- 2,500 plants and animals will go extinct in the USA from habitat encroachment in the next decade. National Academy of Sciences
- World population grew four times in 100 years from 1.6 billion in 1900 to 6.2 billion in 2000. Negative Population Growth

•More than 500 million people worldwide do not have enough clean drinking water. www.populationconnection.org

JOBS

- Up to 14 million jobs are at risk of being shipped overseas. Contra Costa Times 9/30/03
- "We're trying to move everything we can offshore," HP services chief Ann Livermore, Forbes Magazine, December 2003
- As the US economy has shifted toward service jobs, factory jobs have been steadily lost—in fact, in the past 39 months, 2.8 jobs vanished. Christian Science Monitor

ENVIRONMENT

- Humans burn 72 million barrels of oil every 24 hours. Parade 2003
- The USA burns 18 million barrels of oil every 24 hours. Parade 2003
- The United States produces more global warming gases than China and India Combined. Carrying Capacity Network
- 72,000 chemicals have been produced by humans and all have been spread into the water, air and on the land—creating environmental chaos genetically, pollution and destroying major aspects of the planet such as the ozone. Carrying Capacity Network
- Higher populations mean a loss of freedom, loss of natural beauty, loss of personal Identity. Carrying Capacity Network
- Humanity is consuming the earth's resources 20 percent faster that they can be sustained. Carrying Capacity Network
- Between 1982 and 1997, the US developed 25 million acres or an area the size of Virginia, averaging 1.7 million acres annually. Carrying Capacity Network
- Water problems in West will become an unsolvable crisis. "Utah At Risk For Water Wars" May 3, 2003, Desert News, Lee Davidson

DISEASES

- In the past five years, illegal aliens from Mexico have brought 16,000 cases of multi-drug resistant tuberculosis cases into the US. Each infected carrier spreads the disease from 10 to 50 persons. "PATIENT PREDATOR" by Kevin Patterson, Mother Jones News, March 2003
- More than 7,000 new cases of leprosy have been imported into the U.S. via immigrants from India, Brazil and the Caribbean in the past three years. New York Times, Lerner, 2/20/03
- Immigrants both legal and illegal account for 65 percent of communicable diseases in the USA. They include rubella, malaria, dengue fever, west Nile virus, lice, TB and leprosy. www.stoptheinvasion.com
- The US-Mexico Border Counties Coalition estimates that medical treatment for illegal aliens in 2000 exceeded $200 million for 77 border area hospital in California, Arizona, New Mexico and Texas. The costs exceeded over $1.4 billion to US taxpayers. Congressional Record

AMNESTIES AND FUTILITY

- Since 1986, Congress passed seven amnesties meant to stop illegal immigration. Congressional Record
- The 1986 amnesty was meant to crack down on illegal immigration. It added 10 to 13 million illegal aliens to the USA. U.S. Census Bureau, 2000

EMPLOYMENT

- The nation's unemployment rate climbed to a nine year high of 6.1 percent in May, 2003.The number of people who can not find full times jobs is 8.8 million with an additional 4.4 million who have dropped out of the labor force. US Department of Labor
- Immigration costs U.S. born workers $133 billion in job losses annually. Harvard Professor George Borjas
- Some two million jobs have been lost across the country

in the past two years, and 8.2 million Americans can't find work. U.S. Department of Labor

CRIME

- An average of 57,600 cars are stolen in Phoenix, Arizona annually by illegal aliens and drug smugglers for use as transport vehicles. Mostly pick-ups and SUV's. DMV Arizona 2004
- An estimated 75 percent of all illegal drugs in the US come across the Mexican border. It's been estimated that $100 billion is paid out of the US for drugs annually. DEA
- Over two-thirds of the cocaine enters the US from the Mexico border. DEA
- An estimated 50 percent of heroin transported into the US comes over the Mexican border. DEA
- Taxpayers spend $80 billion dollars annually on the 'War on Drugs.' This war on drugs has not stopped the flow of drugs one single ounce in 20 years. LEAP.org
- Human smuggling grossed $9.5 billion in 2002 according to US immigration officials.
- With over three million illegal aliens in California, the number of hit and run accidents has risen dramatically. A greater number of drivers flee the scene of crashes than any other state. California Department of Safety
- A sobering 29 percent of prisoners in federal prisons are legal and illegal immigrants. Federation for American Immigration Reform
- Criminal immigrant imprisoned population costs taxpayers $900 million annually. Carrying Capacity Network

COSTS

- The net costs to American taxpayers over and above what immigrants pay into the US Treasury is $70 billion annually. This includes schools, welfare, ESL, infrastructure, housing assistance, roads, social services and other services. Carrying Capacity Network
- Annual net cost of illegal alien immigration estimated at $20

billion. Carrying Capacity Network
- Immigrant households consume between $11 billion and $20 billion more in public services than they pay in taxes each year. The National Academy of Sciences, 1997
- The nearly 26 million legal and illegal immigrants settling in the USA since 1970 cost taxpayers a net $69 billion in 1997 alone, in excess of taxes those immigrants paid. This represents a cost of $1,030.00 additional taxes paid by each American family of four.   Dr. Donald Huddle, Professor of Economics at Rice University
- Almost every state has a budget crisis. The federal debt exceeds $7 trillion. The Federal deficit spending for 2004 will exceed $500 billion. California is $38 billion in debt with three million illegal aliens. Texas is $10 billion in debt with 1.5 million illegal aliens. Colorado is $1 billion in debt with 200,000 illegal aliens. Denver Post
- Immigrants, both legal and illegal, sent back to their home countries a total of $56 billion of our money. Mexico was sent $15 billion; Central and South America got $25 billion and Asia received $16 billion. All that money was drained out of the USA.
- The lifetime net fiscal drain—taxes paid minus services used—for adult immigrants is $55,200.00. www.stoptheinvasion. com
- Immigrants are 50 percent more likely to use welfare than Americans—with a full 75 percent. CCN Being more likely to use food stamps, medical benefits and housing assistance. Non citizens collect $7 billion annually. CCN
- In 2003, the US government suffered a $544 billion deficit which added to the Current $7 trillion federal debt as of February, 2004. Consumer debt reached $2 trillion. Tom Brokaw, NBC Nightly News
- American taxpayers pay over $500 million daily for interest on the federal debt.United States Department of Revenue
- Immigration costs US taxpayers $24 billion in education expenses annually. The average bilingual education is about $1,200.00 per student. U.S. Department of Education
- An estimated one-third to one-half of illegal aliens work off

the books and pay no taxes. CCN
- $200 million to provide for emergency health care for illegal aliens in the border states in 2000: $79 million in CA; $74 million in TX; $31 million AZ; $6 million in NM. Border Counties Coalition Report www.bordercountiescoalition.com www.advocateoffice.com
- Department of Justice spends $27 billion of taxpayer dollars to provide forms, ballots and brochures for languages other than English. No other country forces such expenditures on their citizens. Congressional Record

POVERTY

- One in five rural American children live in poverty. Population Reference Bureau
- One million Americans are homeless in America. HUD
- American citizens who can't find jobs exceeds 18 million people. Department of Labor
- Home foreclosures grew dramatically in Colorado in 2004. Rocky Mountain News
- Inner city crime and hopelessness continues without pause in the United States
- African-American children's poverty up 50 percent since 1999. "Extreme Poverty Numbers Increase" Elizabeth Levin, Los Angeles Times, 5/1/03

RULE-OF-LAW IGNORED

- We have federal laws against illegal immigration. Between 10 to 13 million foreign nationals have broken into our country against our laws and have not been brought to justice or deported.

EDUCATION

- It costs states more than $7.4 billion a year to educate illegal aliens, enough to buy a computer for every junior high school student nationwide. Federation for American Immigration Reform

Frosty Wooldridge

- California spends $2.2 billion to educate illegal immigrant children. Ranking second and third, respectfully are Texas and New York. Education for American children suffers dramatically. FAIR
- Colorado with only 144,000 illegal aliens spent $140.6 million to educate illegal alien children in 2002. Colorado is nearly one billion dollars in debt. Rocky Mountain News

EXAMPLE OF ONE STATE'S DEBT LOAD: THE GREAT STATE OF TEXAS

Texas' illegal alien population is estimated at 1.5 million. As of August 31, 2001, according to the Texas Bond Review Board, Texas local governments carried a combined total of $86.6 billion debt:

- Texas cities, towns and villages have the most local government debt outstanding at $33.9 billion
- Public school districts have outstanding debts at $24.9 billion
- Health and hospital districts show outstanding debts at $1.2 billion
- Water districts and authorities show debt at $16.3 billion
- Counties show debt at $5.7 billion
- Community and Junior Colleges stand at a debt of $1.1 billion
- Special districts and authorities stand at $3.5 billion
- State of Texas carries a $10 billion debt.   Dallas Morning News 1/26/03 McLemore

EXAMPLE OF GEORGIA DEBT LOAD FROM IMMIGRATION

Net Fiscal Costs of Immigration for Georgia:

- Births of illegal aliens in Georgia cost to taxpayers:
2000– 5,133 births cost: $13 million
2001– 9,528 births cost: $23 million
2002–11,188 births cost: $27 million
- Illegal aliens receiving public assistance in 2002 For 25,000 children of illegal aliens, cost for Georgia taxpayer is $42

240

million annually
- Health care costs to Georgia taxpayers for illegal aliens in 2002: 64,000 doctor visits ran Grady Health System into a $63 million deficit
- Criminals: Gwinnet gang task force estimated 171 immigrant gangs costing taxpayers $15 million not covered by federal government. State Criminal Alien Assistance Program cost Georgia taxpayers $13,166,505.00

Other states spend more or less depending on their immigrant populations.

CHAPTER 26—

BRILLIANT WORDS FROM BRILLIANT MEN AND WOMEN

"We must prevent human tragedy rather than run around trying to save ourselves after an event has already occurred. Unfortunately, history clearly shows that we arrive at catastrophe by failing to meet the situation, by failing to act when we should have acted. The opportunity passes us by and the next disaster is always more difficult and compounded than the last one."

Eleanor Roosevelt

The worst crisis created by immigration forces the United States into being the third fastest growing nation behind China and India. Unless that growth slows quickly—and since tomorrow's population is being determined today—we will be a China-like one billion people later this century.

One of the most sobering letters I've received in years arrived in my email box from a student from Madras, India. He chastised me for writing editorials on the folly of the H-1B visas. He said America should let Asia take over the textile, shoe, tools and other 'manufacturing' jobs. Finally, "You Americans live with an artificially high standard of living," he wrote. "It's time you dropped down to the rest of the world's poverty."

His words stunned me. I wrote back, "Would you consider that you live an artificially substandard level of living and quality of life because you did nothing to stabilize your population when you had the chance. At 1.1 billion, you're locked into a lower standard of living. Tell me your country wouldn't be better off with only 300 million people?"

"You make a good point," he replied. "I never thought of it that way."

Wouldn't China be better off today with only 300 million people? Wouldn't Bangladesh be better off with one million instead of 129 million? What possible benefits can you imagine they enjoy with 129 million people living in a landmass the size of Ohio?

Nonetheless, the writer from India illustrates how humanity, like the frog in the pot of water that keeps adapting until it boils itself to death. In India, China and Bangladesh's histories, they overpopulated themselves into horrible consequences.

America MUST NOT travel in that direction. To do so would be an abrogation of our duty toward future generations.

While Europe is growing at an average rate of 0.1 percent a year, a doubling time of 600 years or more, we are growing at a rate of 1.1 percent a year or 3.3 million annually, or a doubling time of less than 70 years. Some of our states are growing at rates higher than Third World countries, such as four percent a year in California, which will give it over 20 million added people within 30 years. Colorado will hit four to six million by mid-century. Nevada grows by six percent annually causing doubling times of 14 years or less in a region that doesn't have the water to support such massive populations.

With America's population fast approaching 300 million people, we are the third most populated nation on earth in total numbers.

Even Europe with a stable population is being overrun with population numbers from people boiling out of the Middle East and Africa in such numbers as to destabilize what would have been sustainable populations.

Meanwhile, they were making significant strides with environmental problems such as sprawl, global warming, green house emissions and habitat preservations. But they too, will lose those steps as they are overrun.

What every American must ask is, "Do I want my children living in an America with 200 million people added in 50-60 years? One billion by the 22nd century? Why? What is the point? What will they gain? What is the benefit to them, their environment or future generations? At what point will the population stabilize to a sustainable level? Who will make that happen? What if they don't?"

Below are quotes from people who see this monster coming like a giant tidal wave. They come from all walks of life. They think. They study. They write. They investigate. They travel to places where it's already at a crisis point. They are major players on the world stage concerning population and environmental destruction. This population crisis, like a cancer growth, will not go away because we continue ignoring it.

These are quotes from men and women of science or just plain common sense:

"Immigration of the kind and on the scale America has had for the last three decades is in effect a recipe for cultural suicide and the squandering of a rich national heritage." Dr. Lee G. Marland

"The two-generation indirect immigration, i.e., including the births to foreign-born mothers, explained an incredible 98 percent of California's growth between 1990 and 2000." Dr. Leon Bouvier

"Overpopulation can be avoided only if borders are secure; otherwise poor and overpopulated nations will export their excess to richer and less populated nations. It is time to turn our attention to this problem." Garrett Hardin

"Given enough time, any growth rate will eventually exceed the carrying capacity of the entire world." J.W. Downs

"The world will not effectively address the problem of runaway population growth until the United States leads by example and stops its own runaway growth." Dr. Don Spencer, National Medal of Science, Member of the National Academy of Sciences, mentor to 'A BEAUTIFUL MIND' John Nash

"In fact, a stable or slowly shrinking population is not a problem at all—unless we make the mistake of allowing foreigners into our country to displace us. So long as they stay in their own countries, they can breed all they want, as this will only result in their remaining poor and underdeveloped. Many of them, such as the 2.3 billion peasants in India and China, have essentially zero interest in us, anyway." Robert Locke

"The modern plague of overpopulation is solvable by means we have discovered and with resources we possess. What is lacking is not the sufficient knowledge of the solution, but the universal consciousness of the gravity of the problem for billions of people who are its victims." Dr. Martin Luther King

"Each person in the USA has an impact on the environment equal to as low as 10 and as high as 33 in a Third World nation. Therefore, the US population at 292 million is equal in many ways to a minimum of 2.9 billion people in environmental impact." ROYAL ACADEMY OF SCIENCES

"Surviving like rats is not what we should bequeath to our children." Jacque Cousteau

"A really efficient totalitarian state would be one in which the all-powerful executive of political bosses and their army of managers control a population of slaves who do not have to be coerced, because they love their servitude." Aldous Huxley

"Modern industrial society is a fanatical religion. We are demolishing, poisoning, and destroying all life-systems on the planet. We are signing IOUs our children will not be able to pay. We are acting as if we were the last generations on the planet. Without radical changes in heart, mind, vision, the Earth will end up like Venus, dead." Brazilian Minister for the Environment

"Each added American citizen uses 12.6 acres of land to support his/her life. The USA has 400 million acres of remaining farmland. Do the math. At current growth rates of 200 million people by mid-century, we will no longer be able to support our population and, by 2030, will become a net importer of fruits and vegetables." Negative Population Growth

"Rapidly expanding population effectively strangles most efforts to provide adequate education, nutrition, health care and shelter." Population Communications International

"People who take issue with control of population do not understand that if it is not done in a graceful way, nature will do it in a brutal fashion." Henry Kendell

"California in 1965 with only 18 million people stands at 35 million in 37 years and is expected to hit 55 million in 25 years because of immigration. It must build an elementary school every day, 365 days a year just to keep up with its 4 percent growth per year, doubling time of a mere 20 to 28 years." NumbersUsa.com

"'Sustainable growth,' a self-contradictory concept beloved by those who want to continue the same old stands—growth as a solution to all problems—very few people have grasped the simple fact—demographic or economic—is unsustainable." Lindsey Grant

"With twice as many people projected for the next 60 years, we'll need twice as many hospitals, prisons, roads, schools, malls, parking lots and more. This growth will place a heavy burden economic and otherwise on the American taxpayer." Former U.S. Senator Gaylord Nelson

"Population growth is the primary source of environmental damage." Jacques Cousteau

"Immigration is a virtually irreversible decision and it is receiving nothing like the kind of careful scrutiny that irreversible decisions deserve." Economist Thomas Sowell

"Something is fundamentally wrong when we have millions of American citizens and legal residents begging for jobs, yet we are admitting thousands and thousands of immigrants each year with virtually no consideration to our employment needs or their employment skills." U.S. Senator Harry Reid, D-NV (This is an ironic statement because Reid sports a 'F-' and 'D-' grades by local immigration activists in Nevada)

"The massive flows of people across U.S. borders make exclusion of all foreign terrorists impossible." National Commission on Terrorism, June, 2000

"The time has come to risk being politically incorrect, take off the blindfolds, to think the unthinkable and speak the unspeakable...immigration must stop." Environmental writer Harold Gilliam

"The challenge is enormous, and you have to talk about a moratorium. You can't talk about anything short of a moratorium, because, frankly, anything less will never get you one step closer to stabilization." Congressman Tom Tancredo, R-CO

"It is dangerous to offer additional incentives and rewards for illegal immigration while giving only lip service to border security." Representative Tom Tancredo, R-Colorado

"President Bush's plan would move millions of people into a second-class status with no real promise of citizenship." Senator John Edwards, D-North Carolina

"Guest worker programs and gradual amnesty provide cover for terrorists." Representative Lamar Smith, R-Texas

"The demographic consequences of our immigration policy will be considerable. Sixty percent of the increase of our population between 1994 and 2050 will be attributable to immigration and descendants of immigrants. More than 90 percent of the increase of US energy consumption between 1970 and 1990 was due entirely to population growth. The USA continues losing more than one million acres of farmland ever year to urban sprawl and erosion." Mark W. Nowak

"We should have strict laws to identify and deport illegal aliens already in this country. Seventy-five percent respondents agreed." Negative Population Growth

An International Gallop Poll reported that 400 million people around the world want to relocate to the USA.

An Hispanic USA Research Group survey found that 89 percent of its respondents strongly support an immediate moratorium on immigration.

A Wall Street Journal American opinion survey reported that 72 percent of Americans favor lowering immigration.

"We are fast approaching the stage of the ultimate inversion: the stage where the government is free to do anything it pleases, while the citizens may act only by permission; which is the stage of the darkest periods of human history, the stage of rule by brute force." Ayn Rand, The Nature of Government

"In our government, with every decision we make, we must keep in mind the 7th generation to come. It's our job to see that the generations still unborn have a world no worse than ours is and hopefully, better. When we walk upon mother earth, we must plant our feet carefully because the faces of the future generations are looking up at us from beneath the ground. Our connection to the unborn is our responsibility to take action."
Oren Lions, a Native American Poet

CHAPTER 27—

IMMIGRATION AND THE ROAD NOT TAKEN

Former Governor of Colorado

Richard D. Lamm

"Tell me what you will of the benefactions of city civilization, of the sweet security of streets—all as part of the natural upgrowth of man towards the high density we hear so much of. I know that our bodies were made to thrive only in pure air, and the scenes in which pure air is found. If the death exhalations that brood the broad towns in which we so fondly compact ourselves were made visible, we should flee as from a plague. All are more or less sick; There is not a perfectly man in San Francisco."

John Muir, 1874

Imagine if you will John Muir, America's premiere naturalist and one of the fathers of our national parks system. Muir wrote eloquently of our national heritage and the wonders of the natural world. He fought tenaciously to save Hetch Hetchy Valley from being flooded in California. It was as beautiful as his beloved Yosemite. He hated cities and remarked, "The great wilds of our country once held to be boundless and inexhaustible are being rapidly invaded and overrun in every direction, and everything destructible in them is being destroyed. How far destruction may go is not easy to guess. Every landscape low and high seems doomed to be trampled and harried." Today, the founder of the Sierra Club would turn over in his grave if he knew the leadership of his club has stuck its head, like an ostrich, into the sands of denial.

Carl Pope, long time president of the Sierra Club, as of this writing, and his cadre of ostriches have charged 750,000 'trusting' members $35.00 annual dues to carry on John Muir's mission, which was to protect and defend the natural world from human folly. But Pope's refusal to address immigration, as the prime force exploding US population, would not bode well with common sense minded John Muir. I half expect the mountaineer to jump out of his grave to vote for Governor Lamm and the rest of the people running for the Sierra board on a population stabilization ticket.

I was a 20-year member, but quit after Pope would not answer my letters and urging that he address immigration. I swear that John Muir would rush into Pope's office and grab him by the neck while shaking some sense into him.

As Lincoln said, "You can fool some of the people some of the time and all of the people some of the time, but you can't fool all the people all of the time."

Governor Lamm is as passionate about saving this country for future generations as Dr. Martin Luther King was for equality for all Americans. Lamm stands up there with Susan B. Anthony, Eleanor Roosevelt, John Muir, Ben Franklin, Congresswoman Barbara Jordan and other Americans who 'saw' needed changes long before the general population. That's why he's running (as of this writing) for the Sierra board.

Below, Governor Richard D. Lamm writes on the reasons this country must act on population stabilization: IMMIGRATION AND THE ROAD NOT TAKEN

Imagine for a minute that America had taken the advice of President Nixon's Commission on Population and the American Future, which was released in 1972. The Commission recommended, among other things, that America act to end illegal immigration and to freeze legal immigration at 400,000 a year. The Commission found that "the health of our country does not depend on population growth, nor does the vitality of business, nor the welfare of the average person." Strong words. Wise words.

Headed by John Rockefeller, the "Rockefeller Commission" as it was known, strongly urged stabilizing the population of the U.S. and asked Americans to get over their "ideological addiction to growth." America at that time had about 200 million Americans, used far less petroleum and had a much smaller "ecological footprint" on the world environment. But the nation, deep into its "ideological addiction", didn't listen to the Commission.

The Sierra Club of 1970s listened and agreed. The club's policy from the early 1970s to 1996 was: "We must bring about the stabilization of the population first of the United States and then of the world." It is unfortunate that American policy makers didn't listen. Both the Commission and the Sierra Club were making important points about the future of America. We have added approximately 100 million Americans since the Commission's brave and farsighted declaration. As Professor Al Bartlett asks, "what problem in contemporary America was made better by immigration?" That America didn't listen is unfortunate, that the Sierra Club has backed away from their logical environmental/population connection is tragic.

We now have almost 300 million Americans, consume far more non-renewable resources, and our "footprint" is one of the major factors in a deteriorating environment worldwide. Our icecaps are melting, our fisheries disappearing, our water table falling, our coral dying, our soil eroding, our cities metastasizing, our rainforests and open space disappearing.

The Census Bureau's intermediate estimate is that we will add 125 million more Americans in the next 45 years, and approximately 90 percent of that growth will be attributable to immigrants and their descendants. America's "growth" issue is inescapably an immigration issue. Our own fertility rate will stabilize America's population within the lifetime of our children, with the current mass immigration America's population will double and double again. I have a grandchild in utero and that child could live to see an America of one billion people.

Let us also not forget what mass immigration is doing to our own poor. Studies show at the lower end of the economic scale, immigration accounts for 40-50 percent of worker wage loss. Employers love cheap labor. W.E.B. DuBois, founder of the NAACP recognized this when he said, "The purpose of immigration is to lower the wages of labor to the level of subsistence, and to make the corporate interests independent of the labor of descendants of slaves."

Many demographic experts postulate that our current population of 292 million is not itself sustainable, let alone 420 million or a billion. Sustainability looks at the long term: will our resources allow 300 Americans to live at a decent level of living for the indefinite future? Will our children and grandchildren inherit a decent and livable America? I do not expect my children and grandchildren to inherit our consumptive American lifestyles and I frankly don't think they should. Every American wastes enough to support one or more people in the third world. Over-consumption has become a moral issue. The Sierra Club rightly does not try to protect American lifestyles, on the contrary, we argue for reduced consumption, alternative energy, and increased efficiency. But sustainability, if it is ever to fly, needs two wings. We cannot escape calling for stabilizing population if we want to leave a sustainable America for our children.

IMPACT ON THIRD WORLD

The Sierra Club argues for stabilizing the population of the world, but not of the US. This argument takes a number of forms, but mostly it is expressed in moral terms, i.e. the United States is morally obligated to allow immigration for the sake of the Third World. But if that is so, why stop at the current one million legal immigrants? Why not two or five million a year? What is immoral about my proposal (which adopts the proposal of the late Barbara Jordan) to cut legal immigration in half? Why not a moral obligation to take two million a year? At what number does the moral scales shift? Do we have a moral immigration policy at one million, but an immoral policy at 900,000?

Then again, what makes a million immigrants a year so compassionate a proposition? There are four billion people in the world who live under the American welfare standard, and the world adds 75 million more people every year, year after year, after year. America allows one million to come legally, 1/75th of the yearly increase. This has a deminimus impact in alleviating third world poverty, while heavily impacting the United States. We add greatly to the number of consuming Americans with minimal benefit to the rest of the world. We would do far better trying to significantly aid people in these countries rather than to allow a chosen few to immigrate to America. Refugees have, and will have, a reason to seek a safe harbor, but most immigration to the U.S. is people trying to live the American lifestyle. I don't blame them for trying, I might do so myself, but from a macro-standpoint our maximum generosity will hardly dent third world poverty.

It would be my vision that the best role for America is to forge itself into a model of a sustainable society. Jacques Cousteau's wise words apply both to the World and the U.S., "Population growth is the primary source of environmental destruction." It isn't either/or, it is both.

Let us show that an environmentally aware, free people can build a sustainable society. Let us be generous to the world's poor, but by helping them where they live. Most people will grow old where they are born, and we can help far more people by foreign aid than allowing a lucky few to come to America. The Sierra Club needs careful analysis, not jerking knees; it needs a new vision where its solutions will equal the magnitude of the problems it claims to confront. It needs to not let its agenda be controlled by the fear of offending this group or that. We should, in short, be environmentalists, not politicians.

America took the wrong road in 1970 by ignoring the Rockefeller Commission's bold advice. Until 1996 the Sierra Club had it right; then it lost its environmental bearings. We shouldn't let the Sierra Club continue down that wrong road any longer.

CHAPTER 28—

THE ULTIMATE DANGER TO AMERICA—

THE GREATEST CHALLENGE

"Can you think of any problem in any area of human endeavor on any scale, from microscopic to global, whose long-term solution is in any demonstrable way aided, assisted, or advanced by further increases in population, locally, nationally, or globally?"

Dr. Albert Bartlett, Professor Emeritus of Physics,
University of Colorado

Fifteen years ago, I attended a lecture given by Dr. Albert Bartlett titled, "Arithmetic, Population and Energy." His lecture supersedes anything you've ever heard about population dynamics. No matter what you hear from politicians and growth advocates, his facts bring any educated mind to a sobering reality check. This nation and the world are in trouble as populations continue accelerating across the globe.

The more extreme our numbers the more extreme our children's consequences.   Dr. Albert Bartlett brings up the following points in his paper: "REFLECTIONS ON SUSTAINABILITY, POPULATION GROWTH AND THE ENVIRONMENT-REVISITED."

He covers the most profound aspect of this immigration invasion to its ultimate consequence: OVERPOPULATION. He and his publisher gave me permission to repeat the laws that will, in the final analysis, prove what Henry Kendell said, "We can bring about population stabilization graciously or nature will do it brutally."

Dr. Bartlett writes, "The related terms, 'sustainable' and 'sustainability' are used to describe a wide variety of activities which are ecologically laudable but which may not be sustainable. An examination of major reports reveals contradictory uses of the terms. An attempt is made here to give a firm and unambiguous definition to the concept of sustainability and to translate the definition into a series of laws and hypotheses, which will clarify the implications of the use of the concept of sustainability. These are followed by a series of observations and predictions that relate to 'sustainability.' The laws should enable one to read the many publications on sustainability and help one to decide whether the publications are seeking to illuminate or to obfuscate."

It became apparent in the 1960s that we could no longer ignore overpopulation. Bangladesh became the leading edge of a population crisis that had turned China and India into human anthills. In America, cars caused brown clouds over cities, we passed 200 million people, Inter-state freeways opened up, chemical companies polluted the Great Lakes, rivers started on fire, pollutants caused horrific genetic consequences in birds and other wildlife. Disfigured fish, frogs and salamanders begged the question of what we were doing to ourselves.

One look at the brown clouds over our cities that created acid rains, along with environmental degradation of our rivers and oceans—demanded attention. Dams destroyed salmon runs. The first inkling that CF carbons ate holes in the protective ozone appeared in scientific papers. Resources were consumed at unsustainable levels, gridlock and human crowding became more apparent in succeeding years. In 1970, the First Earth Day brought the crisis to our attention.

Politicians, however, jumped all over the word 'sustainable.' They made new terms like, 'sustainable growth,' 'smart growth,' 'managed growth,' 'slow growth' and other palatable terms. They created those terms without regards to limits, accuracy or reality.

Dr. Bartlett wrote, "First, we must accept the idea that 'sustainable' has to mean "for an unspecified long period of time."

"Second, we must acknowledge the mathematical fact that steady growth (a fixed percent per year) gives very large numbers in modest periods of time. For example, a population of 10,000 people growing at 7 percent per year will become a population of 10,000,000 people in 100 years.

"From these two statements we can see that the term 'sustainable growth' implies 'increasing endlessly,' which means that the growing quantity will tend to become infinite in size. The finite size of resources, ecosystems, the environment, and the Earth, lead one to the most fundamental truth of sustainability: When applied to material things, the term 'sustainable growth' is an oxymoron."

Most sobering in this oxymoron is the fact that three babies are added net gain to the planet every second. That creates an added 10,000 per hour, 240,000 per day and 80 million annually. Those numbers escalate global 'goods' production and consumption which increases needs for gas, lumber, water, steel, food, land and thousands of other finite resources.

China's population crisis has a gonad grip on its entire system, which imprisons its people in endless crowding, pollution and subsistence living. Even with Draconian birth control methods of abortion and one child per family, they add 10 million annually via population momentum, net gain. India, with 1.1 billion staggers in the same death grip. Bangladesh, with 129 million people in a country with the landmass the size of Ohio and a bit more— manifests the worst example of runaway overpopulation. They rank near the top in the International Human Suffering Index.

On the international scene, excess population continues pouring into the stable populations of Europe. Immigrants overwhelm France, Holland, Finland, Great Britain and Germany.

Even if the United States hit zero population growth in 2004, population momentum would drive us to add 40 million people.

Dr. Bartlett wrote, "Reports indicate a recognition of the fact that there are serious "long term consequences of human population growth." These consequences could have been explored in simple, concrete, and illuminating detail. However, they refer to the "inevitable increase in population numbers." They indicate nothing can be done. This leads to the question, "If nothing can be done, why bother to educate people about the 'long-term consequences of continued population growth'?"

"Distribution, harmony, and "improvement in the capacity to assess the implications of population patterns" are important, but it seems clear that improvements in the human condition cannot be achieved without understanding and recognizing the importance of numbers, and in particular, numbers of people. As we look at the United States, and around the world, we see the numbers of people are growing. We see places where the problems associated with the growth are so overwhelming as to make it impossible to address the vitally important issues of education of women, distribution of resources, justice, and simple equity."

CARRYING CAPACITY

Dr. Bartlett wrote, "The term 'carrying capacity,' long known to ecologists, has recently become popular. It "refers to the limit to the number of humans the earth can support in the long term without damage to the environment." (Giampietro, et. al. 1992)

"The scale and scope of human activities have, for the first time, grown to rival the natural processes that built the biosphere and that maintain it as a place where life can flourish. An impact on the global environment of this magnitude is properly the cause for alarm.

"The inevitable and unavoidable conclusion is that if we want to stop the increasing damage to the global environment, at a minimum, we must stop population growth."

DENIAL OF THE POPULATION PROBLEM

Most distressing is the fact that President Bush and his cadre of highly educated cabinet minds and advisors fail to grasp the depth and magnitude of this population crisis. They may not comprehend it at all! It may be speculated that they are a group of six-foot tall men and women who didn't learn how to swim and have walked into the deep end of a 10-foot swimming pool.

Everything they do every day of the year demonstrates their lack of comprehension of not only the immigration crisis, both legal and illegal, but also the consequences in the long term as to environment and resources. Along with them, 100 senators speak not a word. Most of the House of Representatives sit idly by as the crisis engages state after state.

A conspiracy of silence muzzles the data on immigration.

Senator Jack Kemp made a comment about population, "Nonsense, people are not a drain on the resources of the planet." He like most quarterbacks, was hit one too many times in the head, which severely rendered him deficient in mental acuity and the ability to extrapolate facts.

Contrast Kemp's statement with the words of the biologist E.O. Wilson who wrote:

"The raging monster upon the land is population growth. In its presence, sustainability is but a fragile theoretical construct. To say, as many do, that the difficulties of nations are not due to people but to poor ideology or land-use management is sophistic."

That begs the question, who would you believe? Jack Kemp, a professional football quarterback who became a senator? Or, a scientist who has studied the issue from top to bottom for a lifetime?

THE WORLD'S WORST POPULATION PROBLEM

Guess who already possesses the world's most dangerous population? The United States, that's who! It's been estimated that an American citizen uses from 10 to 30 times more raw resources and creates that much more pollution than a Third World person. The richer the American, the more he/she consumes and pollutes. When you look at that equation, it's simple to see it. A Third World person eats, grows crops, walks, drinks water, procreates, stays home and dies. An American drives a car, owns a house that burns oil or electricity for heat, flies off around the world, vacations on cruises and drives to work daily. He buys more 'stuff' than can be imagined, eats horrific amounts of food, adds to the trash stream more than any other humans on this planet and a dozen other activities that exceed the carrying capacity of the earth.

By using the low end of the consumption/pollution factor of 10, our 292 million translates (10 X 292,000,000) into 2.92 billion people. That makes us per capita the most prolific consumers and polluters on the planet.

However, China and India chase us as they move to consumer driven societies at lightning speed.

Dr. Bartlett notes, "Because we have high per capita consumption of resources in the U.S., we in the U.S. have the world's "worst population problem.""

We think it is a Third World problem while we are importing that problem into our country via massive immigration. In a speech at the University of Colorado, former U.S. Senator Tim Wirth observed that the best thing we in the U.S. can do to help other countries stop their population growth is to set an example and stop our own population growth here in the United States. We have not done that.

POPULATION GROWTH NEVER PAYS FOR ITSELF

By listening to state governors, builders and Realtors—you'd think growth is a blessing from Heaven. In my state of Colorado, for example, Governor Romer and after him, Governor Owens pushed for growth. In 14 years, they encouraged 1.3 million new residents. Most were refugees fleeing California and the East Coast.   Did it help? We endure a $1 billion debt. We suffer water restrictions. Governor Owens wants to build more dams, but we can't fill the dams we already have. Snow and rain remain constant no matter what our population.

Denver suffered a toxic Brown Cloud in 1990 that is worse today. The gridlock nightmare starts at 6:00 AM and doesn't end until 8:00 PM six days a week. It's so bad, you're lucky if you're not smashed in one of the two dozen accidents daily. To alleviate the daily traffic congestion, Owens spent billions of dollars in cost and confusion for the T-Rex construction project, which will add more lanes to I-25 through the city. But, what he didn't tell anyone is that he's encouraging another one million people into Colorado in ten years to negate everything T-Rex was supposed to solve.

For anyone who has not seen it, the Brown Cloud over Denver is a 'thing' of wonder. It covers the city like a thick brown blanket from horizon to horizon. It's loaded with unending toxic poisons from cracking plants, car exhausts, wood burning, diesel burning, natural gas, fuel oil and more released into the sky 24 hours per day by two million people in homes, cars, trucks, factories and power plants.

Next, fall out from the growth agenda is 'beige blight,' the most popular color of 'cookie cutter' tract homes. From Denver to Boulder and beyond, a sea of rooftops spread across the land like barnacles on the bottom of a ship. Where once beautiful prairie grass waved, Colorado has transformed into one housing tract after another. As you ride into the mountains, thousands of homes dot the hills and jam themselves into the trees.

To make matters worse, population predictions add four million more people to Colorado within 45 years. I wrote an editorial in the Denver Post on May 8, 2003, 'TOO MANY PEOPLE; TOO FEW SOLUTIONS?' In it, I rattled off the four million population prediction. A man from California wrote back, " Mr. Wooldridge, you are incorrect in your population figures for Colorado. I am a 59-year old baby boomer. There are over two million more like me in California and we will be retiring within 10 years. We are leaving this population quagmire in this state and will be moving to the Western Slope of Colorado. You can expect six million added to Colorado."

That brings this discussion to California. Have you seen the TV ads where they use crash dummies showing what happens to the occupants of cars in a head-on collusion? California represents the 'dummies' and the 'car' when it slams into the population brick wall. The people of California are in a hell bent race for disaster. They expect 20 million added people in 30 years. They must build one new school daily, seven days a week to accommodate more than 1,500 people added to their state every 24 hours. They fail and American students suffer. It's an impossible situation with an impossible outcome.

You must wonder who with a brain is leading this country and these states? Who with an ounce of common sense would continue on this deadly path? What is their purpose? Who wants this national suicide? Who will stop it?

Thus far, the only outspoken leaders are former Colorado Governor Richard D. Lamm, Congressman Tom Tancredo of Colorado and Charles Norwood of Georgia. Yet, the elites, media and press daily malign them. Would you believe the elites and corporation-owned major media outlets, or a brilliant scientist?

Dr. Bartlett writes, "There are encouraging signs from communities around the U.S. that indicate a growing awareness of the local problems of continued unrestrained growth of populations, because population growth in our communities never pays for itself. Taxes and utility costs must escalate in order to pay for the growth. In addition, growth brings increased levels of congestion, frustration, and air pollution."

PSEUDO SOLUTIONS: GROWTH MANAGEMENT AND SMART GROWTH

Whether you have 'smart growth,' 'dumb growth,' 'slow growth,' 'managed growth,' it is all growth. It adds up to a disastrous outcome. We must stop trying to solve these problems with "the level of thinking that created them." Are you going to listen to a politician or Albert Einstein?

Dr. Bartlett wrote, "From the highest political and planning circles come various suggestions that are intended to address the problems caused by growth and thus to improve the quality of life. Many of these suggestions are "pseudo solutions" to the problems.

At first glance, these sophistic solutions seem logical. A moment's thought will show that, in fact, they are false.

"The terms "growth management" and "smart growth" are used interchangeably to describe urban developments that are functionally efficient and pleasing. Sometimes these planning processes are advocated by those who believe that we can't stop population growth, therefore we must accommodate it as best we can. At other times, they are advocated by those who are actively advancing population growth. The claim is made that growth management and smart growth "will save the environment." They don't save the environment. Whether the growth is smart or dumb, the growth destroys the environment. "Growth management" is a favorite term used by planners and politicians. With planning, smart growth will destroy the environment, but it will do it in a sensitive way. It's like buying a ticket on the Titanic. You can be smart and go first class, or you can be dumb and go steerage. In both cases, the result is the same. But given the choice, most people would go first class."

USELESS SOLUTIONS: BUILDING HIGHWAYS

California is the perfect example of highway chaos. The more they build the faster they turn into gridlock. It's impossible to escape escalating numbers.

Dr. Bartlett wrote, "It is frequently said that we can reduce congestion and air pollution by building high-speed super highways. This can be proven false by noting that if this were true, the air in Los Angeles would be the cleanest in the nation. The fallacy arises because of the fact that the construction of the new highways generates new traffic, not previously present, to fill the new highways to capacity."

POPULATION GROWTH DESTROYS DEMOCRACY

As stated before, democracy requires an educated population with a similar moral and ethical foundation using a single language while pulling in the same direction.

Democracy is a delicate form of government. It's also one that espouses representation. When this country was formed,

Congress represented a smaller population. In 1963, the Senate with 100 and Congress with 435 members represented 199 million people. The same 100 senators and 435 representatives are now burdened with 292 million people. At current growth rates, they must represent 500 million just past mid century.

It's no wonder this republic no longer serves constituents.

Dr. Albert wrote, "In an interview with Bill Moyers, Isaac Asimov was asked what happens to the idea of the dignity of the human species if this population growth continues at its present rate? Asimov responded, "It will be completely destroyed. I like to use what I call my bathroom metaphor: if two people live in an apartment and there are two bathrooms, then both have freedom of the bathroom. You can go to the bathroom anytime you want to stay as long as you want for whatever you need. And everyone believes in freedom of the bathroom; it should be right there in the Constitution.

"But if you have twenty people in the apartment and two bathrooms, no matter how much every person believes in freedom of the bathroom, there is no such thing. You have to set up times for each person, you have to bang on the door, "Aren't you through yet?"

Asimov concluded with the profound observation: "In the same way, democracy cannot survive overpopulation. Human dignity cannot survive overpopulation. Convenience and decency cannot survive overpopulation. As you put more and more people onto the world, the value of life not only declines, it disappears. It doesn't matter if someone dies, the more people there are, the less one person matters."

LAWS RELATING TO SUSTAINABILITY

Let us be specific and state that both 'Carrying Capacity' and 'Sustainable' implies, "For the period in which we hope humans will inhabit the earth." This means, "For many millennia."

Many prominent individuals have given postulates and laws relating to population growth and sustainability. It has been stated in several magazines that the USA exceeded 'carrying capacity' when it crossed over 200 million in 1965. Everything since then has been like charging a credit card past its credit line with no ability to pay the balance. Either the holder goes broke or the system goes broke when too many people overcharge the limit. At some point, something goes 'poof' or 'boom' or 'the timbers break in the mine.' For a Scuba diver who stayed too long on his reserve and too deep, it means he has no more air and over 100 feet to the surface. For a skydiver, his secondary shoot won't open. For the man without water on a lonely desert road at 115 Fahrenheit. in July, it means his empty gas tank equals the end of his life.

For this country, it means 292 million people are in trouble along with much of the rest of the humans on this planet.

BOULDING'S THREE THEOREMS

Economist Kenneth Boulding created the following three theorems. I can attest to their veracity via my travels in the Third World. Populations in uneducated countries continue human proliferation to the point of misery. Boulding quantified them. Countries like Niger, Mozambique, Somalia and Ghana manifest them in the extreme.

First Theorem: "The Dismal Theorem" If the only ultimate check on the growth of population is misery, then the population will grow until it is miserable enough to stop its growth."

One other check concerning this theorem stems from disease. As uneducated populations grow and their sanitation and personal hygiene habits backfire, epidemics arise. AIDS in Africa kills millions of human beings.

Second Theorem: "The Utterly Dismal Theorem" This theorem states that any technical improvement can only relieve misery for a while. So long as misery is the only check on population, the technical improvement will enable population to grow, and will soon enable more people to live in misery than before. The final result of improvements, therefore, is to increase the equilibrium population, which is to increase the total sum of human misery.

Third Theorem: "The moderately cheerful form of the Dismal Theorem" Fortunately, it is not too difficult to restate the Dismal

Theorem in a moderately cheerful form, which states that if something else, other than misery and starvation, can be found which will keep a prosperous population in check, the population does not have to grow until it is miserable and starves, and it can be viably prosperous."

LAWS, HYPOTHESES, OBSERVATIONS AND PREDICTIONS RELATING TO SUSTAINABILITY

Wouldn't you rather consider a brilliant, compassionate mind such as Dr. Albert Bartlett's than one of a pandering politician? In the first case, a scientist works with mathematics and laws. A politician works with what will get him/her re-elected. He works for money and power. If this contention wasn't true, we would not find ourselves in the $7 trillion national debt we're now in nor would we be suffering from the loss of the rule-of-law as to the chaos and lawlessness of our borders brought on by the power of corporations and money.

Dr. Bartlett wrote, "The Laws, Hypotheses, Observations, and Predictions that follow are offered to define the term "sustainability." In some cases these statements are accompanied by corollaries identified by capital letters. They all apply for populations and rates of consumption of goods and resources of the sizes and scales found in the world in 1998, and may not be applicable for small numbers of people or to groups in primitive tribal situations."

LAWS RELATING TO SUSTAINABILITY

First Law: Population growth and/or growth in the rates of consumption of resources cannot be sustained.

A. A population growth rate less than or equal to zero and declining rates of consumption of resources are a necessary, but not a sufficient, condition for a sustainable society.

B. Unsustainability will be the certain result of any program of "development," that does not plan the achievement of zero (or a period of negative) growth of populations and of rates of consumption of resources. This is true even if the program is said to be "sustainable."

C. The research and regulation programs of governmental agencies that are charged with protecting the environment and promoting "sustainability" are, in the long run, irrelevant, unless these programs address vigorously and quantitatively the concept of carrying capacities and unless the programs study in depth the demographic causes and consequences of environmental problems.

D. Societies, or sectors of a society, that depend on population growth or growth in their rates of consumption of resources, are unsustainable.

E. Persons who advocate population growth and/or growth in the rates of consumption of resources are advocating unsustainability.

F. Persons who suggest that sustainability can be achieved without stopping population growth are misleading themselves and others.

G. Persons whose actions directly or indirectly cause increases in population or in the rates of consumption of resources are moving society away from sustainability. Advertising your city or state as an ideal site in which to locate new factories, indicates a desire to increase the population of your city or state.

H. The term "Sustainable Growth" is an oxymoron.

Second Law: In a society with a growing population and/or growing rates of consumption of resources, the larger the population, and/or the larger the rates of consumption of resources, the more difficult it will be to transform the society to the condition of sustainability.

Third Law: The response time of populations to changes in the human fertility rate is the average length of a human life, or approximately 70 years. (Bartlett and Lytwak 1995) This is called "population momentum."

A. A nation can achieve zero population growth if:
1. the fertility rate is maintained at the replacement level for 70 years, and

2. there is no net migration during the 70 years.

During the 70 years the population continues to grow, but at declining rates until the growth finally stops.

B. If we want to make changes in the total fertility rates so as to stabilize the population by the mid - to late 21st century, we must make the necessary changes before the end of the 20th century.

C. The time horizon of political leaders is of the order of two to eight years.

D. It will be difficult to convince political leaders to act now to change course, when the full results of the change may not become apparent in the lifetimes of those leaders.

Fourth Law: The size of population that can be sustained (the carrying capacity) and the sustainable average standard of living of the population are inversely related to one another.

A. The higher the standard of living one wishes to sustain, the more urgent it is to stop population growth.

B. Reductions in the rates of consumption of resources and reductions in the rates of production of pollution can shift the carrying capacity in the direction of sustaining a larger population.

Fifth Law: Sustainability requires that the size of the population be less than or equal to the carrying capacity of the ecosystem for the desired standard of living.

A. Sustainability requires an equilibrium between human society and dynamic but stable ecosystems.

B. Destruction of ecosystems tends to reduce the carrying capacity and/or the sustainable standard of living.

C. The rate of destruction of ecosystems increases as the rate of growth of the population increases.

D. Population growth rates less than or equal to zero are necessary, but are not sufficient, conditions for halting the destruction of the environment. This is true locally and globally.

Sixth Law: The lesson of "The Tragedy of the Commons" (Hardin 1968) The benefits of population growth and of growth in the rates of consumption of resources accrue to a few; the costs of population growth and growth in the rates of consumption of resources are borne by all of society.

     A.   Individuals who benefit from growth will continue to exert strong pressures supporting and encouraging both population growth and growth in rates of consumption of resources.

     B.   The individuals who promote growth are motivated by the recognition that growth is good for them. In order to gain public support for their goals, they must convince people that population growth and growth in the rates of consumption of resources, are also good for society.

Seventh Law: Growth in the rate of consumption of a non-renewable resource, such as a fossil fuel, causes a dramatic decrease in the life-expectancy of the resource.

     A.   In a world of growing rates of consumption of resources, it is seriously misleading to state the life-expectancy of a non-renewable resource "at present rates of consumption," i.e., with no growth. More relevant than the life-expectancy of a resource is the expected date of the peak production of the resource, i.e. the peak of the Hubbert curve. (Hubbert 1974)

     B.   It is intellectually dishonest to advocate growth in the rate of consumption of non-renewable resources while, at the same time, reassuring people about how long the resources will last "at present rates of consumption."

Eighth Law: The time of expiration of non-renewable resources can be postponed, possibly for a very long time, by:

     A.   Technological improvements in the efficiency with which the resources are recovered   and used.

     B.   Using the resources in accord with a program of "Sustained Availability," (Bartlett 1986)

     C.   Recycling.

D.   The use of substitute resources.

Ninth Law: When large efforts are made to improve the efficiency with which resources are used, the resulting savings are easily and completely wiped out by the added resources consumed as a consequence of modest increases in population.

A.   When the efficiency of resource use is increased, the consequence often is that the "saved" resources are not put aside for the use of future generations, but instead are used immediately to encourage and support larger populations.
B.   Humans have an enormous compulsion to find an immediate use for all available resources.

Tenth Law: The benefits of large efforts to preserve the environment are easily canceled by the added demands on the environment that result from small increases in human population.

Eleventh Law: (Second Law of Thermodynamics) When rates of pollution exceed the natural cleansing capacity of the environment, it is easier to pollute than it is to clean up the environment.

Twelfth Law: (Eric Sevareid's Law) The chief cause of problems is solutions.

A.   This law should be a central part of higher education, especially in engineering.

Thirteenth Law: Humans will always be dependent on agriculture. (This is the first of Malthus' two postulata.)

A.   Supermarkets alone are not sufficient.
B.   The central task in sustainable agriculture is to preserve agricultural land. The agricultural land must be protected from losses due to things such as:
    i.   Urbanization and development
    ii.   Erosion
    iii.   Poisoning by chemicals

Fourteenth Law: If, for whatever reason, humans fail to stop population growth and growth in the rates of consumption of resources, Nature will stop these growths.

    A.   By contemporary western standards, Nature's method of stopping growth is cruel and inhumane.
    B.   Glimpses of Nature's method of dealing with populations that have exceeded the carrying capacity of their lands can be seen each night on the television news reports from places where large populations are experiencing starvation and misery.

Fifteenth Law: In every local situation, creating jobs increases the number of people locally who are out of work.

Sixteenth Law: Starving people don't care about sustainability. (Refer to Human Suffering Index)

    A.   If sustainability is to be achieved, the necessary leadership and resources must be supplied by people who are not starving.

Seventeenth Law: The addition of the word 'sustainable' to our vocabulary, to our reports, programs, and papers, to the names of our academic institutes and research programs, and to our community initiatives, is not sufficient to ensure that our society becomes sustainable.

Eighteenth Law: A society that imports other people to do its work is not sustainable.
(Dr. Bartlett called to say this is his latest 'addition' to these laws.)

Nineteenth Law: Extinction is forever.

OBSERVATIONS RELATING TO SUSTAINABILITY

1. In order to move toward a sustainable society, the first and most important effort that must be made is to stop population growth. This will require the initiation of major comprehensive educational, technical, and outreach programs in the areas of social responsibility, family planning, contraception, immigration and resource use. To get things right, these programs must focus on the goal of stopping population growth and should not be diluted by omitting references to the numbers involved in understanding population growth. The greater the degree to which the carrying capacity has been exceeded, the more probable it is that coercion will become a factor in these programs.

2. The food chain is nature's equilibrium mechanism. It functions to prevent unlimited expansion of populations of flora and fauna. Primitive human societies were able to maintain approximately constant populations and to live within the carrying capacity of their ecosystems. The methods they used to maintain approximately constant populations were often cruel and inhumane. Technology has given many people the feeling that, through our own efforts, we are exempt from the cruel constraints of limited carrying capacities.

3. Ancient civilizations have vanished, in part because they grew too large and their size exceeded the carrying capacity of the ecosystems on which they depended for support.

a. Education notwithstanding, civilizations today show considerable tendency to repeat the mistakes of earlier civilizations, but on a much larger scale.
b. Growing international trade allows the developed countries to draw on the carrying capacity of the entire earth, often at the expense of underdeveloped countries.

4. The complete era of the use of fossil fuels by humans will be a vanishingly short fraction of the span of human existence on the Earth. (Hubbert 1974)

5.   The supplies of all non-renewable resources will effectively expire when the costs (in cash, in energy, in ecological and societal disruption) of making available a quantity of the resource exceed the value of the quantity of the resource.

6.   Comprehensive educational, technical, and outreach programs in the areas of efficient use of resources will be needed in order to help achieve sustainability.

7.   A major use of technology is, and has been, to accommodate the growth of populations, and to remove the recognition of the importance of living within the carrying capacity of the environment.   (See Boulding's "Utterly Dismal Theorem" and Eric Sevareid's Law)

A.   This use of technology has had the effect of encouraging population growth.
B.   This use of technology inhibits an approach to sustainability.
C.   An essential condition for sustainability is that technology be redirected toward the improvement of the quality of life, especially for those whose quality of life is now low, and away from its present use to increase the quantity of life.

TECHNICAL PREDICTIONS RELATING TO SUSTAINABILITY

1.   Peak world production of petroleum will probably occur before the year 2020. Credible sources predict before 2010. (Refer to "END OF THE AGE OF OIL" by Goodstein) Peak production of coal and oil shale, may occur in the 21st Century. Other fuels such as natural gas may not be available in globally significant quantities for more than a few decades into the 21st Century.
2.   If replacements can be found for fossil fuels, especially for petroleum, it will require major technological breakthroughs.
3.   Technological progress in the future is much more likely to be characterized by incremental advances than by breakthroughs, especially in the field of sources of energy.

4. The probability is very small that technological developments will produce new sources of energy in the next century, sources not already known in 1998, that will have the potential of supplying a significant fraction of the world's energy needs for any appreciable period of time.

5. The larger the global total daily demand for energy, the smaller is the probability that a new energy source or technology will be found that will have the potential of being developed sufficiently to meet an appreciable fraction of the global daily energy demand for any extended period of time.

6. The larger the global total daily demand for energy, the longer is the period of time that will be required for a new energy technology to be developed to the point where it will have the capacity of meeting an appreciable fraction of the global daily energy demand.

7. In the event that science and technology find a new source of large quantities of energy, the probability is high that the new source will be technologically very complex, with the result that it will be extremely costly to bring globally significant quantities of the new energy to the marketplace.

8. Children born in 1990 will not live to see 10 percent of the energy consumed in the U.S. generated by terrestrial nuclear fusion. (Bartlett 1990)

9. There will always be popular and persuasive technological optimists who believe that population increases are good, and who believe that the human mind has unlimited capacity to find technological solutions to all problems of crowding, environmental destruction, and resource shortages.

A. These technological optimists are usually not biological or physical scientists.

B. Politicians and business people tend to be eager disciples of these technological optimists.

10. Because population growth is only one of the factors that drives up the cost of living, the rate of increase of the cost of living will probably be larger than the rate of increase of population.

11. The rate of increase of the cost of living will be greater than the rate of increase of family income for a majority of families. This is what is called a "healthy economy."

POLITICAL PREDICTIONS RELATING TO SUSTAINABILITY

1. Local and regional business and political leaders will continue to spend much of their working time trying to attract new industries and populations to their areas, and to spend a prominent few minutes a week complaining and wondering what to do about the consequent increases in taxes, pollution, congestion, crime, costs, etc.

2. Local and regional political and business leaders will continue to use the circular arguments of self-fulfilling predictions in order to generate local population growth. The circular argument proceeds as follows:

i. Quantitative projections of the "inevitable" future population growth in the area are made.

ii. Plans are made to expand the municipal or regional infrastructure to accommodate the predicted growth.

iii. Bonds are issued to raise money to pay for the planned expansions of the infrastructure, and the infrastructure is expanded.

iv. The bonds must be paid off on a schedule that is based on the projections of population growth.

v. The political and business leaders will do everything in their power to make certain that the projected population growth takes place, so that the bonds can be paid off on schedule.

vi. When this results in the needed population growth, the leaders who predicted the population growth will speak loudly of their foresight.

vii. Go back to 'i' and repeat.

3. Some political and business leaders will continue to want to throw away all manner of toxic waste by dumping the waste on the lands of low-income or underdeveloped people, in the U.S. or abroad.

4. Some business leaders will want to continue to manufacture hazardous materials whose sale in the U.S. is prohibited, so that these materials can be sold abroad.

5.   Business and political leaders will continue to find it more attractive to promote growth than to promote sustainability.

A.   It is easy to talk about sustainability.

B.   It is difficult to make realistic constructive progress toward sustainability

C.   Business and political leaders are not attracted to the concept of limits as implied by the term "carrying capacity."

6.   In the U.S., political "conservatives" will continue to be liberal in their policy recommendations in regard to rapid exploitation and use of the earth's renewable and non-renewable resources, with complete confidence that technology will be able to solve all of the consequent problems of shortages, pollution, and environmental degradation. Political "liberals" will continue to urge people to conserve and to protect the environment, to recycle, to use energy more efficiently, etc., i.e., to be conservative.

7.   Entrepreneurs and politicians will continue to use the term "sustainable" for their own personal advantage in promotion of enterprises and programs, whether or not these enterprises and programs are sustainable or contribute to the creation of a sustainable society.

8.   Many members of the academic research and education programs that focus on sustainability issues such as air pollution, global warming, etc. will continue their old ways of generating high per capita levels of pollution.

9.   Many Americans will continue to deny the seriousness of the population problem in America and will focus their attention on population problems elsewhere. They may be motivated in this by their reluctance to accept the fact that immigration accounts for roughly half of the present growth of the population of the United States.

10.   Many Americans will continue to believe that the environment in the U.S. can be preserved without the need of addressing the population growth in the U.S.

11.   Many people who are active in matters relating to population problems will continue their efforts to ignore and to urge others to ignore the quantitative aspects of the population

problem. They will continue to claim that the problems will be more effectively addressed if we focus our efforts on such worthy causes as population growth in other countries, foreign aid, human rights, justice, equity, education of women, the consumption of resources, the distribution of food, etc. Some will even claim that slow growth and sustainability are compatible.

12.   Reports containing the word "sustainable" in their titles will continue to be produced at all levels of government, and these reports will continue to ignore population growth as the greatest threat to sustainability.

13.   There will always be those who reject all limits to growth.

SO WHERE DO WE GO FROM HERE?

The challenge of making the transition to a sustainable society is enormous, in part because of a major global effort to prevent people from recognizing the centrality of population growth to the enormous problems of the U.S. and the world.

The immediate task is to restore numeracy to the population programs in the local, national and global agendas.

On the local and national levels, we need to work to improve social justice and equity.

On the community level in the U.S., we should work to make growth pay for itself.

On the national scale, we can hope (demand) leaders who will recognize that population growth is the major problem in the U.S. and who will initiate a national dialog on the problem. With a lot of work at the grassroots, our system of representative government will respond.

On the global scale, we need to support family planning throughout the world, and we should generally restrict our foreign aid to those countries that make continued demonstrated progress in reducing population growth rates.

A THOUGHT FOR THE FUTURE

"When competing 'experts' recommend diametrically opposing paths of action regarding resources, carrying capacity, sustainability, and the future, we serve the cause of sustainability by choosing the conservative path, which is defined as the path that would leave society in the less precarious position if the chosen path turns out to be the wrong path," Dr. Bartlett said.

"Arithmetic, Population, and Energy" is a profound examination of the overpopulation crisis in America and the world. If you would like a copy of this video, please contact: Mr. Herb Rodriguez

Department of Information Technology Services
University of Colorado at Boulder (80309 - 0379)
(303) 492-2670
herb.rodriguez@Colorado.EDU

As you can see, we're in a whole lot of trouble, not only in the United States, but around the world. If you want to see HOW much trouble, I recommend you view a copy of Dr. Bartlett's video. You will not walk away from it without profound change in your thinking and actions. And, I venture this: we don't have a whole lot of time to turn this population disaster around.

Thank you Dr. Bartlett for granting permission to use some of your brilliant paper and thank you to the editors at Renewable Resources Journal, Vol. 15, No. 4, Winter 1997-98, Pages 6-23 Renewable Natural Resources Foundation, 5430 Grosvenor Lane, Bethesda, MD, 20814

CHAPTER 29—

WITHOUT WATER, YOU AIN'T GOIN' NOWHERE

"Climate change will have a devastating effect on the availability of water in the Western United States. Even as best-case scenario, it forecasts a virtual train wreck, with supplies falling far short of the projected future demands for water by cities, farms and wildlife."

Andrew Bridges, AP Science Writer

It's been said many times that you can't fool your mother. You may think you can fool her in your sagacious 12-year old mind, but she already knows because she's been there. There's another wise entity out there whom you can't fool, either. It's Mother Nature. True, you might be able to get away with a lot of shenanigans for years, maybe even decades. But in the end, Mother Nature will stand you up to a reality check before you can blink an eye. Do you think you're safe? Forget it! Mother

Nature can send a tornado, hurricane, tidal wave, avalanche, blizzard, earthquake, flood, plague, diseases, insects and worse at you any time she wants. She may throw such disasters at you without mercy and she can be relentless. Ask the dinosaurs! Ask the inhabitants of Easter Island or the Mayans. Ask the ghosts of any great nations that fell to ruin on the ash heap of history.

For another consideration, we must look at the most critical resource in America: water. We've enjoyed it in abundance throughout our history. We take it for granted because we've never gone thirsty. If we add 200 million more people, that's going to change.

Again, because China did nothing about its exploding population 50 years ago, it suffers relentless water problems. "China's water shortages are extreme. Of the 640 major cities in China, more than 300 face water shortages, with 100 facing severe scarcities," said, Rob Sanchez in "Changes in China."

Mike O'Brien, is a geologist, University of Minnesota, commercial pilot, flight instructor, Vietnam veteran, was awarded the Air Medal for Valor during combat—and possesses extensive expertise in dealing with water in the West. He won't try to fool you like a developer or politician. As Sergeant Friday on "DRAGNET" said, "Nothing but the facts, sir."

O'Brien writes:

"The weak link in US ecological sustainability is water. A few years ago the USGS began comprehensive, satellite linked, monitoring of our surface and groundwater supplies. Some disciplines have studied water quality and quantity for years. We have been overdrawing and polluting our "bank account" for decades. It was estimated ("Elephants in the Volkswagen" Lindsey Grant, 1992) that the sustainable population of the U.S. was between 40 and 100 million. The reality is that sustainability is going down with our groundwater supplies, increasing drought, and as desalinization/purification become more unaffordable.

"There is an intertwining of other important aspects, which also affect sustainability. One is soil depletion from salinization, micronutrient depletion, desertification, erosion, citification, and heavy metal pollution. This is from irrigation, over-fertilization, and over-use by overpopulation. There is increasing (by up to 10x in 2050) drought from atmospheric pollutants. There is increasing coastal heavy metal pollution, dead zones and over-harvesting.

"In the 1980s and 90s, 375 rivers and lakes were cleaned up. Conservation and re-use measures have gone into effect in many places. Desalinization plants have been built, and have stopped salt water intrusion into many coastal aquifers. Some are temporary fixes.

"The price of water is rising, which helps somewhat improve efficiency and conservation. All our new water supplies come from increased efficiency, conservation, desalinization, recycling and re-use. They all come at a price. The U.S. used 339 billion gallons per day, one quarter of the supply, 65 percent 'used and returned' in 1990. This increased 20 percent in ten years, to 408 billion gallons per day in 2000. We used 262 billion gallons per day from surface water. Forty percent of our municipal supplies came from ground water and 70 percent from the rural drinking-household water. Fifty percent of our crops are irrigated by ground water and 30 percent by surface water.

"Wells are running dry or being or have been shut down due to saltwater intrusion, and persistent pesticide or herbicide pollution. In Colorado in 1994, 35 in Mesa County, while I was there, as an example. As the ground water diminishes, it takes more energy to pump. Major parts of some large aquifers (Snake, Ogallala, Columbia and San Joaquin) will really begin to dry up by 2018, and nearly gone by 2040. This will decrease water supply by over 30 percent and food supply by at least 20 percent.

"The persistent organic pesticides and herbicides, along with pharmaceuticals, are extremely difficult to remove. Nitrates and phosphates are increasingly polluting our water, along with various metals. Salt is expensive to remove, and initial cost outlay of desalinization plants is heavy. We have vast inland salt water aquifers that are very deep and have added problems with sulfates, silicates, or methane in many areas.

"Right now, desalinization plants are putting out water at from below one-half cent per gallon to two cents per gallon, plus amortized building expense. Recycling and re-use systems are also expensive and have heavy maintenance expense. Distribution is quite variable throughout the US and this will be even more variable as climate fluctuates more and more. Generally, floods don't help us, and droughts hurt us. People will tend to migrate to where good water is, and they will fight over it.

"We are at and beyond our limits, yet have a segment of the population that doesn't understand limits or operation, invention, manufacture, and maintenance of complex systems— and is increasing in a hyperbolic curve. It's far beyond the highest projections of a decade ago.

"Demand for jobs reduces wages. Demand for products increases prices (and profits). Scarcity also increases prices. Eventually tax revenue for more desalinization, purification, and recycling systems won't be enough as the poverty rate skyrockets. Overloaded sewage treatment systems will pollute more, especially during floods. Toilets will be plugged up and filled to the brim during times of rationing, when water will be off much of the day in many places.

"This has been the scenario in much of the "Third World" for some time. People who have traveled a lot have seen it. Watch "Cadillac Desert" (1997). Theoretically, we can cut water consumption in half, and thus double population.

"Systems to provide more efficiency, more conservation, purification, and recycling take time and money. Also, remember that groundwater used up is recharged at rates generally so slow as to call them non-renewable. To double our population we not only have to reduce consumption by half, but increase recycling by 40 percent at least. Unfortunately, we're on course for doubling our population.

"Water rates will have to rise dramatically. We are already at deficit spending nationally, and many states are barely making it. People won't vote for tax increases when their income is going down. Half the people will not pay for the other half's water.

"Conflicts are in court right now and will increase. People will kill for water. They've done it in the past and will do it in the future.

"The Colorado River is notable for state to state conflict. California has taken more than its share and this is being stopped as Arizona and Colorado procure their share. Arizona with all its dry rivers that have hardly ever reached the Colorado River is getting more than it should. Colorado, the main source, still doesn't get a fair share.

"Remember that increasing drought amplifies water problems, and we have a drought in the West. Southern California, with its high population growth from immigration and descendants, will only meet 43 percent of demands in 2010 ("Tapped Out" Simon, 1998).

"One by one, cities and towns are coming under the ax of too many people and not enough good water. Skyrocketing water prices, limits to generosity, fighting over water and migration add up to crisis/violence and potential chaos.

"The human body is over 70 percent water. At -1 percent we feel thirsty. At -5 percent we get a slight fever. At -8 percent we have no saliva and many of us turn a blue color. At -10 percent we can no longer even walk, and at -12 percent death occurs. Desert and drought areas get hit first.

"Stopping population growth will buy us 10 crucial years to develop purification recycling systems. Even then we'll have to curb the population already here, or let it happen naturally through higher and higher death rates.

"California isn't the only place that will be hit soon. Southern Nevada then Texas, then other states will have increasing water quantity and/or quality problems, some very costly and nearly insurmountable. Many will not have time to increase quality/quantity of water before high death rates set in.

"Florida is in big trouble, too. There's a lot of desalinization and recycling, but the growth rate is even higher than California's. Seawater influx, contamination from landfills, septic systems and pesticides are reducing supplies.

"Numerous places in North Carolina and Virginia have water restrictions and many communities with poor water quality. West Virginia reported 378 communities with poor water quality in the 1990s. Michigan reported 115 communities, Kentucky 377, and even Oregon had 78 communities reporting water quality problems. This quality problem can be anything from heavy metals, like in Montana, to arsenic, pesticides, herbicides, nitrates, phosphates and saltwater.

"The effects of low, continued doses of many are birth defect and cancer increases. Only so many wells can be drilled in any groundwater source, and only so far from septic systems. This varies from different soils and conditions, but up to 500 feet or more. One way or another, more costs rise.

"All of our states have problems somewhere. Eighteen major watersheds are in the lower 48 states, and numerous aquifers, with the Ogallala the largest and most studied. The USGS keeps real time data from numerous satellite linked reporting points. From my latest download of water-watch current water resources, I can see drought dots in every state except Maine, Alaska and Hawaii.

"Also, the current drought in the West doesn't show on a daily look, there should be a trends map, too. From the ground water climate response network, I see a lot of half full wells, a lot of low ones, and a few that are full. There are many, nearly half, that have insufficient data. Some you can click on and tell exactly when they will be out of water, like Castro County, Texas, beginning of 2018. That's it, and you don't get much rain there either. Others are holding their own, for now. With wells, you can demand all you want, but it only comes out so fast, and there is only so much there.   Over the EPA limits for arsenic? Just up that level, truck in good water, move, or buy a filtration system that might take it out. How about some of those big cities in Texas, sunken over a depleting aquifer and little rain? Or maybe with rain that goes down a river and only very slowly into the aquifer. How long do they have with a geometrically growing population? Probably 20 years, and I bet there are local experts who know and are very worried.

"In 1990 we were using one-quarter of our supply and returning 65 percent of it. It rose 20 percent in ten years. It must be realized that a large amount of water must remain for navigation and for permanently wild rivers. The EPA monitors effluent discharge and sludge deposition. Only 25 percent of U.S. communities return to the Earth's soil the sludge in the form of true compost.

"The flush and forget, let the poor people in attitude is wrong—and deadly. Our best farmlands have seven inches of soil left out of 16 inches less than a century ago, on average. It takes anywhere from 700 years to 10,000 years to naturally form an inch of good farm soil ("Out of the Earth" Hillel, 1992). Half our pasture lands are overgrazed, and all of our good soil, and some marginal, is being used. Soil and water are ecologically intertwined. It is estimated that when the Ogallala Aquifer is, in essence, empty by 2040, that it will take up to 6,000 years to recharge. It takes PVC (a potent carcinogen) 50,000 years to decay in a landfill.

"Phoenix recycles 80 percent of its wastewater (that hasn't evaporated). I pursued a water study when I lived there. In 1989 my study showed that it was already past the ability to withstand a 50 year cycle type drought in 1988. I moved in 1990 and it has grown 40 percent since then. So water recycling is survival in our desert Southwest.

"Evaporation will increase in many other areas as global warming takes more effect. It will have to be that way for much of the rest of the country in 20 years or less. Reduce, re-use, and recycle has been an environmental mantra for 34 years.

"Do we really want to double our population in less than 60 years?

"If it continues growing, we won't have the water we need. Not just the Federal Government, but State and local, too. Where is your water coming from, how much, and of what quality? How much do you use? Will your local area be able to have enough for a 25 percent increase in 10 years? How about a 60 percent increase in 20 years or 100 percent increase in 28 years?

"The riots won't start until the faucets run dry and the toilets are plugged up. Ask yourself when this will happen near where you live, then write, email and talk to friends, acquaintances, the media and politicians. You owe it to your kids and grand kids.

"If you can, think about linear and non-linear factors, accelerated positive feedback loops, heat surges, drought, flood, desertification and one car per minute out of the world's factories ("Thermageddon" 2001). Three to five children are born each second, and three people die each second in the world ("WWIII: overpopulation and the Planet", 1994). Can the U.S. free itself of foreign dependence?

"I have written in the past of "mammal populations in ecological niches, including humans" (1967), of "tubes of probability", and "cascading ecological niche failures." I was asked to examine the economic ramifications and realized they are first, and in fact have been lowering US labor, skilled tradesman, and other wages for 20 years. Now, I have been asked to do the water aspect, specifically for our country, and out of love for my country. It is the second aspect to hit us, and far more deadly.

"Everyone can eventually use a lot less water, and will be forced to. Parts of this country already look like a Third World hellhole. Do we want half of it to look that way? Right now in parts of the world, people are spending half the money they make on water ("Cadillac Dessert" 1997). I sure don't want that to happen in my country. If we don't act, massive consequences will begin—conflict for water, dying of thirst, or starvation from crops that couldn't grow and livestock down to skin and bones, water and crowd borne diseases, accumulated pollution effects and malnutrition.

"We need at least 10 years without massive growth to increase desalinization and purification plants, implement conservation measures, and increase efficiency and recycling. It is the difference between life and death for many millions of Americans."

SECOND SOURCE

Mike O'Brien isn't alone in his projections. Andrew Bridges, AP Science Writer, November 23, 2002, "DROUGHT: GLOBAL WARMING 'TRAIN WRECK' FORECAST FOR THE WEST" writes, "Even as a best-case scenario, it forecasts a virtual train wreck, with supplies falling far short of projected future demands for water, farms and wildlife...the problem in the West is not climate change, it's too many people using too much water...if nothing happens and we keep growing, we're in trouble. If more drought continues, it's worse."

A Department of Energy and U.S Geological Survey found, "Reservoir levels along the Colorado River will drop by more than a third and releases by 17 percent. The Sacramento River will see reduced reliability in the volumes of water available for irrigation, cities and hydropower. With less fresh water, the Sacramento Delta will increase in salinity, disrupting the ecosystem. On the Columbia River system, there will be water in the summer and fall to generate electricity, or in the spring and summer for salmon runs, but not both."

As you've noticed throughout this book, many important points have been repeated. Why? Oftentimes, we humans 'selectively ignore' salient facts when they are not in our faces. For most of us, everything looks okay today. That 'thing' called overpopulation is 'out there.' Global warming is still debated. Massive species extinction doesn't affect us for the time being.

But the fact is, we're all riding that train headed for the edge of the Grand Canyon whether we like it or not. Therefore, I repeat Eleanor Roosevelt's words,

"We must prevent human tragedy rather than run around trying to save ourselves after an event has already occurred. Unfortunately, history clearly shows that we arrive at catastrophe by failing to meet the situation, by failing to act when we should have acted. The opportunity passes us by and the next disaster is always more difficult and compounded than the last one."

After reading this book, especially if you have children, you are invited to take action to prove her right by 'preventing human tragedy,' instead of continuing to ride on this train with no brakes.

CHAPTER 30—

PLAGUE OF THE 21ST CENTURY— TOO MANY PEOPLE

"The problems that exist in the world today cannot be solved by the level of thinking that created them."

Albert Einstein

Dr. Albert Bartlett presented future consequences in America. Those same laws hold true around the world. A quick look shows anyone the horrifying manifestations in Africa, India, Mexico, South America and any land overpopulated by human beings. Once the numbers present themselves on the landscape, they can't be vanquished and they won't vanish. If they could, Bangladesh, India and China would magically wave a wand to reduce their overpopulated societies to one-quarter of their current numbers. Their freedoms and choices in life would become reasonable again. They would not be forced into such draconian birth control measures such as mandatory one-child families in China. Both India and China would love having a mere 300 million people. Instead, they suffer the consequences of their inaction 50 years ago.

One fact about laws: they hold true. You can't escape them. You can't escape gravity. You can't fly a kite in a 100-mile per hour wind. You can't jump off the Empire State Building and expect to live after you hit the pavement. You can't create more gas once you've burned all the world's oil reserve. You can't bring extinct species back to life. Sooner or later, those laws manifest themselves in reality. Nonetheless, this country staggers forward with 'solutions' that accelerate America's population crisis.

Geologist Mike O'Brien painted a "I'm so dry I can't spit" picture of our water crisis in the American West. It extends to many locations in the world. Millions suffer for lack of clean water.

Einstein's quote manifests daily in the folly of our politicians as they pander more and more legal and illegal immigration. Instead of representing American citizens needs, they represent growth. I have contacted Governor Bill Owens of Colorado for the last five years. I've tried to gain an audience with him concerning Colorado's water crisis—to no avail. He assures us, "Colorado needs growth." That's why they call him Governor Pavement.

Colorado dangerously exceeds carrying capacity, NOW, long before we add another four million people. Instead of stabilizing the state's population, he wants more dams to grow our population. He and other leaders never solve the problem. They make it worse. These elected officials follow in the footsteps of the leaders of Bangladesh, China and India 50 years ago.

Their actions provoke a greater crisis when the population outgrows the dams. Colorado maintains a stable rain and snow pack annually. Weather patterns do not evolve into rain forests out of the semi-arid region of Colorado. Therefore, by artificially creating more water storage, which, in turn, will create additional millions in human population, Governor Owens lays the foundation for an even larger disaster in the coming years when a drought hits. It's another example of Third World Thinking. It makes you wonder if our leaders have any common sense? If they do possess common sense, why not use it? Thankfully, Colorado voters voted down the dam building bill. It remains to be seen if Owens begins thinking with a 21st century mind instead of a 19th century mentality. Don't hold your breath.

"Environmental degradation is an iatrogenic disease induced by the economic physicians who attempt to treat the sickness of unlimited wants by prescribing unlimited production. We do not cure a treatment-induced disease by increasing the treatment dosage," said Herman E. Daly in "Selected Growth Fallacies."

The more we grow today, the worse our environmental crisis accelerates.

With all the facts and figures facing our president(s) and Congress, as well as the American public, the majority of us have kept our faith in the proven ineptness and incompetence of our leaders. Few speak out and fewer still do anything. As you've noticed across our nation, when someone does speak out, media experts and politicians condemn them.

But consequences continue building.

California is a whole new nightmare in the making. You might return to Kenneth Boulding's 'dismal theorems' for refreshment of what's coming for the West Coast.

"If present levels of immigration to America continue for two or three more decades, the time frame for a likely dissolution of the United States would in all probability be not in the next century, but in this one," said Dr. Lee G. Marland in "Population/Immigration: One Problem, Indivisible."

Governors in every state are thinking, acting and moving toward the 'suffering' quotient. Instead of thinking and dealing with the reality of limits, they race for more growth, more development, more population, more gridlock, more air pollution, more destruction of farmland and more of everything deleterious for our country. It's like the kid who blows a big, fat, pink bubble gum balloon. It's great while it's viable, but once it 'pops,' the kid must clean the mess off his face. Once the 'water crisis' implodes in Colorado, Arizona and California—we're talking a societal cataclysm beyond description.

Soon past the mid-century, 200 million more Americans will be struggling for dwindling resources, water, food and diminishing quality of life. Soon after that, we will double our population from 292 million to 600 million. In a western state like Colorado or Arizona, a drought in 2050 will become a calamity. When one state suffers such a monumental crisis, all other states will be affected in time.

For graphic examples, one need only look at India and China. In a recent speech, Arun Gandhi, grandson of Mahatma Gandhi, said, "In my country, two million people are born in the streets, live in the streets and die in the streets—never having used a toilet or shower." If massive population is so good, why is India so poor? If overpopulation is so wonderful, why are Bangladesh's people living in such misery? If China's population is the hallmark of happiness, why did two million Chinese risk their lives to illegally import themselves into Canada and the United States in the past two decades? Vancouver, British Columbia is no longer Canadian. They speak Chinese. Why are millions of people from all over the world risking their lives, fortunes and families to come to America? It's simple.

Overpopulation is the "Plague of the 21st Century."

Where is America headed? Do we want such a legacy for our own children? According to the TV program "*60 MINUTES*," we have one million homeless children struggling in our inner cities today. What will be the fate of the percentage of another 200 million people who create homeless children? How about one million homeless adults? Since 1999, 50 percent more African-American children have fallen below the poverty level. If we're such a rich society, why can't we solve those problems? Why won't we address those numbers of people in distress?

How many is too many and when will America address itself to that fact? Who possesses the courage to step up to the reality of overpopulation/consumption/pollution in America in the long term?

At this time, few. Politicians scurry like cockroaches at the mention of population stabilization. Corporations demand larger markets as if nonrenewable resources will appear out of thin air.

Americans face consequences in every corner of our nation. Our East and West coasts, teeming with too many people, strive to deal with escalating water, air and land dilemmas. Deep-water wells, already polluted with industrial chemicals from farmers and manufacturing plants dumping poisons, are drying up. Acid rains pound our lakes with chemicals. Our cities create thick clouds as miles of bumper to bumper cars idle for hours. Humans breathe carcinogens with every breath. The incidences of lung disease set annual records. Farmers kill microbes in the soil with fertilizers and pesticides, which leaves us with contaminated foods. Each year, 1.3 million new cancers are detected in our U.S. citizens. It's an epidemic of our own making.

By failing to act now, what kinds of avoidable consequences will we as a nation face when we hit one-half billion people? States like Colorado will add 100 percent more people to their already drought prone state. That's 100 percent more cars on the road and 100 percent more houses using 100 percent more water. In the U.S. with 200 million added people, that's 77 percent more traffic, 77 percent added planes in the air, 77 percent increased pollution, 77 percent faster uses of already limited resources as gasoline. When we double our population to 600 million people, it will mean a 100 percent doubling of the aforementioned points. If that prospect doesn't make you sick to your stomach, what will?

For example: we're paving over 3000 acres of land each day for homes, roads, and malls! With each new added American, according to Negative Population Growth, 12.6 acres of wilderness is plowed up to support that person. The richer someone is, the more they consume and pollute. In the next 10 years, according to the National Academy of Sciences, 2,500 plants and animals will become extinct in the USA because of habitat destruction via population growth. Why aren't we addressing the moral and biological consequences of such horrific extinction rates?

Additionally, America and the world are fast approaching the end of the "Age of Oil." Sobering indeed is the reality that we have not discovered a viable energy alternative. What if we don't? Can't? If we do find an alternative, the transition will be problematic beyond anyone's imagination.

We are like a car full of drunken college kids racing toward the railroad tracks to beat the on-coming train. President Bush is driving (yes, he was convicted of a DUI at one point) while Karl Rove advises from his 'shotgun' position in the right front seat. In the back seat sit foggy-minded senate and house representatives. Finally, a silent American citizenry fills out the last position. They think the president, his advisors and Congress know what they are doing. The red lights blink on and off, but our leader is too drunk to respond. Suddenly within 100 feet of the tracks while traveling at 90 miles per hour, we realize that we're not going to make it and fumble for our seat belts. Even if we snapped them on in time, well, you know the rest of that story. But in this case, it's our entire nation.

Peak Oil is a term you will become familiar with in the near future. The USA with five percent of the world's population burns 18 million barrels of oil a day. The world burns 70 million barrels daily. Oil supplies will peak at 2020 and some experts think closer to 2010. As oil diminishes, prices will skyrocket. We're describing a disruption of commerce that staggers even the most optimistic economists.

Nonetheless, in the meantime, most Americans and the rest of the world don't give it a thought. It's like taking a 20-mile hike into the desert on a 115-degree day with a pint of water. Once you've run out of water, you are at the mercy of the desert sun. It will kill you.

Most civilizations globally depend on oil. What's the problem? The rate at which we consume oil and gas is outrunning the available rate of supply.

Even if we enjoyed 100 years of oil reserves—and we won't—we're burning up so much fossil fuel as to pour carbon dioxide into the atmosphere by the billions of tons. It's a race to see how fast we can 'cook up' the planet with Global Warming or overrun it with human beings to the point it fights back with horrific diseases, famine or who knows what it will 'think up' to reduce our numbers.

When you add ocean fisheries collapsing, acid rain, ozone destruction, drought, contaminated water supplies, poisoning and sterilization of the soils by insecticides and fertilizers—we're building unimaginable repercussions. Having lived and worked with top scientists in Antarctica, I confirm major ice sheets melting with alarming speed.

How serious is our problem? Upon receiving the Sanger Award for Human Rights in 1966, Dr. Martin Luther King said, "Unlike the plagues of the dark ages or contemporary diseases, which we do not understand, the modern plague of overpopulation is solvable by means we have discovered and with resources we possess. What is lacking is not sufficient knowledge of the solution, but universal consciousness of the gravity of the problem and the education of billions of people who are its victims."

Fifty year ago, Bangladesh, India and China ignored their accelerating populations. Their problems are so gargantuan, they can't solve them and simply suffer. Today, America's leaders follow the same footsteps.

We need an immigration 10-year moratorium and reduction to less than 100,000 people annually before population momentum forces us to an added 200 million Americans and an unsustainable society. We must compassionately promote family planning in other countries by ceasing to be their escape valve. As has been shown in this book, it does not and will not solve their problems, but it will destroy our country. If we don't tame this 'immigration invasion' into our country within the next one to two years, it will grow past our ability to manage it.

Historical comparatives abound. The Greeks gave us the Trojan Horse that destroyed Troy. Easter Island's extinct human population comes to mind. Look at the misery of Bangladesh, China, Africa and India. Look how France is being overrun. Just as the Titanic sunk from taking on too much water, the United States will sink from taking on too much population.

"Time is running out for humankind to implement either ecological ethics or sustainability ethics. If not implemented, nature's laws will become evident, whose consequences are not humane," said John Cairns, Jr. in "The Unmanaged Commons."

If we do nothing, we commit our children and all living things to a difficult future by neglecting overpopulation in 2004. It's a disservice to ourselves, our nation and future generations.

CHAPTER 31—

How to Save America

"Will you surrender, sir?"
"On the contrary, I have not yet begun to fight."

Captain John Paul Jones

This country is in trouble. After reading this book, you know how much, how far-reaching and how critical it is. This massive invasion has gained a huge foothold in our country. It's like cancer that spreads to the lymph nodes and infects the entire body.

We can't blame millions of desperate people for crashing onto America's shores. My compassion runs deep from my own experiences around the world. Africa is a nightmare for millions. Asia grinds on daily under its teeming masses. Mexico broils under the sweat of desperation. China's problems magnify beyond solving. South Americans destroy their rain forests at one and a half acres per second while they cause the extinction of thousands of creatures. Americans burn oil as if there is no tomorrow. Where does it end?

296

What is the point of devolving our First World country into the morass of Third World misery? Do you want to leave your offspring the same legacy as children suffering in Africa? In China? In Latin America?

The option is yours, while you still have a choice, to steer toward a reasoned destination. We must transit away from the iceberg that sank the Titanic. We can change directions away from this immigration calamity.

As citizens of a First World country, we are eminently capable with our powerful educational system and electoral process to avoid the demise that has visited all great civilizations before us. We DO NOT have to commit national suicide as the historian Arnold Toynbee observed.

What else can we do? First, good old Yankee ingenuity is alive and well in America. Questionnaires were sent across the Internet requesting citizens to give their top ideas on how to save America. Some were angry because they were sick of the invasion. Some had lost their loved ones to illegal aliens via drugs, car crashes, crime in their communities, violence, lost jobs, raped daughters, language crisis in their schools, diseases killing their kids and a host of other consequences brought into their lives by immigration.

Nonetheless, their ideas streamed in my computer from Americans of every walk of life. College professors submitted their ideas as well as teachers, college students, carpenters, janitors, bus drivers, truck drivers, bartenders, professionals, housewives, restaurant owners, principals of schools, farmers and pilots. They care about America. After all, this is their home. This is their country.

This is what they submitted on 'HOW TO SAVE AMERICA.' It is an essential strategy for victory if we are to preserve and maintain our nation:

A TEN-YEAR MORATORIUM ON ALL IMMIGRATION: This would allow our country to regain its collective breath. It would allow us to regain our schools, language, medical facilities, financial balance, ecological viability and order, which is necessary for a First World country to operate for all its citizens.

We must employ a linkage strategy. Congressman Tom Tancredo said, "The challenge is enormous and you have to talk about a moratorium. You can't talk about anything short of a moratorium because, frankly, anything less will never get you one step closer to population stabilization."

It's absolutely essential in every contact with legislators that activists push for an immigration moratorium. We must leverage to get 'good' bills passed and stop 'bad' bills such as amnesty for illegals. Thus, link your support for a 'good' bill or opposition for a 'bad' bill with a call for a moratorium. For example: "Senator, we want you to sponsor a bill enacting a moratorium on mass immigration, and sponsor a companion bill to H.R. 687 or H.R. 946 outlawing Matricular I.D. cards."

You want to stop anchor babies, diversity visas, chain migration, H-1B visas, L-1 visas, illegal alien migration and push for a moratorium.

DEPORT ILLEGAL ALIENS: We need mechanisms in place whereby illegal aliens are deported slowly and effectively or begin self-deporting. We must enforce our immigration laws 100 percent. That means arresting employers who hire illegal aliens. Enforce steep fines so all employers get the message that the rule-of-law is to be abided by all citizens in America and not selectively. This would force employers to pay living wages to American citizens and not 'slave wages' to Third World immigrants, which only depresses wages and living conditions for all Americans in the long run.

No judges, no lawyers. Their anchor babies go with them. We must get rid of the Executive Office for Immigration Review. This office is responsible for over 400,000 illegal aliens absconding when they were scheduled to be deported. We need to place 7,000 illegal immigration lawyers in the unemployment lines where their actions have forced Americans.

PASS THE CLEAR ACT: Senator Charles Norwood of Georgia presented the CLEAR ACT (Bill S. 2671) which would give police officers authority to enforce Federal Immigration laws. We pay 650,000 police officers in the United States that could help immigration law enforcement. All law enforcement officials must be able to arrest, detain and transfer illegal aliens to the Bureau of Immigration and Customs Enforcement.

In addition, illegal immigration must be completely eliminated by increasing the number of B.I.C.E. and Border Patrol officers on the streets, going out into the communities and detaining and deporting illegals, just as truant officers walk the streets in various cities of the United States. In other words, there must be a dramatic lowering of legal immigration quotas and the full elimination of illegal immigration.

LIMIT LEGAL IMMIGRATION: Once the ten-year moratorium is up, we will only allow 100,000 immigrants per year or as many that can maintain replacement levels for a stable U.S. population. We do not want to become like China, India, Bangladesh or any overpopulated country. Legal immigration must be managed with common sense. If our country's social services--schools, hospitals, clinics, and prisons are too crowded to handle additional people, then it only makes sense that legal immigration be curtailed. If the country's infrastructure--roads, utilities, airports and housing are over extended, legal immigration must be curtailed. If unemployment exists in certain geographical areas, then bringing in more people to sit in line or to collect funds is counter productive.

NO BENEFITS FOR ILLEGALS: As shown in this book, illegal immigration costs Americans debilitating amounts of tax dollars for schools, medical, housing and other services—at the degradation of educating our own children. That is what draws them. We must cut off all social services and education funding for illegal aliens and their children. This will help them self-deport or not come to the USA in the first place. Their own countries need to take responsibility for their own citizens. Mexico would be an excellent place to start.

It will also stop the 'escape valve' allowing foreign countries to use us as a dumping ground for their lack of family planning practices.

FAMILY PLANNING WORLDWIDE: The United States and other First World countries need to assist other countries with family planning methods. Birth control is a major aspect of family planning. Without it, Third World countries are doomed to endless population increases and degradation.

The Catholic Church, Protestants, Islam and other religions that continually work against family planning must step out of the Dark Ages and into the 21st century. We can promote education that spotlights their entrenched thinking based on concepts that were founded 2,000 years ago. Humans must work in harmony with nature and that means we must stabilize our numbers. We must maintain one or two children families worldwide.

It's not logical to think any of these great religions would flip to a rational action by accepting family planning any time soon. Therefore, we are obligated to take care of our citizens first to ensure our country's viability. After that, we may continue our assistance worldwide.

DEVELOPMENTAL ASSISTANCE: First World countries need to assist with development, housing, education, fresh water, family planning and health care/education for countries that suffer from this planet-wide population crisis. Help them in their own countries.

ENGLISH: It is imperative that all immigrants speak English before coming to America. It's not our responsibility to spend our money to teach them. Further, all education, all state and local documents, newspapers, radio and TV must be in English in order to preserve America as a unified nation with a single language. No more foreign languages allowed on our TV or radio stations. This is America and we speak English.

MILITARIZE OUR BORDERS: Borders must be militarized, especially during this time of terrorism. We enforce borders in Korea, Iraq, Afghanistan, Bosnia, Germany and other countries. We must put troops on our borders for national security. We have the technology for camera-carrying remote controlled miniature planes that can stop human encroachment easily. This journalist has seen them in action. Once the word gets out that we're serious about our national sovereignty, this invasion will abate.

AMERICANIZING IMMIGRANTS: Using common sense in limiting the numbers of immigrants who can enter the country and dispersing those immigrants are only two parts of the formula for successful assimilation of immigrants into the United States. This sounds like a simple task; you may think that immigrants only need to look around them to see how we live in America.

However, if you live in Southern California, an immigrant would see so much diversity in ethni-cities and behaviors that he or she would have no clue as to how to behave. The result is that we native-born Americans must define the values that are essential to the ideals of America and then we must teach those American expectations and values. We can't have them throwing their trash which has happened all over California and other states with large immigrant populations. If we cannot define the values and expectations that represent America and if we, ourselves, do not live by those expectations, then we can hardly expect immigrants to assimilate into the American way of life.

STOP DESTRUCTIVE PROGRAMS: We must stop programs such as 'chain migration,' 'Diversity visas,' 'anchor babies,' 'H-1B visas,' 'L-1 visas' and pass a law that no legal immigrant can access the welfare office until after five years of residence in the United States. Those sponsors of legal immigrants should be held strictly responsible for their expenses and not American taxpayers.

DO WHAT IKE DID: Do what Dwight Eisenhower did back in the 1950's. He called his program, "Operation Wetback." Eisenhower sent the illegals back across the border. Approximately 1,000,000 Mexicans were forced to leave the United States. America maintained itself without the help of one million Mexicans doing the "jobs Americans wouldn't do." If Mexicans or other legal immigrants want to apply for a green card to work here lawfully, Americans are in favor of lawful entry.

NO MEXICAN TRUCK DRIVERS IN AMERICA: With the Mexican truck drivers potentially gaining the 'green light' to drive in the near future, this is going to be easier for the drug cartels to transport drugs. This is another alarming ramification among all the other wretched problems. Sadly, the drug cartels swing a lot of weight as to illegal immigration. Seventy-five percent of drugs brought into the United States come in from Mexico. Additionally, it's an extreme risk and safety crisis to allow Mexican trucks and non-English reading or speaking Mexican drivers on America's highways. How do I know? As a summer job from my teaching years, I was a head trainer and safety officer for one of the top agents for United Van Lines. I wouldn't let one single Mexican truck driver into the United States. They can't speak or read English. They don't have the education or judgment needed to drive an 80,000-pound rig safely down our highways at 70 miles per hour. The operative word in that sentence is: SAFELY.

ENFORCE LABOR SANCTIONS: Laws established by Congress must be enforced. In 2003 only 37 companies were fined for hiring illegal aliens with 200,000 or more known to be flagrant violators. Jobs for the working class people in the U.S. should be a priority. This would ensure wages rose to meet the needs of the jobs. Instead of sinking to the depressed wages of the Third World, Americans would maintain higher wages and living standards.

ENFORCE RICO LAWS: (Racketeer Influenced and Corrupt Organizations Act) Law (18 U.S.C. Sections 1961-68 1982 & Supplement 1111985). The original 24 federal felonies that were considered as racketeering activities were murder, intimidation of witnesses, kidnapping, obstructing justice, counterfeiting, theft of interstate shipments, white slavery, embezzlement of pension funds, certain federal drug offenses, bankruptcy fraud, mail fraud and wire fraud. In 1984, obscenity was added as a predicate act.

If you know anyone who hires illegal aliens, they are in violation of federal laws. If such employers have taken your job, they are in violation of federal law. You may sue them.

This pertains to violation of our immigration laws:

(F) Any act which is indictable under the Immigration and Nationality Act, section 274 (relating to bringing in and harboring certain aliens), section 277 (relating to aiding or assisting certain aliens to enter the United States), or section 278 (relating to importation of alien for immoral purpose) if the act indictable under such section of such Act was committed for the purpose of financial gain.

ENFORCE IMMIGRANT RESPONSIBILITY ACT OF 1996, Section 642. When cities choose to remain sanctuary cities for illegal aliens, they lose their federal funding. Special Order 40 that allows illegal alien sanctuary must be abolished immediately. It serves illegal aliens and criminals to the detriment of American citizens. It is one of the BIG reasons for the illegal alien crime wave engulfing our cities. Refer to the Chapter 14 where a police officer tells it straight from his squad car.

ENFORCE LAWS: Enforce laws relating to Human Trafficking, 8 USC 1324. The Anti-Smuggling Units of B.I.C.E are making arrests and disrupting aliens smuggling organizations in larger cities with some additional manpower. We must arrest illegal aliens inside our country. Additionally, it's utterly ridiculous that we catch them and release them back on the border where they try again. We need to arrest those who hire them. THAT would stop this invasion quickly when the jobs dried up for illegals.

CHURCH AGENDAS: Catholic, Islamic and Protestant churches openly encourage legal and illegal immigration without taking responsibility once their clients arrive in the United States. We cannot and must not allow them to sponsor thousands of incompatible/violent cultures from around the world. It is a disservice to take them out of their native lands and it's a financial and social crisis to introduce them into our society.

1) Honor the U.S. Constitution in its entirety.
2) Enforce all existing laws for everyone.
3) Elect a president and Congress that understand that this great nation is more than an economy and will abide by numbers 1 & 2 above.

STOP GLOBALISM: GATT and NAFTA were the early embodiments of globalism. The big hammer ready to drop is the Free Trade of the Americas agreement. Bush wants this to come into effect in 2005. See http://www.stoptheftaa.org/ This one, from my perspective, may be impossible to stop.

ELECT SENATORS AND CONGRESSIONAL REPRESENTATIVES WHO REPRESENT AMERICANS: One of the reasons Congress and our President have created this national nightmare stems from their being members of the 'good old boy' network. They are the 'elites' who never worry about mortgages or car payments like the rest of us. As long as they represent illegal alien immigration and massive legal immigration as well as corporations who pander this nightmare, you will not see change. You must elect leaders who will take action on behalf of Americans.

A scant 50 percent of Americans vote in national elections. Local elections rate less than 20 percent participation most of the time. More Americans see this crisis and more Americans are stepping up to the plate. They are running for office in many states.

Get out and support them! Instead of sitting on the couch with a beer in one hand, a remote in the other and a pizza on the coffee table—it's time to take action in the political process. If you don't, you can bet the illegal immigration lawyers, MALDEF, LULAC, LA RAZA, Senator Orrin Hatch of Utah and Mark Udall of Colorado are working against you. Also, Chris Cannon of Utah, Nancy Pelosi of California, Representative Berkley of Nevada, Senator Harry Reid of Nevada, Flake and Kolbe of Arizona and dozens of others aid illegal aliens by doing nothing while creating your worst nightmare.

STOP REGISTRATION OF ANY ILLEGAL ALIENS OR NON-CITIZENS FOR VOTING IN U.S. ELECTIONS: This means no driver's licenses for illegal aliens. It means no voting cards for illegal aliens. It means no citizenship until an individual stands in line and lawfully awaits his or her turn into becoming an American citizen.

PASS THESE BILLS: Call, write, fax your senators and representatives to pass S. 1906 and S. 2671 (Clear Act) which will allow police to round up and deport illegal aliens. Additionally, demand they pass HR 946 (Immigration Reduction Act) that reduces legal immigration to under 300,000 annually. That's AFTER a 10-year moratorium and the best number will be under 100,000 annually.

You must demand they pass bills that arrest immigration and do not pass any bills that encourage immigration such as the Dream Act, which gives illegal aliens in-state tuition. Demand your senators and representatives to withdraw 'chain migration,' 'diversity visas,' 'anchor baby' citizenship, H-1B and L-1 visas.

Mass immigration and resulting population growth is one manifestation of globalization, which has an agenda of eliminating national sovereignty and borders and making workers interchangeable units in a commodities market.

THE MOST IMPORTANT WAY TO SAVE AMERICA: You! Use the Internet with web sites that create collective action. Connect with all Americans. Use your money and your time. Stand up. Write. Call. Radio talk shows. Call on TV networks and express your anger. Express your ideas. Be heard. Be seen. Be passionate. Demand. Expect action. Become action in motion.

CHAPTER 32—

TAKE ACTION FOR YOUR COUNTRY

"Whatever you can do, or dream you can do. Begin it. Boldness has genius, power and magic in it. Begin it now."

Goethe

If you think someone else is going to save your country, think again. It's up to you to save your country. How? By banding together with groups that exert power in the halls of Congress. You must band together with like-minded people who will create a force so powerful that radio, TV, Congress and even the president will be compelled to change. It's called a 'consciousness shift.' Once there are more of us than there are of 'them,' we will succeed in gaining a 10-year moratorium on all immigration and eventually reduce immigration to a total of 100,000 per year, no exceptions.

How can you do this personally? First start where you are—with what you possess. Remember that Betsy Ross started with the first stitch to create the American flag. Thomas Jefferson started with, "We the people." John Paul Jones said, "I have not yet begun to fight!" Jack Kennedy said, "Ask not what your country can do for you, rather, ask what you can do for your country." Dr. Martin Luther King said, "I have a dream." Second, make your intention known by writing it down. Make it a solid goal with accompanying supports. Lock on to your vision. You can't 'want' something to happen. You must 'intend' it to happen. The universe can't do anything with a 'want.' However, it will set into motion an 'intention.' Finally, take action toward your intention. Maintain determination until final success. What is your intention?

Keep a positive attitude and keep moving forward. Remember that many Americans before us struggled for this nation. They didn't give up. They moved forward with a resolute patriotic passion.

You are going to change the disastrous course of immigration into America. You are working to gain a 10-year immigration moratorium, stop all illegal immigration, deport illegal aliens, stop anchor babies, halt diversity visas, lower legal immigration limits to less than 100,000 annually, stop chain migration, stop H-1B and L-1 visas, stop outsourcing, insourcing and offshoring, push for English as our only language and more ideas only you can give birth to from your passions for your country.

Below are the organizations to help you:

www.numbersusausa.com
Roy Beck, a man I admire and respect heads this grass roots organization that gives you maximum power by offering you free pre-written faxed letters to political leaders. They provide a weekly action items list to keep you informed. I HIGHLY recommend you become a member of this group of citizens who are making a HUGE impact on this crisis. It's easy, quick and effective to fax their pre-letters to your senators and representatives. Encourage all your friends to join.

www.asapcoalition.org and www.balance.org

Alliance to Stabilize America's Population Coalition. Over 50 organizations support common programs for a moratorium on legal immigration and deportation of illegals.

www.AmericanBorderPatrol.com and www.AmericanPatrol.com
This is an organization attempting to stop illegal immigration at our borders. Glenn Spencer is a front line patriot who has invented a spotter plane that locates illegal alien movement. His web site informs you daily on this invasion crisis.

www.BetterImmigration.org
Better Immigration lobbies Congress and provides congressional report card ratings, an essential tool for Americans.

www.CommonSenseOnMassImmigration.us
A pocket-sized booklet contains a number of short articles on immigration. Excellent material to hand out to politicians and interested parties. Vast network dealing with this crisis. This is a highly informative web site.

www.CarryingCapacityNetwork.org
This organization works for immigration reduction, resource conservation, population stabilization, national revitalization and sustainable economy. Excellent and highly effective!

www.CIS.org
Center For Immigration Studies provides extensive research and reports on the various implications of Mass immigration into America.

www.CivilHomelandDefense.us
Civil Homeland Defense organization works for immigration reform.

www.DeportAliens.com
Working to deport illegal aliens and stopping further illegal aliens. Go to this web site to find out how to report illegal aliens and have them deported. Very effective.

www.DesertInvasion.us
National parks at our southern border are being overrun by an overwhelming number of illegal aliens. This web site will keep you informed and give you action plans.

www.DiversityAlliance.org
This organization works for a sustainable America.

www.EnglishFirst.org
Is an organization that realizes and promotes the use of English as the language of America and its importance in keeping this country cohesive.

www.911fsa.org
9/11 Families for a Secure America. All those who suffered the devastation of 9/11 have banded together to bring this crisis to the forefront of American citizens.

www.fileus.com
Friends of Immigration Law Enforcement. Excellent organization that pushes for enforcement of our immigration laws.

www.fairus.org
Federation for American Immigration Reform dedicated to changing immigration policy to help the USA.

www.house.gov/tancredo/Immigration/
Congressional Immigration Reform Caucus.

www.ImmigrationControl.com
Americans for Immigration Control is a grassroots organization developed to help you help our country.

www.IllegalAliens.us
An illegal immigration primer whose goal is to provide information on illegal immigration prevention, enforcement, and attrition.

www.IMMIVASION.US
Immigration political cartoons.

www.ImmigrationsHumanCost.org
Dedicated to telling the stories of forgotten citizens who still hope that their American dream will not be extinguished.

www.KrisEggle.org
This organization is run by Bonnie and Bob Eggle, the parents of the National Park Ranger, Kris Eggle, who was gunned down by Mexican drug smugglers. Her story is being repeated for millions of mothers whose kids suffer from the billions of dollars of drugs being smuggled across our borders.

www.LimitsToGrowth.org
This organization exposes the crisis of immigration via incompatible cultures, overpopulation and consequences.

www.MICHNews.com and www.washingtondispatch.com and info@alternet.org
Organizations featuring top writers addressing the immigration crisis into America.

www.NPG.org
Negative Population Growth supports lowering the population in America and the world to sustainable levels in the long term.

www.Balance.org
Population-Environment Balance concerns itself with overpopulation issues. They champion worldwide population stabilization for all humanity.

www.populationaction.org and www.prb.org
Informs on the crisis of overpopulation and reports on demographic statistics.

www.ProEnglish.org
Is an organization advocating English as the language of America.

www.ProjectUSA.com
Project USA is run by Craig Nelson, a man with impeccable credentials who is working for the future of our country. I recommend you join him in his efforts nationally. He provokes national discussions with his commentaries and billboards addressing illegal immigration.

www.PropertyRightsResearch.org
Works on maintaining property rights in the face of massive immigration.

www.rense.com
Jeff Rense is a powerful speaker, commentator and leader in exposing this immigration crisis and offers his radio listeners top speakers and experts who are working to solve this crisis.

www.enteract.com
Midwest Coalition for Responsible Immigration is headed by top people in the area of the Midwest.

www.npg.org
Negative Population Growth leads the field in reducing population in the USA.

www.ReportIllegals.us
Quickly and easily report illegal aliens and this site shows you to deport them.

http://www.rescueamericanjobs.org/
Rescue American jobs. Our jobs are being stolen by immigration. This web sites shows you how to take action. You may wish to enforce RICO laws.

www.SecuredBordersUSA.com
Lawrence Pappas and his staff are working to secure our borders. Excellent and powerful organization. It's important to obtain, sign and notarize their petition, which is being carried to the Congress

and president when 50 million are obtained. It demands immediate action to stop illegal immigration as well as deportation. You won't find a more outstanding American patriot than Lawrence Pappas along with his staff.

http://www.stopimmigrationnow.org/
Stop Immigration now petitions.

www.stoptheinvasion.com
Stop the Invasion in the North Carolina area.

www.TheAmericanResistance.com
A national organization based in Georgia dedicated to stopping illegal immigration. This is run by one of the finest patriots in the South, man I admire and respect.

www.TheSocialContract.com
This is a think tank organization of the finest American minds working to alert the public to the ongoing immigration invasion. It possesses information on everything from A to Z on immigration and overpopulation. Subscribe to their quarterly magazine that includes concise research and exceptional commentary.

www.TheTerryAndersonShow.com
The Terry Anderson Radio Show – "If you ain't mad, you ain't payin' attention!" Listen live on the Internet.

www.canadafirst.net
Canadian Immigration Reform Committee.

http://www.secureamerica.info/
United to Secure America.

www.LetsTakeBackAmerica.com
United Patriots of America works to stop this immigration crisis on the East Coast and across our country. Ron Bass works tirelessly with Americans across this country.

Info@usbc.org
This is one of the oldest web sites promoting border security.

www.proenglish.org
If this nation is to survive, it is imperative that English remain the national language spoken, written, taught and learned in this country by all Americans.

www.VDare.com
Is an organization featuring top writers concerning the crisis over immigration into America. Excellent source to keep you informed on what is really going on with our
borders and government.

www.fileus.com
Exceptional organization as Friends of Immigration Law Enforcement.

www.LimitsToGrowth.com
Sobering commentaries that will shock and enlighten you as to this invasion.

www.webhighlights.org
Outstanding organization working for the benefit of humanity. Al Sanchez works tirelessly with his staff to promote betterment of all humanity.

www.ZaZona.com
Is a jobs destruction newsletter keeping people up to date on the outsourcing and offshoring of jobs to other countries and the inequities of H-1B and L-1 visas that give jobs away to foreign countries or bring foreigners into our country and take away American jobs.

STATE ORGANIZATIONS:

Arizona— Citizens Against Illegal Immigration - www.citizensaii. org

Ranch Rescue - www.RanchRescue.com
www.pan2004.com
This organization works tirelessly to stop illegal alien invasion of Arizona.

California—Californians for Population Stabilization - www. capsweb.org. Californians for Population Stabilization includes dedicated citizens working to bring immigration into the spotlight as it destroys California and the quality of life once famous in that state.

California Coalition for Immigration Reform - www.ccir.net - a California based organization dedicated to stopping illegal immigration. This is the most powerful and active group in California. It is run by one of the finest patriots in America today.

Colorado— Colorado Alliance for Immigration Reform - www.cairco. org Florida— - Floridians for a Sustainable Population (FSP) - www. flsuspop.org - a Florida based organization dedicated to stopping illegal immigration.

Georgia—Georgians for Immigration Reduction - www. breathingroom.us
www.theamericanresistance.com
This is an outstanding action group headed by D.A. King who is an American patriot.
Illinois— Midwest Coalition to Reduce Immigration - www. immigrationreform.org
Massachusetts - Massachusetts Coalition for Immigration Reform http://www.massimmigration.com
Minnesota— Minnesotans for Sustainability - www.mnforsustain. org
Nevada— Emigration Party of Nevada - www.sendemback.org
New Hampshire—New Hampshire Citizens for Sustainable Population - www.homestead.com/SustainablePopulationNH/NHSUSPOP.html
New Jersey, New York, Connecticut— Tri-state Immigration Moratorium - www.trim.org

New York—Sachem Quality of Life - www.sqlife.com
North Carolina - Carolinians for Immigration Reform -www.nclisten.
com
Oregon— Oregonians for Immigration Reform - www.oregonir.org
www.agoregon.org
Alternatives to Growth Oregon
Tennessee - Tennesseans for Responsible Immigration Policies -
www.Tnrip.org
Texas—Texans for Immigration Reform - www.texansforimmigrati
onreform.com
Utah— Utahns for Immigration Reform and Enforcement - www.
ufire.net

Excellent News resources:

www.rense.com
Washington Dispatch www.washingtondispatch.com
Alter Net info@alternet.org
Lewis News http://www.lewisnews.com/main.asp
Most In-depth Concise Honest News and commentary www.
michnews.com
News With Views http://www.newswithviews.com/
Covenant News http://www.covenantnews.com/
Idaho Observer http://www.proliberty.com/observer/
The Citizens Review On-Line http://www.citizenreviewonline.
org/current_news.html
Glenn Spencer's American Border Patrol http://www.
americanpatrol.com/
Buy AMERICAN - http://www.buyamerican.com/
Judicial Forum http://www.judicialforum.org/

Books that inform:

POPULATION POLITICS by Virginia Abernethy
TOO MANY PEOPLE by Lindsey Grant
A BICENTENNIAL MALTHUSIAN ESSAY by John Rohe
THE END OF NATURE by Bill McKibben
OUT OF GAS: THE END OF THE AGE OF OIL by David Goodstein

OUR PLUNDERED PLANET by Fairfield Osborn
THE SIXTH EXTINCTION by Leakey and Lewin
FOOD, ENERGY AND SOCIETY by David and Marcia Pimental
ONWARD MUSLIM SOLDIERS by Robert Spencer

USING THE INTERNET AND LINKING ARMS

Send this letter out to all your friends. Write me at www.
frostywooldridge.com
I will send you the following letter for your network:

Dear Whomever:

Things you can do:

Each of us follows in the footsteps of Thomas Jefferson, Lincoln, Madison, Franklin, Washington, Susan B. Anthony, Ike, Dr. Martin Luther King, Eleanor Roosevelt or any American who cared about the future of our country. The hour is late, however, the hour is not up. Where would this country be without their actions? Declare yourself an American citizen who inherited the same responsibilities that Jefferson or any foot soldier from Valley Forge all the way to the deserts of Iraq, accepted. It's your responsibility as a citizens. Below are some of the ways you can do something.

Most people don't realize it, however, it's growing into a huge crisis for our country. We've got over 10 million illegal aliens in this country with around another 800,000 pouring over our borders each year in addition to the 1.5 million who come in legally. We're headed for an added 200 million Americans in 50 years which will leave us struggling with an unsustainable society. Our kids are going to inherit a mess. What can you do? Plenty.

1. Nationally, join www.numbersusa.com.   This organization works to stop illegal immigration and reduce legal immigration to a sustainable 100,000 per year. You may join for free and you can send pre-written faxes weekly. You'll enjoy up to the minute

information. Pass this web site on to all your friends and have them pass it to their friends. We are in danger of losing our country, our language and our way of life.

2. Go to info@numbersusa.com and ask for a local contact in your state In California, California Coalition for Immigration Reform at:
www.ccir.net.   We're gaining thousands of ordinary citizens each week who are sick and tired of our officials doing nothing about massive illegal immigration and no one is thinking about the world our children will inherit from our irresponsible actions today.

3. Call your senators and congressmen today. Tell them what you want.

4. Web sites that explain diseases: www.fairus.org and www.cis.org
www.thesocialcontract.com and www.balance.org and
www.carryingcapacity.org

6. Also, you can go to my web site for all my editorials and send them around to your friends to wake them up. www.frostywooldridge.com

7. Write the president and share your concern: president@whitehouse.gov Ph. 1-202-456-1111   For Congress: 1-877-762-8762

8. Pass this letter on to all your networks.

9. The phone number for reporting illegal aliens at work or anywhere is: Bureau of Immigration, Customs and Enforcement—1-866-347-2423.

10. You may anonymously report illegal alien employers by going to www.reportillegals.com

Thank you,
Your name

References:

"America Extinguished: Mass Immigration and the Disintegration of American Culture" by Samuel T. Francis

"Along U.S. Border, a Third World is Reborn" March 3, 1988, Colonias, New York Times

Border Security: "Chiefs of Police: Border Security A Sham"— WorldNetDaily.com 2004
http://www.worldnetdaily.com/news/article.asp?ARTICLE_ID=36780

"Can Immigrants Save Social Security: Many Are Not Paying Into The System" by Edwin S. Rubenstein, president of ESR Research, The Social Contract, Winter 2003

www.CommonSenseOnMassImmigration.us
This is a comprehensive booklet covering all aspects of this immigration crisis.
Call toll free: 1-800-352-4843

"Changes in China: Global Developments Impact the U.S." by Rob Sanchez, The Social Contract, Winter 2003

Crime: "ILLEGAL-ALIEN CRIME WAVE" by Heather MacDonald, City Journal, published by the Manhattan Institute, Winter 2004, http://www.junomsg://03884650/

"Defining Chicano Culture" by Marc Cabrera, MonterreyHerald.com

Dog fighting: "Many Lost Pets Stolen—Investigators Link Recent Thefts To Illegal Dogfights" by Kimberly Matas, Arizona Daily Star, 1/10/04
http://www.dailystar.com/dailystar/dailystar/5356.php
http://www.azstarnet.com/sn/border/5356.php

Dog fighting: "See Spot. See Spot Killed" by Sergeant Steve Brownstein, Chicago Police Department (Warning: This is a disturbing article on animal cruelty)
http://www.vaguepolitix.com/crime/jokers/index_03.htm

Dog fighting: "Dogfighting Is On The Rise, But So Is Enforcement Effort" by Doug Simpson, AP, January 11, 2004
http://www.thestate.com/mld/thestate/news/nation/7682924.htm

"Drought: Global Warming 'Train Wreck' Forecast For The West" November 23, 2002, by Andrew Bridges, AP Science Writer

"Europe's Islamist Wake-Up Call" by Val MacQueen, FrontPageMagazine.com, February 27, 2004, http://www.frontpagemag.com/Articles/ReadArticle.asp?ID=12372

Facts on cockfighting: http://www.philippineshotelresort.com/leyte/info.html
http://www.artocock.hypermart.net/
http://www.spca.bc.ca/Factsheets/factsheet_cockfighting.htm

FORBES MAGAZINE, "PREYING ON HUMAN CARGO" by Michael Maiello and Susan Kitchens, June 7, 2004, page 74-84. www.forbes.com

Gangs: "California Police say MS-13 Is Responsible for Rapes and Killings" by Michelle Nicolosi, Globe Correspondent, 2002, Boston Globe

www.washingtontimes.com
"Gang Violence Rages Across Jurisdictions" by Matthew Cella, August 7, 2003

Gangs: www.streetgangs.com

"Globalization and Its Inconsistencies" by Herman E. Daly, School of Public Affairs, University of Maryland, The Social Contract, Spring 2003

"Guilty Plea In Kentwood Horse Killing" by Brenda Walker, Sonoma Index-Tribune 2/13/04

"Horse Tripping Not Cultural" by Karen Cerro, San Gabriel Valley Tribune, 12/29/03

International Human Suffering Index by Sharon L. Camp, Ph.D., Population Crisis Committee, 1120 19th Street, NW Ste 550, Washington DC 20036

"Immigrant Enclaves and Balkanization" by Paul Pringle, Dallas Morning News, September 21, 1999 Huntington Park, California

Job loses: "Losing America's Livelihood" by William F. Jasper
http://www.stoptheftaa.org/artman/publish/article_109.shtml

Language: "ONE LANGUAGE, ONE TONGUE" by former Colorado Governor Richard D. Lamm

"Leprosy Rising in U.S." by Sharon Lerner, New York Times, 2/20/03

"Land, Energy and Water: The Constraints Governing Ideal Population Size" by David Pimental and Marcia Pimental, 1991, NPG

Mass Immigration: "'Mass Immigration Said Swamping US Cities" by Jon Dougherty, January 13, 2004, NewsMax.com
Click here: Mass Immigration Said 'Swamping' U.S. Cities
http://www.newsmax.com/archives/articles/2004/1/12/224428.shtml

"MEXIFORNIA" by Victor Davis Hanson
www.amazon.com

"Mexican Rodeo Contests Enrage Local Horse Lovers" by Mark Waite, Pahrump Valley Times, 9/17/03. Violent cultural activity known as Horse Tripping is an offense under Texas law for "Torturing an Animal," section 42.09(a) (1) of the Penal Code

On Aztlan and Reconquista movement:
"Pushing Out Whitey" (March 2000)
"We Have been Warned" (June 1998)
"Reconquista Update" (January 2002)

"Onward Muslim Soldiers" by Robert Spencer
Expose' of basic Islam's Jihad quest around the world

"Paving the Way to Aztlan" by Linda Bentley, reporter, Sonoran News, June 11, 2003, Vol. 9, No. 24

www.carryingcapacity.org
Population consequence figures: "Ecosystems, Food and Energy Supplies Threatened by Population Growth" April 2004

www.populationaction.org
Population figures: "People in the Balance" by Richard P. Cincotta, Bonnie Dye, Tom Gardner-Outlaw, Jennifer Wisnewski—Population Action International
"Why Population Matters" by Population Action International

Population Facts, Figures and Charts:
www.balance.org and www.populationconnection.org

"Population/Immigration: One Problem, Indivisible" by Lee G. Marland, Ph.D., The Social Contract, Summer 2003

"Reflections on Sustainability, Population Growth and the Environment—Revisited" by Dr. Albert Bartlett, CU Professor of Physics. Permission given by Dr. Bartlett to use portions of his paper and permission from editors at Renewable Resources Journal, Vol. 15, No. 4, Winter 1997-98, Pages. 6-23 Renewable

Frosty Wooldridge

Natural Resources Foundation, 5430 Grosvenor Lane, Bethesda, MD, 20814

"The Trouble With Islam: A Muslim's Call For The Reform of Her Faith" by Irshad Manji, St. Martin's Press

"The Kiss of Death" by Carlos Bastien. Chagas Disease infects 16 million in Latin America with 50,000 deaths annually

"The Patient Predator" by Kevin Patterson, Mother Jones Magazine, March/April 2003, Tuberculosis kills two million worldwide annually

"The Unmanaged Commons" by John Cairns, Jr., Professor of Environmental Biology Emeritus at Virginia Polytechnic, The Social Contract, Winter 2003

"There Is No Global Population Problem" by Garrett Hardin

"Selected Growth Fallacies" by Herman E. Daly, The Social Contract, Spring 2003
"TIMEBOMB: GLOBAL EPIDEMIC OF MULTI DRUG RESISTANT DISEASES" by Lee Reichmann, MD

"U.S. and Mexico Agree Immigrant Plan"—BBC, August 10, 2001 http://news.bbc.co.uk/2/hi/americas/148365.stm

"World's Ten Worst Dictators" by David Wallenchinsky, Parade, Denver Post, 2/22/04

Cover photograph: By Border Patrol Special Agent John W. Slagle from 'Operation Shorty.' International case involving exploitation of Guatemalan nationals utilized as indentured slave labor in California, Oregon and Florida. This group, one of an average of 2,200 crossing the borders daily walks through the bush on the Mexican/U.S. border on their way to pick up points.

ABOUT THE AUTHOR

Frosty Wooldridge is a graduate of Michigan State University. He is an environmentalist, mountain climber, triathlete, dancer, Scuba diver, racquetball player, skier, writer, speaker and photographer. He has taught at the elementary, high school and college levels. He bicycled 100,000 miles on six continents and six times across the United States. His feature articles have appeared in national and international magazines for 25 years. He is the author of 'HANDBOOK FOR TOURING BICYCLISTS' Chockstone Press; 'STRIKE THREE! TAKE YOUR BASE' a teen novel, The Brookfield Reader; 'ANTARCTICA: AN EXTREME ENCOUNTER' Author House, October 2004; 'BICYCLING AROUND THE WORLD' Author House, August 2004; 'INTO THE WIND' a teen novel, Author House, September 2004; 'SALTY TIGHTS: A SLICE OF HEAVEN, TASTE OF HELL—BICYCLING THE CONTINENTAL DIVIDE' Author House, October, 2004. Web site: www.frostywooldridge.com

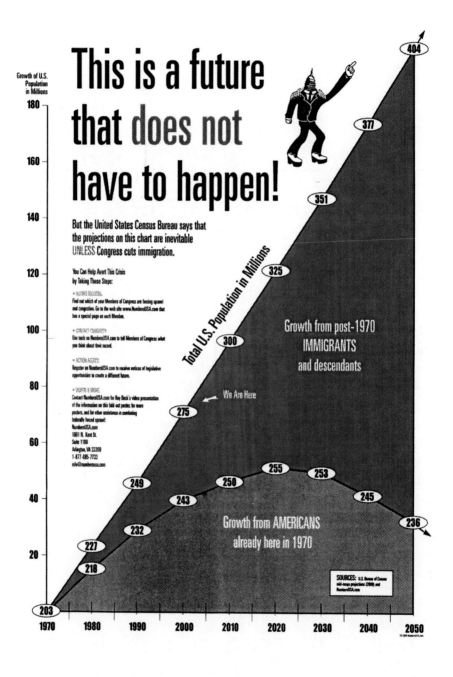

Printed in the United States
87442LV00001B/163-174/A